The *Coasts* of *Canada*

Other Non-Fiction by Lesley Choyce

Edible Wild Plants of Nova Scotia (1977)
An Avalanche of Ocean (1987)
December Six: The Halifax Solution (1988)
Transcendental Anarchy (1993)
Nova Scotia: Shaped by the Sea (1996)

The COASTS
of Canada

A HISTORY

by
LESLEY CHOYCE

GOOSE LANE

Edited by Laurel Boone and Angela Williams.
Jacket design by Julie Scriver.
Book design by Julie Scriver and Paul Vienneau.
Cover images, reprinted by permission: Front, top to bottom: "Americae pars borealis . . . ," Cornelis de Jode, 1593 (detail), National Library of Canada, NMC 6579(+c); "Tofino, British Columbia," Alison Hughes; "Icebergs in Otto Fiord, N.W. Ellesmere Island," Monica Bernard, GSC, A94P0010; "Cousin's Shore, Prince Edward Island," Alison Hughes; "View of the Arctic Sea, from the Mouth of the Coppermine River, midnight 20 July 1821," tinted engraving by Edward Finden after the painting by George Back, © National Maritime Museum, London, PBC5004, D9751_2. Back cover, left to right: "Hunting Seal," by Pierre-Narcisse Tetu, February 18, 1871, NLC, Website Images in the News: *Canadian Illustrated News* (3:7, p. 108); "Americae pars borealis . . . ," Cornelis de Jode, 1593, as above; "The Grand Banks Fishing Schooner Bluenose," W.R. MacAskill, NSARM, 1987-453/98.

Printed in Canada by Friesens.
10 9 8 7 6 5 4 3 2 1

National Library of Canada Cataloguing in Publication

Choyce, Lesley, 1951-
The coasts of Canada : a history / Lesley Choyce.

Includes bibliographical references and index.
ISBN 0-86492-360-0

1. Atlantic Coast (Canada) — History. 2. Pacific Coast (B.C.) — History.
3. Arctic Coast (Canada) — History. I. Title.

FC164.C56 2002   971'.00946   C2002-903377-2
F1026.C56 2002

Published with the financial support of the Canada Council for the Arts, the Government of Canada through the Book Publishing Industry Development Program, and the New Brunswick Culture and Sports Secretariat.

Goose Lane Editions
469 King Street
Fredericton, New Brunswick
CANADA E3B 1E5
www.gooselane.com

*For those Canadian writers whose shared passion and concern
for the environment has alerted us to the beauty and
fragility of the natural world in which we live.
I dedicate this book to David Suzuki, Elizabeth May,
Harry Thurston, Farley Mowat, Pierre Berton,
George Woodcock, and Michael Clugston, as well
as to the many other writers who refuse to give
up the fight to save the wildlife, the seas,
the rivers, the forests, and the shores.*

The Coasts of Canada – A History

CHAPTER ONE

Where the Land Stops and the Sea Begins

Salt Air and Arctic Ice

ON A COLD, RAW DAY IN APRIL, 1990, I stood on the shore of the Strait of Belle Isle, in the southeast corner of Labrador, near the town of L'Anse-au-Clair. I had been away from home for a while, travelling through small coastal communities on the Lower North Shore of Quebec. Winter, I knew, was giving up its grip down south in Nova Scotia, but here in the north, it still had control of the land and the people around me.

Vikings had visited this shore where I stood. John Cabot had probably passed by here. Jacques Cartier had sailed along this coast and stared at the shores of what he considered a forbidding land. Like them, perhaps, I was feeling a little bit homesick and still somewhat overwhelmed by the power of northern elements.

But I was standing on a sandy shore. I was on a beach — not what most people think of when they think of beaches, but a beach nonetheless. That gave me some small comfort. I love all beaches, anywhere, north or south. I began to hike along the shoreline, this minuscule fragment of the coastline of Canada, and I savoured the lusty aroma of salt air and subarctic ice. Before me was not open water but a beautiful frozen jumble that stretched thirty kilometres to Newfoundland. In the hazy distance, I saw what I thought were hills of that shoreline, but it might have just been clouds.

Everyone I had met here in coastal Quebec and Labrador had been hospitable in the extreme: from Arctic char, caribou steaks, and bake-apple pies to homemade beer and homemade music, I had been treated royally. The people who live on the margins of this vast land know how to treat strangers. But I'd been away for too long, I ached for home, and there was a problem about how soon I might get there.

11

My morning flight from nearby Blanc Sablon to Quebec City had been cancelled. An early-morning squall accompanied by sheering winds had closed the tiny airport. By afternoon, a major spring snowstorm was expected to ground all air traffic, and the weather office promised six or possibly seven days of non-stop storms.

Beside me a L'Anse-au-Clair resident named Dave, a friendly Labradorean who had been shuttling me around in an ancient Chevy with a stone-cracked windshield, said that he loved watching the ice on the strait. "When she finally breaks up, sometimes she goes all at once. You go to sleep one night and it's there — big junks of it and pans big enough to put a tractor-trailer on. Then you wake up one morning and she's gone."

The ice, I admitted, was beautiful. Although I could see open water in thin ribbons here and there, there looked to be plenty of solid ice, even though I knew there must be a raging current beneath the surface. I wasn't really serious when I asked, "Could you walk to Newfoundland from here?"

"It's been done, but you'd have to know what you're doing."

Small foolish fantasy on my part: walk to Newfoundland on the other shore and catch a bus south to Deer Lake, fly to Halifax, be home by tomorrow.

"I'd take you over on my Ski-Doo if you want."

"Really?"

"I've done it once before, but it was earlier in the year. Spring's a bit chancy. If you want to try, I guess I'm up for it."

"I don't know."

"We'd have a fifty-fifty chance of making it. It's up to you."

I wasn't that desperate, and I would never know if he was serious or just teasing me. I stared out across the fascinating wasteland of flat pans and jutting peaks of pure blue-white frozen sea. "Let's call the airport one more time."

"No problem." Dave drove me to a phone in a bar with three forlorn moose heads on the wall over a fireplace. There was no news about the arrival of the plane that was scheduled to take me back south. But the man at the airport said there was a small commercial plane still hoping to take off for St. Anthony, Newfoundland, in about thirty minutes.

"What about the weather?" Outside, I could see the snow had started up again.

"This is a little one. Supposed to stop soon. Window of maybe half an hour. They figure a few planes can go out."

Dave seemed a little disappointed as he drove me to the airport. I found a seat on the plane to St. Anthony with about twelve other passengers. We waited on the runway for the snow to stop and a hole to open up in the clouds, then taxied and took off.

I saw snow falling to the north and snow falling to the south. I looked down at the strait beneath us, saw some kids standing on one ice pan jammed up on shore, then we were swallowed by the clouds. The small aircraft was pummelled by the wind — left and then right; we dropped abruptly and then suddenly bobbed up. It felt just like the roller coaster at Upper Clements Park. A woman across the aisle from me began to cry, and I offered her a piece of gum. We never made it above the clouds, and the plane shuddered all the way to St. Anthony, until it landed on a flat piece of scrubland where incorrigible relatives of Leif Eriksson may have harassed and fought the native Skraelings.

I changed planes and flew to Deer Lake, where I found my way onto a larger jet and retreated homeward through empty blue skies above sparkling waters. The west coast of Newfoundland from this altitude looked like an endless strand of sandy beaches. The north coastline of Cape Breton appeared rugged but somehow friendly. I finally found my way home to Lawrencetown Beach on the Eastern Shore of Nova Scotia and saw my own ocean, unfettered by ice, scintillating beneath a starry night sky.

A Seal on the Road

In the winter of 1997-1998, with the continent teased, drenched, iced over, vexed, taunted, and terrorized by El Niño, Nova Scotia was still cold, the ground seized hard as granite and the half-salt, half-fresh water in the lake beyond my garden frozen hard enough to skate on. One evening just after dark, driving down the ice-slicked gravel road that leads to my home, I hit the brakes and slid to a greasy stop just inches in front of something that I thought was a big chunk of ice that had fallen off the back of somebody's pickup truck.

A closer inspection revealed that it was a seal pup, a harbour seal to be

The coast of Nova Scotia. (ALISON HUGHES)

exact, in his beige-to-nearly-white winter coat. He was about one and a half metres long and probably weighed more than me. My daughter and I got out and asked the seal to move; we tried to explain that the next resident coming home from work might well run him over. There was plenty of frozen marsh and ice to the east and west — all he had to do was slide off the same way he got here. His big, weepy, beautiful eyes were focussed on me there in the glare of my headlights, and he looked tame enough to pet, but, as I moved my mittened hand near his back, he bared a set of fine stiletto-like teeth and made hissing noises like you'd expect from some kind of giant snake.

He appeared to have no intention of moving, road ice no doubt as comfortable as any other form of ice, so I went home and came back with equipment. First I tried prodding him with a plastic sled. He punctured it in several places and whipped it out of my hands. I went back to simple humanitarian harassment to get him to move, but he'd have none of it. Finally, I threw an old blanket over him and used a snow shovel to push him out of the road. He never did get the point that I was a fan of seals (some of them my surfing companions) and had no hakapik axe to spike his brain, no intention of selling his valuable fur.

"Probably got lost chasing smelts," my neighbour said, when I was

The COASTS *of* CANADA

called back out much later that night. The seal had wandered out onto the paved road, where the traffic increased the chance of his demise. We used the snow shovel and blanket trick again and coaxed him into a frozen ditch. He was seen the next day sliding over snow-covered dunes, and he probably did make it back to the sea. For me, the seal was a good reminder that we still share the coasts of this country with creatures who were here long before we were. Occasionally, seals have been known to come up out of Halifax harbour and scoot out into the traffic of Dartmouth. Not far from the mouth of the harbour, whales get ploughed into by container ships, and the sad carcasses of the great beasts float ashore.

A Coastline of Instability

Peter Gzowski caught me off-guard the first time he interviewed me on *Morningside* nearly two decades ago. I had told him that I had surfed both coasts of Canada. "Only two?" he chided. "But Canada has three." It was a mistake I would not make again. Yes, there are three coasts, and like other Canadians, I grieve that I am not as intimate with the northerly coast as I'd like to be.

No, I had to admit, I had not surfed the north, although I imagined it could be done, under the right conditions. In one respect, however, I think now that Gzowski may have been wrong. Canada does not have three coasts. It has either a thousand or it has just one. One long coastline, beginning south of Seal Cove on Grand Manan Island, New Brunswick, and ending not far from Victoria on Vancouver Island, a coastline interrupted by Alaska, yes, but a single coastline nonetheless. This coastline is a long one — 71,262 kilometres, or 243,792 kilometres if you count the shoreline of every island that is part of this wild, undisciplined country. The British Columbia coast alone is almost 900 kilometres long as the crow flies, stretching from the Washington state border to the southern tip of Alaska, and much, much longer if you measure the shoreline of each inlet, every nook and cranny.

Everything about Canada's coastline suggests instability. The land was born of ice and rock. Much of the ice is gone, but it left whole islands of red soil like Prince Edward Island, and it dumped fine roundish drumlins outside my back door in Nova Scotia. It gouged magnificent fjords into the land on the west coast of Newfoundland, on Baffin and

Ellesmere Islands, and on the shoreline of British Columbia. Melting glaciers and ice caps have inundated ancient shores, which we know as continental shelves; these extend underwater for up to 180 kilometres in the east and about half that distance in the west. The sea continues to chew away at our edges, reshaping Canada daily, sculpting the land, leaving sea stacks and arches and jagged cliffs. We have plentiful beaches of soft, smooth sand — rocks ground down by the sea, slathered by foamy waves. A sandy summer shore is a fine place to smooth a beach towel and lie down for a while, yet some of our finest beaches, far to the north, are cold in all seasons and, in winter, dark as well.

Tsunamis and Politics

Seas and bays and gulfs and straits endorse the planetary politics of the three great oceans along Canada's coasts: the North Atlantic, the Arctic and the North Pacific. The Beaufort Sea and the Labrador Sea are separate from their mother oceans only in name or because of current patterns. Bays suggest enclosure: Hudson and Fundy are tucked into the land. The straits of Canada, like rivers of the sea, divide island from island and island from continent. Wind and gravity conspire to create waves, some mere ripples and others head-high and perfectly formed for surfing, like those of Lawrencetown Beach in Nova Scotia or Cox Bay on Vancouver Island. Sometimes, at sea, waves collect their locomotive energy and create staggering rogue waves over thirty metres high that can swamp the largest ships. If you're bobbing about on the Pacific south and west of Vancouver Island, keep a keen eye open for these monsters. Even more deadly are tsunamis, often misnamed "tidal waves." Early in the twentieth century, the sea floor off the East Coast moved, and although most of the world paid no attention, sudden enormous waves swamped Newfoundland outports and Nova Scotia harbours. In 1964, an even more powerful wave travelled south from the coastline of Alaska, causing several million dollars worth of destruction on Vancouver Island and killing a hundred people along the length of the Pacific Coast.

Ocean currents move relentlessly along our shores, making them both colder and warmer. People living on the West Coast were once fond of the theory that the climate was warmer there because of a current that pulled warm water in from as far away as Japan. An exotic idea, but a wrong one.

Instead, the warmth of the British Columbia coastline comes, oddly enough, from the Subarctic Current. Air moving over the enormous warm mass of the Pacific pulls warmth from the sea towards the Subarctic Current and dispenses it generously on the land.

In the Atlantic, the Gulf Stream pulls warm water north. My home would be a tropical paradise were it not for the obdurate Labrador Current. Draining down from the top of the world, its frigid waters push the Gulf Stream warmth away to the west to favour continental Europe. Fortunately, however, the mixing of the Labrador Current and the Gulf Stream southeast of Newfoundland creates a sumptuous mix of nutrients that once made for the richest fishing grounds in the world. Overfishing has upset the balance, but those two immense currents could, in time, probably repair this enormous life support system; it's in their relentless nature and their immaculate design.

Not long ago I heard on the news that fishermen were meeting on Prince Edward Island to discuss the fact that a five-year moratorium on cod fishing has not resulted in the return of the cod to the Gulf of St. Lawrence. It may take another fifteen years before cod can be harvested again. But the fishermen worry that the burgeoning seal population may not allow that to happen. Half a million seals in the Gulf, possibly five million in the whole region, all feed on fish. What's to be done? I think of my lost, feisty friend lounging on a public road in winter. The best I could do was shove him out of the way of immediate harm. As soon as he found his way back into the sea, he was in direct competition with my own species for whatever fish the Atlantic has left to offer us for nourishment. Must we destroy our competitors in order for fishermen to earn a living from the sea? In the Arctic, the hunting of wolves near coastal communities is done with snowmobiles and rifles, tradition mixed with gasoline and bullets. On the West Coast, fish stocks are in decline, just as they are in the east. Battleships and merchant ships ply all three coasts now, the dream of the Northwest Passage a reality that troubles coast dwellers and politicians alike. We continue to live in an uneasy balance with our oceans, if there is any balance at all.

The Coasts of Canada

When I face the sea, I look south, directly towards Antarctica. But it is the North Atlantic that controls our environment. In summer I feel warm, damp winds spawned by hurricanes and tropical storms. I know that there is a continent over my shoulder to the west, but more importantly, there is the Arctic directly to my back. I see myself as truly Canadian, in that I believe I am significantly shaped by the forces of cold and the power of the north. But I am more precisely a *coastal* Canadian. I am intimately tuned to weather, to tides, to freezing and thawing of water both salt and fresh. I ride waves in this sea in summer or winter. I am in love with and in awe of the elemental forces of coastal life.

And so the story I find myself ready to tell is the history of the three coasts of this country. Much of inland Canada now ignores the sea and the legacy of these coastlines, as if our history is only the tale of politics and industry, as if what happens in an Ottawa caucus or a Toronto boardroom is the primary story of who we are. For once, let the mid-continental tales of Canada be relatively mute, and let the narrative of a coastal people reshape our visions of who we are. This is the history of coastal Canada, told by one writer living on one those shores. This is a book of discoveries heaped upon one another. Adventurers and followers. Winners and losers. It is the story of those steadfast, hardy souls who persevere in difficult realms, who live with the companionship of sea things, whose lives may be marginal figuratively as well as literally. Like any history, *The Coasts of Canada* is a record of misunderstandings, errors, and bad judgement. It is a also a plea to preserve the good things of coastal communities and natural shorelines.

In 1986 I set out to hike the entire coastline of Nova Scotia, a little at a time. I spent several summers enjoying the exploration of mostly untouched, unspoiled beaches of stone and sand, mud, shells, and driftwood. But I gave up after having travelled no more than seventy kilometres. I gave up on the idea of completion and settled on an endless series of sojourns along fragments of the glorious coast. I have been rewarded with vivid images, fresh air, abundant wildlife, and an intimacy with the edge of land that will forever haunt me. Where the land stops and the sea begins, whether on my coast or on the coasts of other Canadians, there is a place to stand and look both seaward and landward and dream. It's a place of beginnings, of change, of expectation, and sometimes a place of fear, a place to face gargantuan planetary forces, a shoreline of renewal and rebirth.

CHAPTER TWO

First to Arrive

By Way of Siberia

WE'RE STILL GUESSING, but the ancestors of Canada's Aboriginal peoples probably originated in Africa or Southern Asia not more than ten million years ago. The cold and ice of the early Pleistocene era kept homo sapiens in Africa and the southern areas of Asia and Europe, slowly evolving in a somewhat hospitable climate. But as the glaciers retreated, ancient humans travelled north and eventually east across a land bridge which is now water — the Bering Strait. A hefty chunk of the world's water was still locked up as ice in those days, causing sea levels to be much lower than they are today.

In fact, we may be living in a relatively short stretch of time right now where ice does not dominate the planet. Despite short-range global warming, another ice age may be just around the corner in geological time, and we'll be able to walk to Siberia on dry land if we care to reverse the trek of those distant Canadian forefathers and mothers.

Eastern Asia was actually somewhat free of ice during those periods when America and Europe were blanketed by it. It was drier over there 80,000 years ago, and as recently as 20,000 years ago (a mere blink into the past), the Bering Land Bridge was ice free and so was a surprising chunk of Alaska, the Yukon, and the northerly coastal plain of Canada. Almost all of the rest of Canada, except for a big piece of the Labrador coast, was buried beneath a massive block of ice over a kilometre thick in some places. The ice-free region of the far west, which was connected to Siberia, allowed animals to wander east and west, with human hunters in hot (or, should we say, cold) pursuit.

The tyrant ice began to loosen its grip around 15,000 years back. A kind of ice-free highway opened up east of the Rocky Mountains, and it is likely that the first North Americans started following it south and eventually east to spread out across the continent. Three thousand years later, the glaciers were in full retreat, and ancient native peoples were living along the giant lakes left by the glaciers as well as along coasts and rivers.

While the land bridge concept seems the most likely means by which humankind found its way to Canada, there have been other theories put forward. Explorers (or possibly lost fishermen) in animal-hide boats may have come this way during Palaeolithic times, before the Bering Land Bridge appeared, skimming along the southern edge of the ice pack. It would have been a rugged, cold trip, but macho chest-thumping has driven men to such daunting tasks. Unfortunately, there's little hard evidence to build a case for these intrepid travellers, and most speculation is based upon legends.

Similarities in Neolithic stone tools suggest that Scandinavians may have come to Canada around 4,000 years ago, and some theorists even conjure the possibility of people from northern Russia trekking across the ice to Greenland and then beyond. Much later, in the eighth century, Irish monks seem to have walked the pebbly, volcanic shorelines of Iceland. They, too, made animal-skin boats, but they were still a long way from North America, and to get here, they would have had to avoid the Gulf Stream or fight its current, which tended to sweep them back to Europe.

While cold and current opposed Europeans trying to find their way west to Canada, the situation on the Pacific coast was different. A west-to-east current and the prevailing winds from the west suggest that sailing ships from Asia may have had help from environmental forces if they wanted to explore this way, or sailors may have accidentally reached these shores without a clue as to where they were. In modern times, empty fishing boats from as far away as China have washed up on the coast of British Columbia. It's fun to entertain the idea that earlier explorers had arrived this way, but the fact of the matter is that such a voyage would have been nearly impossible. Whether intentional or not, drifting on favourable winds and currents from Asia to British Columbia would have been an ordeal so long that any crew would have died from thirst or starvation. Historians, however, have not completely written off the possibility that some such event may have happened during several thousand years of sailing activity. Individual Asians or even Africans finding their way to the Americas by sea may have survived, but it is unlikely they had any significant influence on the people they may have encountered.

The Great Northern Hunters

Canada's Siberian ancestors traversed the Bering Land Bridge, chasing reindeer and other arctic mammals. Along the northern coast, they began to hunt seal and walrus, and some discovered that this change gave them a more stable life of plentiful food and relative comfort, despite the cold and the long, dark days of winter. Now known as the Paleoeskimos, these people spread out across the north over several generations and had this coast of the continent to themselves 3,000 years ago.

The Paleoeskimos used harpoons to hunt seals and bone-tipped spears to fish and hunt birds. James Tuck, a Memorial University archaeologist, has found arrows of chipped stone dating back nearly 2,000 years, suggesting that these ancient arctic folk had bows and arrows. There's no hard evidence that they used boats. Instead, they attached their harpoons to handlines, so they could haul their prey to land. They kept their footing safely on shore or ventured onto hard ice. Wasn't that the reason they were given the gift of all that ice, after all — so they didn't have to take dangerous rides in skin boats and possibly fall into the freezing water?

Animal skins, cleaned with flint blades, were made into clothing or sewn together to create tents with needles made from bone. Although snow probably banked itself up around the tents, the Paleoeskimos did not build the familiar igloo-style snow house. Stone fireplaces were at the centre of their homes, but they may not have been glowing all the time, since there wasn't much in the way of firewood to be burned. Heather, low-lying Arctic willow, and animal fat might have provided a modicum of warmth, but body heat and plenty of animal skins for protection would have had to suffice for day-to-day survival, even in the winter, when temperatures dipped to minus thirty or minus forty degrees Celsius.

Some of the stone fireplaces still remain along the coasts of northern Canada. Near these humble monuments to a people long gone from the face of the earth, archaeologists still find piles of bones that show what Paleoeskimos ate: mostly seal, but also all kinds of birds, especially ducks, fox and, in the High Arctic, musk oxen — a quarry that would have required great courage and skill to bring home for Sunday dinner. If there was a poor hunting season, they either moved on or starved, but clearly the Paleoeskimos were used to moving on. Did they wonder if there was promised land, an easier life, just up beyond the next bay? Or did they crave adventure, yearn to explore? Such curiosity seems unlikely; they probably moved on only because of a desperate need to find enough food to feed their children. Whatever the case, these were hardy and highly adaptive people. However distant from ourselves, however unconnected to modern life, they may have learned lessons our descendents will have to figure out when the next age of ice swallows up our backyards.

Over a period of 1,500 years, beginning 2,500 years ago, the Paleoeskimos' descendants, known as the Dorset people, spread out across the Arctic to Labrador and across the Strait of Belle Isle to Newfoundland. In the far north, they lived in homes of snow and turf, using soapstone lamps that burned oil from sea mammals. Their diet included seal, walrus, and narwhal, and they may have developed early versions of dogsleds and kayaks. The Dorset disappeared less than a thousand years ago. They are portrayed as strong but gentle, qualities that were important for tranquil family life but not of value when they had to confront a more aggressive immigrant.

Homes with Whalebone Rafters

The Thule people, the ancestors of the Inuit who live today in far northern Canada, arrived about a thousand years ago, travelling east from Alaska. They had been skilled hunters of the Chukchi and Bering Seas, and, unlike the Paleoeskimos, they hunted from boats as well as along the shores. They had perfected the one-man kayak and the larger umiak, a skin boat as much as ten metres long and capable of carrying several families. From these large boats, the Thule hunted the bowhead whale, undaunted by its size or the dangers of capsizing and drowning in arctic waters.

From their hunting forays, they stockpiled meat from seals and whales. They used oil from the whales to heat their relatively comfortable homes, which they dug into the earth. The houses had wood frame roofs sheathed with animal skins and covered with sod. Although the

An Inuit family in a large leather boat, Hudson Bay, 1897. Photo by A.P. Low.
(GSC, 18690)

amount of heat given off by a whale oil lamp sounds minimal by modern standards, the insulation provided by the earth walls and sod-covered roof was probably better than that of the modern homes constructed in the far north in the twentieth century. With ample food and well-insulated homes, the Thule people lived in some degree of comfort.

The Thule people followed migrating bowhead whales eastward and eventually discovered an abundance of them, which lured the hunters even further east to Baffin Bay and eventually to Labrador. Some Thule families had carried with them knives and tools made of smelted iron that had originated in Siberia, handed down through several generations. They searched for iron throughout the north, and eventually they came across large fields of fallen meteorites on Ellesmere Island and in northwestern Greenland. It is possible that news of these iron finds spread west with travelling hunters and encouraged more and more Thule people to move into the High Arctic of the east. Stone implements were replaced by tools made of processed iron, and there is also some evidence of tools made of copper and bronze that may have been forged from local materials.

The Thule of the eastern Arctic built their homes with whale bones instead of driftwood for rafters; these homes were extremely well built, almost airtight, with stone slabs inside for beds. Although the abundance of food and the quality of these homes afforded these early people a good life, the climate began to grow colder by the fourteenth century. From the middle of the sixteenth century to the middle of the nineteenth century, the earth underwent what is called "the Little Ice Age." Written records in Europe and China indicate that cold winters made for dramatic changes in agriculture and lifestyle. In Canada's High Arctic, ice cover restricted the migration of the whales, diverting them further to the south. As the world grew colder and the number of whales diminished, the descendants of the Thule migrants became more dependent on seals, fish and caribou. The whalebone-raftered homes of the past were replaced by igloo-style ice block houses.

The sophisticated culture of the Thule brought an end to the people descended from Paleoeskimos. Researchers believe that the benign Dorset were either absorbed into the new culture, driven back from the coasts that sustained them, or killed by the more aggressive hunters. Or perhaps their disappearance was the result of all of these factors, working in various combinations in various times and places. The Thule people are the ancestors of the Inuit. Although there is a multitude of regional variations, modern Inuit languages seem to have a common source whose origin lies among the people of northeastern Siberia. The Inuit appear to be more closely linked to those ancient Siberians than to the rest of North America's First Nations people.

CHAPTER THREE

The People of the Raven

Cities of Cedar

TWELVE THOUSAND YEARS AGO, Aboriginal explorers from the north
and west were finding their way south along the coast of what is now
British Columbia. The ice was in retreat at that point, and the Siberian
people seemed anxious to move on to whatever might be ahead.

Coastline living was relatively comfortable compared to the harsher
habitat in the north. Tools made of stone were used to build boats and
canoes designed for catching the ever-abundant fish. Harpoons were
used to kill seals and whales at least 6,500 years back, but information
gathered at the Namu site near Burke Channel suggests that salmon was
probably the mainstay of the diet.

Archaeologists think that the culture known today as the Locarno
People existed on the British Columbia coast for about 1,000 years, beginning around 3,500 years ago. Carvings have been found of animal skulls
worn by shamans, as well as labrets — oval-shaped discs made of bone or
stone worn by women — and replicas of killer whales. During the Marpole
Phase (from 1,500 to 2,400 years ago), the people developed wood-
working tools. Wedges made from antlers have been found, as well
as hammers and adzes with blades of polished jade. The forest and the
territory inland were unfamiliar to coastal dwellers and often thought to
be populated by hostile spirits, although there is evidence that they traded
fish for meat with inland people. Hides, ornamental spoons, and the goat
horns from which they were made also found their way to the coast.

All Pacific coastal societies were centred on obtaining food from the
sea. This led to the establishment of permanent settlements close to salmon stocks, although seasonal camps followed the spawning fish inland.
Distinct cultures grew up around places where rivers emptied into the

sea — where the best salmon fishing was, of course. Among the major groups of Northwest peoples were the Tlingit in the north, the Haida of the Queen Charlotte Islands, and the Tsimshian, Haisla, Bella Coola, Kwakiutl and Coast Salish of the southern mainland. Winter villages consisted of up to 1,000 people. Giant cedars were cut down with stone axes, and the logs were split with great precision to create cities of wood. In the summer, many coastal dwellers moved out of the big plank houses and into more open summer camps where they fished and gathered shellfish and seaweed.

Before European contact, west coast dwellers spoke a wide range of distinct languages. Although there were five main families of languages, there was considerable variation in vocabulary and pronunciation from one group to the next. Some languages would be as different, for example, as French is from Swahili. Early European explorers had little knowledge of just how varied these people were and tended to group them together, calling them names that had little to do with how the people referred to themselves. In 1778, for example, James Cook asked some folks on Vancouver Island who they were; they replied "Nuu-chah-nulth." Cook's hearing was not good that day, perhaps after spending so many weeks with the sea wind trumpeting in his ears. He thought he heard "Nootka," and the misnomer stuck.

An Abundance of Riches

Unlike many other North American First Peoples, the inhabitants of the West Coast had an overabundance of food. It would be hard to imagine any place on earth where the sea provided greater bounty. They ate herring and halibut, cod, oolichan, clams, abalone, crabs, mussels, seals, porpoises, and sea lions. Salmon was the dietary mainstay of many if not most communities, but George Woodcock notes that shellfish was the true staple of some coastal diets because it was a reliable source of protein through those months when the salmon were not around, and the small mountains of shells discovered on the outskirts of villages support this idea. The people also ate the whales brought ashore by the warrior hunters. One of their hunting methods was to drive harpoons by hand into the animal's flank. The harpoon was attached by rope to an air-filled buoy made from animal skins. The buoy would force the whale to surface, where the hunters would keep wounding it until it died.

Aside from whale hunting, satisfying life's basic needs required relatively little time and energy, and so the people had plenty of time for religious observance and for art and arguing. Cultural activities and community politics were important components of this comfortable life.

Rank and privilege were strongly emphasized in west coast communities. The chief of a village had total command, not just over his own wealth but over anything involving the people of his village: their destiny, their art, and even their names. Totem poles made by master carvers often incorporated the family insignias with bold graphic art. The Salish people were fond of dogs, and the upper class wore clothing woven from dog fur. While important families had considerable time for sport, art, and leisure activity, commoners did not have the same privileges. They fished for salmon, while upper-class hunters pursued whales, harpooning them at sea or chasing them into sheltered beaches for the kill. The common people were better off than slaves, however. Taken in raids of other villages, slaves could be killed, sold or given away at the whim of their masters. Slaves could not marry, but slave women were occasionally taken as concubines. Otherwise, most upper-class Haida and other coastal peoples were expected to be monogamous.

Sea otter pelts were used as a form of currency in early times, and the value of other items such as canoes or slaves might be expressed in numbers of these pelts. Copper was a symbol of prestige, and anything made from copper might be displayed to show status or given away to demonstrate influence and generosity.

At the same time, potlatches redistributed wealth in a community. These ritual parties or feasts might celebrate a new memorial pole to a dead chief or commemorate a daughter's or son's coming of age. The potlatch was a form of generosity, but it was also designed to show off the sponsor's wealth and status. It involved music, dancing, and theatrical performances involving masks. A chief held a potlatch to impress people, to show off his own importance and the riches his family had accumulated. Almost anything might be given away if it garnered prestige for the giver: copper jewellery, impressive amounts of food, hand-hewn canoes, even slaves. If a nearby chief happened to hear of a significant potlatch, or if he happened to be around to receive some of the largesse, he might

"The Strike," by artist Bill Holm, 1995. (CMC, I-A-631)

become envious and try to throw a bigger, better potlatch, giving away even more wealth than his competitor. When Europeans arrived on the scene, they considered the potlatch ceremonies so bizarre that they declared them to be satanic; the British were downright frightened by the idea of nobility freely giving away their possessions. Eventually, in 1884, the government of Canada made potlatches illegal, and they weren't legalized until 1951.

Cedar trees were an important part of everything in the lives of west coast dwellers. They needed whole cedars for totem poles and dugout canoes, and they made formidable houses from cedar planks. Since matrilineal or patrilineal kinship was a integral part of the societal structure, their houses — truly giant wooden buildings — would accommodate several families. Cedar was used for fish smokehouses, dishes, and sacred ornaments. Clothing was made by weaving shredded cedar bark or dog and mountain goat wool. As Norman Newton suggests in his book, *Fire in the Raven's Nest*, Haida communities integrated their villages so fully with the natural world that they seemed to be "growing out of it."

Wild plants were allowed and even encouraged to grow in the midst of controlled spaces or incorporated in play areas for children.

The Northwest people were ceremonial. Formal group activities marked the move between summer and winter villages. Spirit dances commemorated the relationships between people and animals or other spirits of the natural world. At the Kwakiutl winter festivals, songs were created and sung for dead ancestors, and the singing was followed by feasting, partying, and ritual cleansing of the body and the spirit. The coastal people's religion was full of interplay between people and animals, and their petroglyphs attest to this interaction. Even though they killed fish and animals for food, they gave thanks to the spirits of these creatures for providing human sustenance. To dignify the sacrifice made by a fish, for example, they might return its bones to the river it came from. They believed that tricksters appear often and have powerful influence over human history. They attributed sickness to the soul's having escaped from the body or to the spirit turning against the individual. When a person died, they performed ceremonies to keep the departed soul from interfering too heavily with living people.

Shamans played a major role in the complex rituals that evolved to govern daily life. To become a shaman, a young man had to contact a supernatural entity while in a deep trance. This guardian spirit would take the shaman to the underworld, where he would be dismembered by spirits, put together again, and sent back into the world of the living. He would then be able to undergo transformation into animal form when necessary to connect himself to that older, happier state of being. While shamans were the professional keepers of the faith, other spiritually sensitive individuals with special skills believed they had received them through contact with a guardian spirit. A curious and effective memory device helped pass on ideas or past events. They used a knotted cord or rope on which each knot represented an event, story, or idea. History and other forms of knowledge could be shared by reciting the accounts represented by each knot, and each person recounting the information might enhance or embellish it.

There are many variations on the creation stories of the west coast people. One Haida version goes something like this:

In those big, stormy, grey clouds of the North Pacific lives the ruler, Shalana. He has a servant named Yealth the Raven. Raven, a bit of a meddler, is eventually booted out of the sky kingdom and dropped into the sea. Wanting to get back up into the heavens, Raven flies up and down, beating his wings against the water and pushing it up into the sky. As the water falls back down, it turns to rocks that begin to pile up below, creating the rocky backbone for Haida Gwaii, the Queen Charlotte Islands.

In need of company, Raven makes a pile of clam shells on a beach of Haida Gwaii and transforms it into two human beings, both of them women, whom he considers slaves. When they complain about being the same sex, a toss of shells changes one into a man, thus creating the first two Haida people.

Raven wants to take the female for his wife, but she isn't interested, so he flies back up into the heavens, transforming himself into a bear along the way and digging his way back into the grey cloud kingdom. While up there, he transforms himself into an eagle and steals fire from the Great Chief as well as kidnapping the chief's son. Raven then returns to earth. He drops the child into the sea, where the fish rescue him and bring him back ashore to Raven. So Raven has now brought fire to earth and also a new leader — one saved by fish and raised by Raven. The female slave agrees to live with Raven and help take care of the boy, but she and the grown boy eventually become lovers. Raven gets angry and the lovers flee, stealing Raven's sacred possessions, the fire stick and the sun. They go south and have a daughter. The original male slave meets them and wants to marry the daughter, but her father forbids the marriage. The frustrated lover takes revenge by smashing the sun into pieces on the floor. Those pieces then leap up into the sky to become sun, moon, and stars.

Next, the male slave wanders north, still trying to figure out how to attain a wife. He is sure there is one in the grey cloud kingdom for him, so he starts shooting arrows at the newly minted moon, one arrow after the next, straight into the notched tail of the one before. He does this, one each day, for 364 days, and on the following day, a full year after he began,

"The Raven and the First Men," by Haida artist Bill Reid, 1980. (MAV)

he climbs the arrow ladder up into the sky kingdom. There he is fortunate enough to see a naked woman bathing in a crystal-clear lake; he kidnaps her and returns to earth. Raven, observing this, steals the woman and punishes the man by turning him into an invisible spirit that must wander until the final days of earth.

The legacy of west coast Aboriginal stories is rich and vast, providing lessons in spirituality, psychology and models for explaining natural phenomena. A Tschimopse myth seems to relate to the El Niño cycle: it describes a man-eating monster who ravages the human world every fifteen years, bringing on sickness, famine and hardship. According to another story, tsunamis are caused by three powerful sisters who become angry on occasion and send monster waves to drown the coastline and smash canoes; sometimes they can be appeased and disaster averted by payments and sacrifices. A Haida tradition says that killer whales are drowned people returning to earth in an altered form. The appearance of a killer whale near a family home is an indication that someone there is about to die. Included among traditional Native stories are legends of people arriving from afar in boats, examples from the distant past of the apocryphal reports about sailors drifting east from China and Japan.

CHAPTER FOUR

Civilizations of the East Coast

Large Spirit and Strong Will

THERE WERE PEOPLE living in Labrador at least 9,000 years ago. The accepted notion is that they came from the west, generation after generation, a parade of nomadic peoples searching for more comfortable living arrangements and more food. There is evidence of their habitation along the Strait of Belle Isle, not far from where I turned down the offer of a Ski-Doo ride across the uncertain ice. April was probably even colder in those days, but the glaciers were retreating of their own accord to begrudgingly provide a little room for human survival. These early Maritime Archaic Indians hunted mammals from the land and sea. Some 3,000 years later, Paleoeskimos moved down from the Arctic and replaced them.

About 2,500 years ago, however, the Paleoeskimos had been displaced by their descendants, the gentle Dorset people. They had the run of Labrador until the Thule people, the forebears of today's Inuit, and the Innu moved into the rich hunting grounds half a millennium later. The Innu were related to other North American Aboriginals, and there were two groups, the Montagnais and the Naskapi. Both were hunters. Along the coasts, they pursued walrus, seal, bear, caribou, beaver, and various kinds of birds, and they supplemented their diet with the plentiful fish and berries. They used bows and arrows and spears tipped with sharpened bones. Like many North American First Peoples, they believed in the spirits of the land, the sea, the sky, and the creatures around them. They danced and sang before the hunt to communicate with these spirits. The Innu families lived reasonably well off the land until the Europeans began their clumsy and often hostile intrusions.

The Inuit, the descendants of the Thule people who had migrated east from distant Alaska, lived further north than the Innu. They had much in common with other arctic peoples, including the roots of their language. In the summer, they moved inland to camp and feast on caribou steaks over an open fire, with wild berries for dessert. By fall, though, the Inuit returned to the coast to hunt seals and to fish for char, salmon, and cod. In their kayaks, they also chased and killed Greenland (bowhead) whales. Walrus, polar bears, and puffins were the main prey for winter hunting.

Although food was plentiful, life was never easy. Doing battle with large mammals required a large spirit and strong will. But it also required a great degree of patience. An extended trip for seal or walrus called for the construction of a temporary ice igloo. Trying to catch a seal in winter meant long hours sitting by a round hole cut in the ice, luring and then spearing the creature. Back in the comfort of the family home of sod and animal skins, an Inuit hunter would tell the story of his adventures at night by the light of an efficient lamp, complete with a wick, that burned seal oil.

The People of Red Ochre

The first humans to live in Newfoundland are known today as Maritime Archaic Indians, and the oldest evidence of their presence appears to date from about 7,500 years ago. Like the Maritime Archaic Indians of Labrador, these people were superseded by the Dorset and then by the ill-fated Beothuk, descended from ancestors who had migrated north.

The Beothuk understood the use of the basic elements around them, making spears and tools from chipped stones (chert). In the summers, they lived in small villages of no more than fifty people along the north and south coasts of Newfoundland. Using canoes carefully crafted to withstand journeys out onto the open sea, they fished, harpooned seals, whales, and porpoises, or hunted sea birds. A favoured food was the eggs of the flightless auk, and, in order to gather them, brave men would paddle canoes to the Funk Islands, nearly sixty kilometres from shore.

At the close of summer, the Beothuk built fresh-water canoes and travelled inland to hunt the migrating caribou. They created ingenious fences to funnel entire herds into narrow passages, where they could easily slaughter as many animals as they wished. Since land and sea provided them with sufficient food, the Beothuk did not practice any form of agriculture, although, not relying wholly on the vagaries of the hunt, they preserved meat by smoking it.

The Beothuk carved bones and antlers for jewellery and art objects. They used a powdered form of the mineral hematite to make a red paste, known as red ochre, which they used to paint both their canoes and their skin. As Kevin Major notes, "For the newly born the ceremony was an initiation, for the older a renewal of their identity as part of the land that sustained them. With this same red ochre they covered their dead." It was this red colouring that led early explorers to refer to them (and ultimately all North American Natives) as "Red Indians."

Their homes, called *mamateeks*, were made of deer skin or birch bark. Some were as large as six metres across, and a dozen or so people could live inside. Summer homes were light in construction, covered with animal skins or thin layers of bark, but winter homes were more substantial, sometimes formed around upright tree trunks, built into the sides of hills, or dug at least partially into the ground. The cone-shaped top structure consisted of several layers of bark or skins.

Chiefs rose to power in the small villages through their hunting prowess, and occasionally, when hunting paths crossed, different bands of Beothuk would hold a council and talk the politics of canoes, fur trading and food. Like the Innu, they had ceremonies to consort with the animal spirits that sustained their culture.

Although their numbers were never great — some say fewer than 1,000 — the Beothuk had fashioned a means to live a relatively comfortable life in a harsh environment. Eventually, the colonizers drove them from the shores, hunted them down, and took the last few individuals prisoner; the last Beothuk, a woman named Shanawdithit, died of consumption in 1829. All that may be seen today of the Beothuk people are their coastal burial sites in caves and rock structures, two of the most prominent being at Port au Choix and Notre Dame.

The Mi'kmaq and Maliseet

The Mi'kmaq probably first settled in Nova Scotia 10,000 years ago, after their restless ancestors had migrated eastward from their Asian origins for many generations. Dan Paul, a contemporary Mi'kmaw historian,

*This Mi'kmaw petroglyph at George's Lake, Kejimikujik National Park, Nova
Scotia, seems to show couples dancing around a central hand.* (PC)

reports that Mi'kmaw culture became highly organized, with a fairly
sophisticated legal system, a democratic political process system, and
social practices that placed high value on cooperation and sharing. Leaders
were chosen based on their knowledge, their hunting and fishing skills,
and to some degree, their social skills. At the core of community life was
a pantheistic religion, a personal and spiritual connection to the earth
and everything upon it, from rocks and trees to fish and geese. It was a
generally monogamous culture, although polygamy was permitted and
the attitudes toward sex were quite liberal. In the early days of European
settlement, Chrestien LeClercq reported that the Mi'kmaq were very
emotional people and that their society had a high degree of dedication
to family and community.

Characteristically, Mi'kmaw villages of fifty to 500 people developed near an inlet, bay, or river, and most people lived in coastal settlements. There were seven clearly defined Mi'kmaw districts along the coasts of the Maritimes and the Gaspé Peninsula; pre-contact Mi'kmaw sites have been located in Nova Scotia at Debert, Dartmouth, Yarmouth, and Amherst, and at Souris in Prince Edward Island. The huge complex of sites at Red Bank, New Brunswick, reveals that Mi'kmaq have lived near the mouth of the Miramichi River, where the fresh and salt water meet, for nearly 3,000 years.

Although the villages were located along the Atlantic shores, families migrated inland in the winter to avoid the harsh weather. In spring and summer, they ate mainly salmon, trout, cod, lobster, and clams, and they used harpoons to kill seals as well. The retreat to the winter forest meant a change in hunting tactics and a change in diet. Moose, caribou, and smaller mammals then became the most common foods. The early European visitors were quite confounded by the Mi'kmaw diet. According to Nicholas Denys, "They often ate fish, especially seals to obtain the oil, as much for greasing themselves as for drinking; and ate of the whale which frequently came ashore on the coast, especially the blubber on which they made good cheer." Apparently this fare kept the Mi'kmaq in good health; according to ethnologist Ruth Holmes Whitehead, they commonly lived to be more than a hundred years old.

The Mi'kmaq were excellent builders of canoes, nimble craft for use on inland lakes, rivers, and streams, as well as large, seaworthy vessels. So sturdy were their ocean-going canoes that in 1659, Father Charles Lalement wrote, "Savage Mariners navigate so far in little shallops, crossing vast seas without a compass, and often without sight of the sun." Mi'kmaw canoeists were indeed quite capable of navigation out of sight of land. On occasion they travelled from the shore of Nova Scotia all the way to Newfoundland. Beginning around the end of the sixteenth century, they began to share Newfoundland with the Beothuk, enjoying the riches of life on Newfoundland's south coast.

Although the arrival of Europeans and the long string of treaties that followed would steal the land and the livelihood from the Mi'kmaq, they would always hold onto a powerful, intimate connection to the land and to the sea.

Malti Pictou, Jerry Lonecloud, and John McEwan, all noted guides, pose with a woman and a child in front of a Mi'kmaw wigwam, Bear River, Nova Scotia, about 1900. The canoe has the typical shape of Mi'kmaw vessels. (NSM 97.31)

The heritage of New Brunswick's Maliseet is similar to that of the Mi'kmaq. The Maliseet live west and south of the Mi'kmaq. Many of the ancient Maliseet communities, sustained by their hunters and fishers, were on or near the shores of the Bay of Fundy and along the St. John River. Their own name for themselves is *Welustuk*, "People of the beautiful river."

There is little evidence of hostility between Mi'kmaq and Maliseet, nor between the Maliseet and the Pasamaquoddy, who live along the southern Fundy coast. The same cannot be said of the Mohawk, who lived to the north and west. The Mohawk, a more warlike people, sometimes invaded Maliseet and Mi'kmaq territory, terrorizing villages.

The rivers of what is modern-day New Brunswick opened up the interior of the province to Europeans, who found their way from the shores of the Fundy and the Gulf. The newcomers relied on information from Mi'kmaq and Maliseet who had canoed the rivers and portaged the lakes for centuries by the time the French and English arrived. The interior was laced with highly navigable water highways, all leading to and from the coast.

CHAPTER FIVE

From Across the Atlantic

Of Saints and Sailors

THE MOST INTERESTING of the European explorers from the distant past is probably St. Brendan of Ireland. Towards the end of the fifth century, maps began to include a land called St. Brendan's Isle, far away from Europe out in the Atlantic Ocean. St. Brendan's Isle looks hauntingly like Nova Scotia. St. Brendan is said to have set out from Ireland on a quest for a peaceful place to live, but he failed several times before finding his desired refuge. In the twelfth-century version of the story, Brendan sails with thirty men to live in his new-found paradise. An angel leads the way, but on the journey Brendan has to fend off sea monsters, whales, mermaids, and even semi-human devils. He fails in his first attempt to find the island, and he concludes that the reason for his failure is that his boat is made from the skins of animals his men have killed. So he returns home, builds a wooden boat, and sets off again with sixty men, encountering more sea monsters as well as pygmy demons on the voyage. At last he arrives at an island where one lone Irishman lives, the survivor of a shipwreck. This castaway directs Brendan further on, and he arrives in a land where a man wearing white feathers greets him. We'll never know for sure, of course, if St. Brendan's journey represents a dream, a legend, or a somewhat embroidered version of actual events. Did Brendan arrive in heaven, in Cape Breton, or in some earthly paradise combining the two?

Around 780, another Irishman by the name of Bran has a dream about beautiful women that sends him and his friends off in three ships made from animal skins — curraghs. Sure enough, he finds the place that he calls "The Land of Women." He is captured by the queen and held hostage. When he finally escapes and returns to Ireland, he discovers that he's been in some kind of time warp, and centuries have passed. When one of his crewmen steps on Irish soil and dissolves into nothing, Bran takes a hint, returns to the sea, and is never heard from again.

We may never know for sure who were the first Europeans to find their way to the New World. In 871, Norse sailors who landed on the shores of Iceland found an Irish monk there along with other Irish settlers. The belligerent Scandinavians drove the Irish away toward Greenland and maybe even as far south as the shores of the Gulf of St. Lawrence. And then there's the ninth-century story of the Icelandic merchant Gudleifr Gunnlaugsson. Storms drove his ship far across the Atlantic, where he was supposedly captured by people with dark skin. They debated amongst themselves whether the foreigner was dangerous and if he should perhaps be put to death, but Gunnlaugsson was apparently saved by a local white man, who came to his rescue and sent him back on his way to Iceland.

Archaeologists poking around on Baffin Island in 1978 uncovered a wooden carving they believe to be European in origin. The figurine, possibly dating back to the ninth or tenth century, is one of a number of fragments of evidence suggesting that the far reaches of the North American Arctic were visited before the Vikings found their way to these shores. In his 1998 book *The Farfarers*, Farley Mowat pulls together some convincing threads of a story that shows how sailors from the Shetland and Orkney Islands could have travelled far to the west to hunt walrus and to get clear of the belligerent Norse raiders. Mowat contends that they made a home around St. George's Bay in Newfoundland in the tenth century and travelled yet further to the north and west to hunt and live on Baffin Island. Known as the Albans, these hardy sailing and hunting people left ruins of their homesteads in the western Arctic — stone houses that used their overturned ships for winter roofing. With these intriguing possibilities, Mowat reminds us that history must continually be rewritten as new information shreds our over-confident, even smug understanding of the past.

Blood on the Shoreline

Norse explorers were a brave and proud but obsessively violent people who ventured west across the cold seas looking for new lands to inhabit and unknown villages to raid. Their sagas tell of voyages to a place known as "Vinland the Good," a land perhaps as far south as Massachusetts or as far north as the coast of Labrador. The name "Vinland" refers, not to a land of vines, but simply to a land of grass. In northern Newfoundland, in the grassy fields now called L'Anse aux Meadows, archaeologists have uncovered evidence of Norse homes inhabited by women as well as by men.

The ancient stories tell of encounters with "Skraelings," Native people who may have been Inuit, Beothuk, Mi'kmaq, or some other group. The Norse considered the Skraelings hostile and dangerous, but the Norsemen themselves were anything but amiable tourists. They were easily aggravated, aggressive, and often made enemies, and the Skraelings probably recognized their imminent danger and defended themselves.

Written in the fourteenth and fifteenth centuries, the Icelandic sagas are full of half-truths, exaggeration, and even contradiction. Nonetheless, the Vikings certainly came this way; they settled, they fought, and they died or retreated. A northern people, turbulent but resilient, they differed from other Europeans who would follow; they were probably better prepared, both physically and psychologically, for what awaited them on the coast of North America. The harsh environment was not their worst adversary. Their greatest enemy was their own fiery temperament and the feuds it caused.

Sometime after 986, Erik the Red left Iceland to create a settlement in Greenland, where his two sons, Leif and Thorstein, lived. In that same decade, another Norse sailor, Bjarni Herjulfson, was blown far off course and sighted some wooded land that could have been Newfoundland, Labrador, or Nova Scotia. Bjarni sold a ship to Leif Eriksson, and Leif set off to find this place that Bjarni had sighted. He went north and saw glaciers, and then sailed south, where he saw the forested coast (this time most likely Labrador) and, further along, Vinland. Leif spent the winter there at L'Anse aux Mead-ows and headed back to Greenland in the spring. On the way back, he rescued fifteen men who had been shipwrecked on a reef.

Leif was held in high esteem as a result of his forays into the unknown. One of his brothers followed in his footsteps and was reportedly killed by

The western half of a map of Vinland, showing the lands visited by Leif Eriksson and a companion and later by Bishop Eric (Henricus) of Greenland. The map is said to date from 1440. (YU)

the Skraelings. His brother Thorstein set off in 1008 for Vinland but was driven back by bad weather.

In 1013, two brothers, Helgi and Finnbogi, were preparing to sail for Vinland when Erik the Red's illegitimate daughter, Freydis, proposed that they all sail their ships together. Freydis would move into the house left behind by Leif in Vinland. Apparently the two brothers arrived first and moved into Leif's old abode, but when Freydis arrived, she gave them the boot. They moved out, but there were hard feelings. A domineering woman, Freydis had her husband gather their men and fight for a ship that the brothers had refused to sell her. The men succeeded in killing Helgi, Finnbogi, and their crews, but they spared their women. Dissatisfied with this arrangement, Freydis took an axe and slaughtered the women herself. Eventually, after all this bloodshed, Freydis and her crowd returned to Greenland, where half-brother Leif eventually found out what had transpired. He cursed Freydis and her progeny with bad luck thenceforth. And so ends the ignoble and gruesome tale of early Europeans' first attempts to "civilize" Atlantic Canada.

The next recorded voyage occurred in 1020, when Thorfinn Karlsefni left Iceland with 160 men and women, a migration of such commitment that it even included livestock. Retracing Leif's voyage, Karlsefni sailed to Greenland and beyond to a place they called Bear Island, intending to populate the new land. They endured a hard first winter, with poor fishing, and so they moved southward to another location, where they found wild animals and abundant offshore fish. A second winter passed. Then, according to the saga, a large party of Native people arrived to trade with them. Things were going well until one of Karlsefni's bulls ran out of the woods and scared the Skraelings, who fled but returned later in great numbers to fight the Norse settlers. The village survived the battle, but apparently Karlsefni decided that they would be better off to return home.

There's a good chance the Vikings found their way to Nova Scotia as well. The so-called Yarmouth Stone, discovered in a field near that town, seems to bear a message in ancient Icelandic that researcher Henry Phillips deciphers as "Harkussen men varu," meaning "Harko's son addressed the men"; Harko reportedly travelled with Karlsefni. In 1939, Olaf Strandwold translated the message as "Leivur Eriku Resr," or "Leif to Erik raises," a record of praise from Leif Eriksson to his father. A critic, however, describes Strandwold as a man "able to find runes in any crevice or groove and decipher them." Others believe the markings are not Norse at all but more likely of Mi'kmaq origin.

Whalers and Princes

Basque whalers and fishermen travelled to the Grand Banks and the coast of Newfoundland as early as 1199. By the thirteenth and fourteenth centuries, the Basque people had created a monopoly on whaling and had thinned the herds off the coast of Europe. Thus they were forced to travel more often to the waters off Nova Scotia and Newfoundland for

Ruins at L'Anse aux Meadows. (PC, 39900001)

their prey. Basque sailors were tough, stalwart men, willing to put up with great discomforts as they crossed the Atlantic in primitive boats. Port-aux-Basques, in the southwest corner of Newfoundland, is named for these early whalers. Here they prepared whale flesh for the journey home and dried and salted their catch of cod; indeed, they called Newfoundland "Ile de Bacaillau," Island of Cod. The season over, they returned home aboard ships that had no real sleeping quarters and little in the way of protection from the elements. On board, they faced the cold, pelting storms of rain and ice amid the pervasive smell of salted fish and the stench of deteriorating whale blubber.

Two European princes with colourful careers may have visited Canada's Atlantic coast well before Columbus crossed the Atlantic. Prince Madoc, who lived in Wales in the twelfth century, is reported to have travelled all the way to the coast of Nova Scotia and on down to Mexico before returning home to bring colonists back to the new world he had found. Some American colonists later claimed they encountered Indians who spoke Welsh — conceivably the descendants of Prince Madoc and his people — although the evidence is slim at best.

The COASTS *of* CANADA

Another prince, Henry Sinclair, was the son of Isabella, Countess of Orkney, and Sir William Sinclair, who was killed in an attempt to take Robert the Bruce's heart to the Holy Land. As a young man, Prince Henry dreamed of sailing across the Atlantic. In 1398, he heard a story about a fisherman who disappeared far to the west and then returned home after twenty-five years to tell tales about plentiful fish near a land inhabited by people he claimed to be cannibals. With little fear of cannibals, Sinclair and a loyal crew set sail for the west and discovered an island they called Estoilanda. Here he met an Icelander who informed him and his men of yet another island called Icaria, ruled by an Irish king. When Henry and his men arrived in Icaria, they became involved in some kind of a scuffle with the Native people and were forced to move on. Further along the coast, they spotted smoke on a hillside, and the men explored what was probably the northern shores of Nova Scotia. They reported that the smoke came from the burning of a pitch-like substance bubbling up in local springs. The inhabitants lived in caves and were considered to be friendly, although somewhat shy. Several of Sinclair's men stayed on, while others returned home. Some writers, such as Frederick J. Pohl and Michael Bradley, believe that Henry Sinclair was a member of the Knights Templar, a society that claimed to have inherited the Holy Grail, the cup used by Christ at the Last Supper. This society had been suppressed since 1312, and these writers believe that a desire to find refuge from persecution motivated Henry's voyages to the New World. Some go so far as to suggest that Sinclair brought the Grail to Nova Scotia, where he hoped to found a new society — a New Jerusalem — and where the Grail may remain.

"Christopher Columbus," by Johannes Strandanus. (MM, PAF7099)

CHAPTER SIX

The Northern Coast of the New World

Prima Terra Vista

THE LEGACY OF Christopher Columbus is well known. Although twentieth-century revisionists have tarnished his achievements, his explorations permitted an enormous increase in European knowledge about the western shores of the Atlantic, including knowledge of Canada's east coast. The son of a Spanish-Jewish weaver living in Genoa, Columbus schooled himself on the seas as a pirate. When he survived a shipwreck off the coast of Portugal, he became convinced that he was destined for some great discovery. As every schoolchild now knows, he believed he could reach the Orient by travelling west. He had ventured as far north and west into the Atlantic as Iceland, and it is reasonable to believe that, had his political alliances been more northerly, his ambitions might have found favour in the English court. Perhaps then he would have advanced even further along a North Atlantic route.

Instead, Columbus pledged his loyalty to Spain. In his extensive voyages to the South Atlantic, he found what he believed to be evidence of westerly lands: floating pieces of large cane plants and the trunks of pine and other trees. After jumping through a long sequence of bureaucratic hoops in Spain, Columbus convinced the Holy Brotherhood to put up some funds, and he borrowed money as well. This backing enabled him to set off across the ocean by a route that was much longer than the fairly well-travelled path from continental Europe by way of Iceland to the Atlantic's western shores.

Columbus made four voyages in all, putting Spain well on its way to finding the long-sought trade route to China and its wealth of spices and precious metals. As well, he saw himself as an evangelist intent on bringing Christianity to the heathens he encountered. Like so many explorers who followed him, though, he saw everything new as a potential commodity, including the many Caribbean people whom he enslaved. King Ferdinand and Queen Isabella of Spain appointed him Viceroy of the Indies, but Columbus turned out to be such a poor leader that they eventually revoked his title.

The French became envious of the Spanish and more than a little worried about their looming access to China. King Francis I enlisted another Italian, Giovanni da Verrazano, to lead an expedition west from Rouen in 1524. Verrazano reached the Outer Banks of North Carolina, and beyond this thin sliver of land, he saw another wide body of water, probably Pamlico Sound. He believed Asia to be on the other side of that. The Natives he met were friendly. Instead of exploring further to the west, which would have resulted in the disappointment of not finding the route to Asia, he sailed north, the first European to describe what is now New York harbour and the Hudson River. Verrazano continued north to Maine and skirted the coast of Nova Scotia, then sailed on past Newfoundland. His was the most extensive survey of the coast to date, and it laid the groundwork for the French to claim a massive chunk of North America.

Like Columbus, John Cabot was born in Genoa. He arrived in England between 1484 and 1490 and settled in the port of Bristol. There he nursed his ambition to sail westward to parts unknown. Stormy weather terminated his first voyage to the New World in 1496, but he was not overly discouraged. Cabot was an optimist, an adventurer, an excellent navigator, and a man with a head for business. By the time he set off on a second foray to the New World, King Henry VII had given him permission to claim and become governor of whatever new territory he found, as long as he paid one-fifth of all profits to the Crown. No one else would even be allowed to visit these projected new-found lands without Cabot's consent. Like Columbus, Cabot believed he was headed toward Asia, where he expected to find spices, jewels, and all manner of riches. The *Matthew*, a fairly small ship called a navicula, had a crew of eighteen, including Cabot's thirteen-year-old son, Sebastian. Off the coast of Newfoundland, Cabot saw vast quantities of fish. Although he didn't fully recognize it, here was the wealth he was looking for. In June of 1497, he and his party landed on unknown shores and found evidence of tools used for trapping animals and fishing. Today, both Newfoundland and Nova Scotia claim to be the site of Cabot's landing, and monuments erected in both provinces assert his presence. No matter which claim is true, Cabot had arrived in a new world, and his trip set in motion English land claims that lasted for centuries.

It is estimated that Cabot's Atlantic crossing took fifty-five days, the *Matthew* sometimes sailing at a speed of only 2.5 kilometres per hour. Cabot's son, Sebastian, created a map of the coastline they discovered. He describes the section he labelled *Prima Terra Vista* as being "very sterile," yet also recording, "There are in it many white bears, and very large stags like horses, and many other animals. And like in manner there are immense quantities of fish — soles, salmon, very large cods, and many other kinds of fish."

On the voyage back to England, John Cabot gave away an island to a friend from Burgundy and another piece of land to a barber-surgeon from Genoa. Once back in England, he was rewarded with an admiralty and a pension of twenty pounds per year, a whopping sum at the time. Richard Hakluyt, in his *Divers Voyages*, claims that Cabot brought three Aboriginal people back to England. It is unclear whether they were guests or prisoners, but the chronicler reports that "these were clothed in the beast skinnes, and ate raw flesh, and spake such speech that no man coulde understand them, and in their demeanor like to bruite beasts, whom the king kept a time after."

In 1498, John Cabot left Bristol again to visit the land he supposedly ruled. He took five ships this time, although terrible weather drove at least one of them back to Ireland. Cabot himself continued, sailing past icebergs before turning south in July into excellent sunny weather. On the Grand Banks, he again encountered vast quantities of fish. There is some uncertainty about whether Cabot returned to England; having failed to find a route to the riches of Asia, he may have fallen into some disgrace. Even so, as a result of his journeys, maps surfaced in England and Spain showing a fairly detailed coastline from Cape Breton to Long Island. There was no great enthusiasm for racing off to this unfamiliar territory, and it would be a while before other adventurers found their way to the West. Nonetheless, Cabot piqued the formerly dormant English interest in the new territory and its land and sea resources.

The Elusive Waterway

The Portuguese had a head start on exploring the northerly coasts. King Manuel I sent Gaspar Corte-Real looking for the Northwest Passage, and in 1500 he stopped in Greenland, claiming to discover land already familiar to Aboriginals and Vikings. He might have nicked the North American coast as well, perhaps setting foot on the bald rocks of Newfoundland. On a second voyage the following year, with his brother, Miguel, Gaspar explored more extensively and sent his brother home with reports about the coastline. Gaspar, however, was never heard from again, and later, when Miguel went back to look for him, he, too, was lost.

Disappearing sibling explorers may have suggested to the Portuguese that they'd have better luck snooping around towards the south, and the nobility concluded that such forbidding territory in the north probably wasn't worth the investment of money and time. While the potentates gave up on claiming and exploring the northwest coast of the Atlantic, maps resulting from the Corte-Real adventures show the coast of Labrador and capes Bonavista, Spear, and Race in Newfoundland.

Jacques Cartier, too, sought the elusive avenue to Asia that might lead him to gold, spices, and wealth. He left the Brittany port of Saint-Malo in April of 1534 with two ships and sixty-one men, and they sailed to Labrador and then down the Strait of Belle Isle and around Anticosti Island. On the first day of July, 1534, the Mi'kmaq of what would be Prince Edward Island probably had their first glimpse of white-skinned people: Jacques Cartier and some of his men coming ashore in longboats to stretch their legs. The locals, as if they had some intuition that this was the beginning of a very long streak of bad luck, left the beach and didn't hang around for cordiality. They had a good life on their island of Abegweit, and they probably hoped that the bearded strangers would turn around and sail away — which they did. But, of course, they did not stay away.

Cartier received a warmer reception from the Mi'kmaq on the Bay of Chaleur. On the Gaspé Peninsula, he met an Iroquois band led by Chief Donnacona, and he took two of the chief's sons aboard his ship. Conflicting reports suggest that he either persuaded Donnacona to send his sons along with him or simply kidnapped them to show off upon his return to France that September.

The famous portrait of Jacques Cartier, painted in 1860 by Théophile Hamel, which is probably more imaginary than documentary. (NAC, C-011226)

The next year, Cartier set off again with three ships, 110 men, and the two Iroquois. He went as far as Donnacona's home village (now the site of Quebec City). From here, with the help of Iroquois guides, he ventured further up the St. Lawrence until he struck the rapids near the island of Montreal, a sad indication that this was not the ultimate waterway to the untold wealth of Asia. During the ensuing winter, twenty-five men died of scurvy; those who lived were cured thanks to the Iroquois, who taught them to make a medicinal tea from tree bark.

In the spring, when conditions for travelling improved, Cartier prepared to return to France. He repaid Donnacona's hospitality by abducting him and nine others, including four children, and took them back to France. Donnacona continued his service to his betrayer by telling him of a land further west, "where there are immense quantities of gold, rubies, and other rich things." Cartier persuaded Donnacona to tell this to the French monarch, and thus he fanned even higher hopes of riches to be found in the new land.

On this second return voyage to France in 1536, Cartier made a curious diversion as he was sailing homeward out of the Gulf of St. Lawrence. East of the Magdalen Islands, he noticed the striking mountainous coastline of Cape Breton. He sailed south and then north in a sort of hairpin turn to take a better look at the coast from Inverness to Cape North. But that was probably as close as he came to Nova Scotia. Having already made his way up the St. Lawrence, he was much more interested in what he had found there, and he was anxious to return to France with his observations, his disappointed expectations, and his cargo. Cartier's expeditions whetted the political and expeditionary appetites that would lead France into a power struggle for North American lands, a struggle that continued for well over two centuries.

In 1541, Cartier set off from France a third time, now under the command of Jean-François de La Rocque, Sieur de Roberval. Cartier's ships arrived at Quebec before Roberval's. He told the Iroquois that Donnacona had died but that the other captives were living like princes in Paris; in truth, most of the abducted Natives had died. Cartier went as far as Montreal once more but went no further, failing to realize that, once past the rapids, he could have continued into the immense lakes and waterways in the heart of the continent.

Cartier suffered through another bad winter and provoked the Iroquois to outright hostility. He was convinced, however, that he had discovered gold and diamonds, and he was returning to France in the spring with evidence when he met Roberval's ships along the Newfoundland coast. Roberval ordered him to return to Quebec, but Cartier slipped off in the night and headed for France. At home, he proved himself a fool: the riches he had brought back turned out to be merely quartz and iron pyrite instead of diamonds and gold. Roberval spent a chilly winter in Quebec before returning to France, and Cartier eventually retired to a quiet life in Saint-Malo. King Francis saw the whole business as a failure, but later voyagers profited greatly from Cartier's knowledge of the St. Lawrence River, the greatest inland extension of the Atlantic coast.

Love in a Cold Climate

The hardy Basque whaling men slaughtered whales for their precious oil along the Labrador coast in the 1500s, and as early as 1540, they had settled into a quasi-permanent year-round station at Red Bay. Whaling had become big business, with nearly two dozen ships sailing out of Red Bay and two thousand workers employed on ships or processing the catch on land. The men harpooned the whales from small craft, a fearsome job; if an offended whale capsized a boat, the icy waters were most unforgiving. On shore, the work was less deadly but certainly unpleasant. Men cut the fat off the giant carcasses, boiled it, and extracted the valuable oil. Funnelled into barrels and shipped off to Europe, the whale oil made a handsome profit for the financial backers and merchants collaborating in this complex industry.

The Portuguese, Spanish, Basque, English, and French had all come to fish the waters around Newfoundland and stopped ashore for supplies or to settle for a few months to dry fish in the begrudging sun of summer. Sometimes St. John's or another harbour was just a stopover for supplies on the way to another destination. Roberval, however, had other uses for Newfoundland. While Jacques Cartier was leaving Quebec and heading home in 1542, Roberval was guiding his own shipload of French immigrants to the colony he was trying to set up on the lower St. Lawrence River. Roberval's niece, Marguerite, was on board and destined to marry a man she did not love. Instead, she fell for one of the lowly sailors aboard Roberval's ship. Her uncle savagely punished anyone who did not follow his orders. He put her ashore on an island — Fogo, perhaps, or some other inhospitable rock — with her nurse as her only companion. Her sailor lover escaped from the cruel captain to be with her; he died a few short months afterwards, but not before he had made Marguerite pregnant. The baby died, too, on that hostile, lonely island, and so did the nurse. Marguerite spent a lonely and terrifying year there before the smoke from her fire was spotted from a passing French ship and the generous captain returned her to France.

Roberval's colony, which he ruled through brutal punishment for even trifling offences, lasted only a few months. The demoralized survivors of that experiment returned to France with tales about the their leader and the winter weather that were horrific enough to deter the French from settling the northern coastline of the New World for well over half a century.

"The last voyage of Henry Hudson," after a painting by John Collier. (NAC, C-2061)

CHAPTER SEVEN

In Pursuit of the Northwest Passage

The Gold of Meta Incognita

MARTIN FROBISHER and I have at least two things in common. We both felt like explorers when we came to what is now Canada, and we both found some shiny rocks that we thought would make us rich. When I immigrated to the Eastern Shore of Nova Scotia in 1978, I began to dig a well behind our old farmhouse, chipping away at loose stones and bedrock with a pickaxe until my hands bled. I had abandoned the suburbs for the good, humble life in the wilderness. When my pickaxe suddenly revealed a large, sparkling array of gold chunks embedded in the slate, I was sure I had inadvertently discovered gold.

Since I had moved "back to the land" to avoid money and material things, this bonanza posed an entirely new set of ethical problems. Fortunately, before I had wrestled too strenuously with my moral dilemma, I learned that I had discovered, not gold, but iron pyrite. Blissful voluntary poverty would be mine for at least a few years more. Martin Frobisher and his English backers of the sixteenth century were not quite so relieved, however, when they learned that "all that glittered" in the wilds of the New World was not gold.

When he was only fourteen, Frobisher barely survived an expedition to West Africa that whetted his appetite for danger and adventure. Joining what passed for the navy, he became a bloodthirsty "sea dog," rampaging the oceans against any vessel thought to be unfriendly to his queen. A true Elizabethan adventurer, he was as skilled at plundering as he was at following his nose into distant and unfamiliar territory.

Like his more sedentary but equally rapacious backers, Frobisher hoped to find a route to China that was quicker than the long, tedious plough around Africa used by England's enemies, the Spanish. In June

Cornelis de Jode's 1593 map showing the Northwest Passage as an obvious and easily navigable channel along the north shore of North America. (NLC, NMC 6579)

of 1576, he braved icy storms on a voyage that led him as far west and north as Baffin Island.

It was August 1576, when Frobisher and a few of his men rowed ashore. Blind faith in the dream of the Northwest Passage prevailed: he climbed a hill and thought he was looking out over the rugged coast of some part of Asia; to the west, he was sure he saw Cathay — China. He made contact with some Inuit living in the area, and, much to everyone's greedy delight, one of his men found gold — or at least a rock that looked as if it contained gold.

On the hike back to the shoreline, Frobisher exchanged cursory salutations with some local Inuit. The ship's master, Christopher Hall, went ashore again later, gave them some gifts, and even lured a few aboard the *Gabriel.* The trading had begun: animal skins for "belles, looking glasses, and other toyes." One brave Inuit hunter even agreed to sail on the vessel far enough to guide it through the tricky passages ahead. Five sailors rowed him home to prepare for the journey, and that's when something went wrong. Nobody knows what happened — maybe the sailors offended

Gerard Mercator's 1595 map shows the North Pole as a magnetic rock around which the oceans of the world drain back into the centre of the earth. (NAC, NMC 16097)

the Inuit in some grave way. In any case, the men did not return to the ship. Believing they were being held hostage, Frobisher proceeded to take his own hostage. The intended Inuit guide, who was still seated in his kayak, was snatched aboard ship. Frobisher hoped that another shore dweller would come out to strike a deal so he could get his men back, but he had no such luck. His sailors were "tyred and sik with laboure of their hard voyage." It was late August, and Frobisher felt it was too much of a gamble to hang around longer or to proceed further west. Instead, he decided to take his Inuit captive and his "gold" back as a present to Queen Elizabeth.

Frobisher had the opportunity to tell the Queen personally about his discoveries. Bolstered by Frobisher's optimism, she dubbed the new territory "Meta Incognita," the unknown goal, as if to imply that maybe it wasn't the route to Cathay after all but someplace of value in its own right — which it would be if indeed it had a vast storehouse of gold on its shores. In England, Frobisher was a bit of a hero. As far as everyone was concerned, he *had* probably discovered the beginning of a new route to China, and cartographers began to revise their maps to accommodate the hypothesis.

However, the idea of searching for the Northwest Passage dimmed in light of the riches at hand; Frobisher's next trip was to mine the rock. In 1577, he sailed to Baffin Island with 120 men, five of whom were miners. These unlucky men chipped away 200 tonnes of the New World, and it was promptly shipped back to England.

The English assayers may have been either dead wrong or puzzled or outright liars, but it seems that no one came right out and said that a whole lot of time, trouble, and expense had gone into hauling worthless rock. Frobisher returned again to the North in 1758, driven there by the ambitious and costly illusion that he had found a whole continent of gold. It all seemed too good to be true, and, of course, it was just that. This time, a hefty 2,000 tonnes of rock containing no gold whatsoever was loaded aboard ships. Frobisher did a little more venturing around Hudson Strait, but it was the big load of fake gold that held his interest. For his trouble, he received a stone-tipped arrow in the buttocks. Inuit hunters were provoked, no doubt, not only by the foreign men who liked to scar the earth to rob it of shiny rocks, but also by the insufferable arrogance that defined their leader. Nearly 300 years later, in 1861, archaeologist Charles Hall travelled north to find the remains of a building Frobisher's men had erected. He discovered that the Native people in the area told stories about the ill-mannered Englishman's visit as if it had happened just last week.

The Warm and Fertile North

In Elizabethan times, geographers and other creative thinkers liked to speculate about what was at the top of the world. One favoured theory suggested that all channels between northerly islands led to a massive whirlpool at the North Pole, at the centre of which sat a huge dark magnetic rock. A vortex sucked the water from the channels down into the planet, a thought guaranteed to terrify arctic explorers: not only might they freeze to death or get chewed up by a polar bear, they might get sucked — ship and all — right down to the centre of the earth. George Best, a writer of sorts who had travelled north with Frobisher, had an overwhelming desire to be published, and, in 1578, he had his opportunity. With some conviction, he wrote that there were just four great arctic islands north of mainland America, and that the channels between them "runneth in headlong bye that deepe swallowing sincke, into the bowels of the earth."

Europeans at that time had latched onto the delightful thought that they were taller than the other peoples of the world, and Best claimed that one of those northerly islands was inhabited by pygmies. Equally removed from reality was his claim that one island was warm and fertile — a good place to plant crops and live comfortably year-round. Best had his day in print; his publisher sold out the print run of a book containing much more fiction than fact. But the author was right about one thing that deeply annoyed his old captain: Frobisher's voyage had taken him only through polar islands, not islands off the coast of Asia.

Some Englishmen still believed that Frobisher's pretty rocks contained gold; it was just that no one could figure out how to extract it. Frobisher had bankrupted his backer, Michael Lok, but he held onto his dignity and reputation, retired from gold digging, and, instead, accompanied the bloodthirsty Sir Francis Drake to the West Indies to sink a handsome part of the Spanish Armada and slit the throats of Spanish enemies. For this service, the Queen forgave him his gold boondoggle and knighted him for bravery. Even so, he died in 1594, at the ripe old age of fifty-five, as a result of wounds received in a battle at the Spanish fort at Crozon, France.

Sailing to Brobdingnag

In 1579, Frobisher's fighting comrade, Francis Drake, had sailed the long southerly route all the way to the west coast of the Americas; he may or may not have ventured north as far as Vancouver Island. He reportedly sailed up the picturesque coastline of Central America, feeling considerable pride over stealing jewels, gold, and silver from the Native people. Not satisfied with the glory of having liberated enough riches to make him a hero back home, he continued northward to look for the western terminus of the Northwest Passage, perhaps hoping for a shortcut back home to save himself the interminable and dangerous voyage around South America. A celebrated thief and murderer, a courageous mariner and adventurer, and a dutiful servant to his country, Drake was also something of a naive optimist. Having lost only one of his three ships on this leg of the voyage, he encountered bad weather and took shelter in a bay somewhere around the forty-eighth parallel. Drake noted that it was unseasonably cold for June 4. Some believe that he was in or around Vancouver Island — if it was cold and the weather was bad, he must have been in Canada, so the defenders of this theory suggest. But Drake didn't encounter any of the locals, a stroke of good fortune for them. Had Drake sailed into Georgia Strait, he might have believed he'd found the Strait of Anian, which appeared on his map. Of course, there was no such strait and no inland sea at the end of it. The interior of what is now British Columbia lay to the east, the edge of a wide continent impervious to the whims of mapmakers or adventurers.

Strangely enough, when Jonathan Swift published *Gulliver's Travels* nearly 150 years later, in 1726, he illustrated Lemuel Gulliver's trip to Brobdingnag, the land of giant everything, with a fictitious map of the west coast of North America. Just south of Brobdingnag and north of a cape named for Sir Francis Drake is the "Streights of Annian." The idea of this strait remained in the public imagination for a long time; indeed, George Woodcock's interpretation of that map leads him to be-lieve that Swift situated Brobdingnag where the Queen Charlotte Islands are in reality.

In 1592, thirteen years after Drake's voyage, Apostolos Valerianos, an adventurer of Greek origin better remembered as Juan de Fuca, sailed north from Mexico under the Spanish flag. Although his claim has never been fully verified, he said that he found a large island that fits the description of Vancouver Island and that he talked with its inhabitants. On the island were gold, silver, and pearls — or so he declared in order to spice up his story. He also took credit for having sailed through a passage to a northerly sea. Juan de Fuca died in 1602 with many of his reports unsubstantiated, but his name was given to the strait that separates Washington State and Vancouver Island.

It seemed inevitable to the explorers now jabbing away at the continent from both sides that someone would find the Northwest Passage. In

1585, John Davis "rediscovered" Greenland; most Europeans had ignored or forgotten about this massive island near the top of the world that the Vikings had claimed and even settled. Then he sailed across Davis Strait (named for himself, of course) and bumped into Baffin Island. He must have liked this corner of the world, because he returned on two other occasions, slipping into Frobisher Bay and exploring north into Baffin Bay. A great observer of plants, rocks, and even people, he wrote a fair and plausible account of meetings with the Inuit, who, as far as anyone knows, never shot him in the behind or anywhere else. He was one of the few Englishmen of his day who could claim that he summered along the shores of Baffin Island, but instead of persisting in this pastime, he decided to test his navigating skills by sailing around the world. On one hazardous attempt, he discovered the Falkland Islands and established the claim that led to a short but expensive war in the late twentieth century. In 1605, while working for the East Indies Company, Davis was killed by Japanese pirates near Singapore.

To Heaven by Sea

Born in Dartmouth, England, in 1537, Sir Humphrey Gilbert became fixated on the idea of an undiscovered route to the Far East. He was enamoured with colonizing in general and approved of the notion that England could profit from going just about anywhere and claiming what it found, then doing something with the new found lands to make money. He was a leading proponent of the Northwest Passage, and in 1578, Queen Elizabeth respected his heady ambitions by giving him authority to sail west, find what he could find, and claim it — a dream come true for an ambitious empire builder.

Planning the expedition turned out to be far easier than actually making it, and Gilbert's first foray was poorly organized. Storms battered his ships, and some of his men deserted, preferring the landlubber's life to an icy sea death. But Gilbert had swallowed his own hype wholeheartedly and was ready for a second try. Either the Queen had taken a personal fancy to him, with his plucky moustache and clever goatee, or she thought he was a great schemer who simply had bad luck around boats. She wanted to send another party of explorers but thought Gilbert should stay home

Sir Humphrey Gilbert, about 1584.
(PANL, B 16-18)

safely in England where he belonged. Gilbert was too enthusiastic about his vision to sit and sup at home while his men had all the fun, so he insisted he was ready to sail again. Hot-blooded and driven by vanity, he was reputed to be a harsh, even cruel captain. His crew undoubtedly wished the bull-headed dreamer had heeded the queen's plea as they sailed off in June 1583, this time with five ships: *Delight, Raleigh, Golden Hind, Swallow* and *Squirrel.*

The men on the *Raleigh* realized soon enough that the trip was foolish and turned back, but the other four ships pressed on. Gilbert fulfilled his dream when his own ship approached the craggy coastline of New-foundland and slipped into the protection of what would be St. John's harbour. With the Queen's approval in hand (now known as Gilbert's Charter), he claimed what he had found for his Queen and for himself. No one, not even most of the English sailors with him, cared about documentation, but Gilbert was pleased that he had done the deed properly and officially. Not all of Gilbert's men were as impressed by what they found as was their leader. Grumbling and sickness dampened much of the expedition. The worst offenders were sent packing aboard the *Delight* on August 20, but they were swept far to the south and foundered on the sandbars off Sable Island, starting that island's long career as "The Graveyard of the Atlantic."

By September, Gilbert himself was ready to return home to receive the glory that was his due. Heavy winds and heavier seas could not inspire caution in the belligerent captain; chin jutting towards the salty blast, Gilbert reminded his men that they were "as neare to Heaven by sea as by land." Soon afterwards, the North Atlantic claimed the ill-prepared *Squirrel* and drowned all those on board, including Humphrey Gilbert himself. The *Golden Hind*, however, returned safely to port, and so began England's tenure over Newfoundland, its first colony in the New World. England felt it had a just claim on virtually all of the New World as a result of the travels of John Cabot, but it had almost seemed like too much trouble to actually invest money, men, and time in settling this curious but perhaps inconsequential foreign land. Now that Queen Elizabeth had sacrificed Sir Humphrey Gilbert in order to take possession of Newfoundland's rocky shores, however, further talk and pamphlets about the Northwest Passage proliferated; Gilbert's publicity campaign lived on well beyond his watery demise.

Other European nations had taken notice of Newfoundland and remained curious if not fully informed. Venetian mapmaker Pietro Andrea Mattioli knew next to nothing about the Native inhabitants of Newfoundland, but in 1547, he had noted on his beautiful map, "The inhabitants are idolaters, some worship the sun, others the moon, and many other kinds of idols. It is a fair place, but savage." Despite its remoteness, by 1583, one English Captain, Edward Hayes, regretted the fact that people were settling along the Newfoundland shores and noticed that the island was becoming "pestered with inhabitants." Some Englishmen regarded Newfoundland, not as a mere dot in the distance, but as a place of the utmost significance. Philosopher and essayist Francis Bacon wrote, "The fisheries of Newfoundland are inexhaustible and of more value to the Empire than all the silver mines of Peru . . . greater than the gold mines of Golconda, there is none so rich." Here was a man prepared to take fish over gold as sustenance for his greedy empire.

After Gilbert had gone down in the *Squirrel*, Sir Walter Raleigh continued to explore and claim lands on behalf of his Queen. Raleigh helped establish a settlement on Roanoke Island in what is now North Carolina. He went back to England, but when he returned three years later, the settlement had entirely vanished. Nonetheless, the London and Plymouth Trading Companies received the right to rule over a vast portion of the Atlantic Coast from Acadia far south to Cape Fear, while another new organization, the Virginia Company, was granted the right to create an outpost in Newfoundland in 1610. From here John Smith (of Pocahontas fame) explored much of the region by ship and charted the coast. He told his people back in England that he had encountered fair weather and good land for farming, but even so, few people were eager to leave England and settle on these distant shores.

Desperate Men in Distant Lands

Henry Hudson died in 1611, but nobody seems to know exactly when he was born. Like Gilbert before him, he hoped to find some secret pathway to the East. Working for the Dutch East India Company, he first tried to chart a Northeast Passage north of Russia. His crew was not fond of polar ice, however, and they mutinied. Taking the hint, Hudson sailed west instead of northeast later that year, voyaging up a river not far from what would one day be the site of Yankee Stadium, Nathan's hot dogs, and the United Nations headquarters.

It wasn't the shortcut to the Orient he was hoping for, but he had investigated a sizeable chunk of a continent; he returned to try a more northerly route in 1610, accompanied by his son and a crew of the most seaworthy of men. Aboard the *Discovery*, Hudson was not deterred by the cold as he sailed past Iceland and Greenland and into Ungava Bay. Baffin Island blocked him from tacking north, and he observed more barren and apparently hostile land to the south, but in June he found open water to the west and entered what would be named Hudson Strait. Islands of ice ground against each other, and fog settled in to mute the crew's elation over this possible route to the tropics. They could see no lush vegetation on the easterly shores of Hudson Bay; no smell of flowers or spices reached the ship as they hugged the coast, sailing south all the way into James Bay. They found rivers, to be sure, but no thoroughfares, no blessed passageway further on, just the bulk of the massive unknown continent of North America. Hudson had almost persuaded himself that they had reached some arm of the Pacific Ocean before sullen despair set in, along with the realization that they were stuck for the winter.

The *Discovery* was run aground, and all hands went ashore to tough out a miserable winter in this alien land of fog and ice. Suffering was the lot of every man through long, brutal months of sickness and hunger, with never enough heat to stave off the ravages to their bodies and souls. When some semblance of spring arrived (nothing like what they were

Henry Hudson. (NAC, C17727)

used to in England), Henry Hudson informed his sorry lot of sailors that he intended to float the *Discovery* and continue the search for a route westward.

Rebellion broke out among the crew. Led by William Wilson, Henry Greene, and Robert Juet, the ravaged survivors put Hudson, his unlucky son, and seven loyal sailors into a dinghy and set them adrift on James Bay. The *Discovery*, navigated by Robert Bylot, left for home, but not before Greene and Wilson got into a battle with Native people along the shores and Juet died of disease brought on by starvation. Eight or nine men survived to see England again; four of them were tried for murder but were not convicted. However scurrilous, the crew had some valuable knowledge of northern waters that might still be of use to westward explorers looking for profit, and courts could be persuaded to turn a blind eye towards crimes committed by desperate men in impossibly distant lands.

Another would-be discoverer of the Northwest Passage was William Baffin, born in 1584. He'd scouted around Greenland and Spitsbergen, and eventually he joined Robert Bylot in 1615 to find that elusive route to riches aboard the *Discovery*. They saw lots of ice and tacked around the entrance to Hudson Strait, but they couldn't hit the jackpot. Baffin went back the next year with Bylot on the *Discovery* again, and they sailed further north than any European had ever gone: up to the northern tip of Baffin Island and into Lancaster Sound. This actually *was* the entrance to the Northwest Passage, although they didn't recognize it. Like John Davis,

Baffin devised some technical improvements for navigating in the north, and also like Davis, he ended up being killed in a warmer clime. Baffin died at the hands of a Portuguese soldier who felled him with a musket shot in the Gulf of Oman. His discovery of Lancaster Sound, which indeed did lead to the Pacific, was unheralded and more or less forgotten. No other explorer traversed that far north again for more than 230 years.

CHAPTER EIGHT

Privilege, Politics, Greed, and a Plague of Mice

The Aid of Neptune's Favour

GIOVANNI DA VERRAZANO used the term "Arcadie" to label a large chunk of the northeast coast of North America. It reminded him of Arcadia, that legendary land of beauty and tranquillity, and the name stuck for many years. Eventually, Arcadie was mixed with "cadie," the Mi'kmaw word for "safe harbour." The result was a French adaptation: *Acadie* came to include present-day Nova Scotia, New Brunswick, Prince Edward Island, and easterly parts of Quebec.

Both England and France began to see the potential for profit in the New World right around the beginning of the seventeenth century. King Henry IV of France gave special permission to Pierre du Gua de Monts to establish French colonies between the fortieth and forty-sixth parallels of latitude. He granted de Monts the right to trade with Native people there and to harvest whatever he could from the land or the sea. De Monts looked at a number of prime locations for his first colony but was most interested in the area around the Bay of Fundy and the nearby St. Lawrence waterway, which he hoped would prove to be the desired route to the Far East. In 1604, de Monts headed west from France, along with a nobleman named Jean de Poutrincourt and Samuel de Champlain. Champlain, the son of a sea captain, was born in 1567; he had crossed the Atlantic before, and in his lifetime he would make many voyages to the New World. His trip with de Monts, however, was a particularly tough crossing. Their ships endured devastating storms and a near-fatal incident involving icebergs. They almost ran aground on the sandbanks near Sable Island before reaching Cap de la Have on the south shore of Nova Scotia. They sailed into the Bay of Fundy, then known as Baie Française, and discovered a smaller body of water that Champlain de-

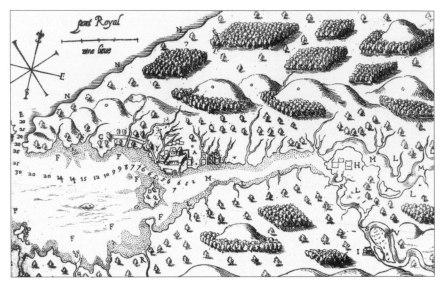

Champlain's map of Annapolis Basin, with the Habitation at Port Royal on the north shore. (NLC, NL 15325)

scribed as "one of the finest harbours that I have seen on all these coasts"; Port Royal would eventually be established here. Unfortunately, de Monts, Champlain, and their companions decided not to stop here, but to sail further on across the Bay of Fundy and spend the winter on an island in the mouth of the St. Croix River (which today divides Canada from the United States). It was a bad move. Probably they all would have died without the help of the local Maliseet, who provided food and herbal medicines to ward off disease. As it was, just over half of the seventy-nine men barely survived the winter. The rest succumbed to scurvy.

In the spring, Champlain went looking further down the coast for a more hospitable place to build a fort, but, in the end, the leaders agreed that they had already discovered the most desirable location and returned to the site of Port Royal.

The Mi'kmaq welcomed the French visitors. Chief Membertou, their leader, was described as "of prodigious size, and taller and stronger-limbed than most, bearded like a Frenchman while not one of the others had hair on his chin." Membertou claimed to be over a hundred years old, and he told them that he had previously exchanged words and gifts with Jacques Cartier.

De Monts went home to France to tell the king about both the bad fortune and the good, leaving behind a colony of forty survivors under the leadership of Lieutenant Françoise Pontgrave. The winter at Port Royal was not as bad as the previous one on St. Croix Island, but in the spring of 1606, Pontgrave set off to find a warmer place further to the south for a permanent colony. Along the way, Pontgrave had a heart attack, and his ship ran aground and broke up. The bad luck discouraged almost everyone, and all but two of the Frenchmen planned to return to France on fishing boats. While at Cape Sable, the Port Royal refugees learned that supplies and more men were on their way from France in the hope that the new colony might yet survive. The ships arrived as planned, with Poutrincourt in command, aided by lawyer-poet Marc Lescarbot and the de la Tour brothers, Claude and Charles. The newcomers and refugees sailed together to Port Royal to keep the settlement alive.

By November of 1606, however, Poutrincourt felt like a failure. On his voyage to explore more of the New England coast, he had faced strong, unfavourable winds, unsafe harbours, and unfriendly Natives. Lescarbot decided to cheer everybody up by putting on a play, which he described as "French rhymes penned in haste." Lescarbot played Neptune, standing in a boat and accompanied by four French "Indians." He tried to put a good spin on what had so far been a dismal undertaking:

If man would taste the spice of fortune's savour,
He must needs seek the aid of Neptune's favour.
For stay-at-homes who doze on kitchen settles
Earn no more glory than their pots and kettles.

Lescarbot had mounted the first theatrical production in the New World.

Winter was coming on, and it was clear that more than a few lines of poetry were needed to keep everybody happy. To that end, the Order of Good Cheer was established. Extravagant meals consisting of great volumes of drink and vast quantities of food would be held regularly. On the menu were wildfowl, sturgeon, moose, beaver, otter, wildcat, and raccoon. Chief Membertou took part in the feasts, and sometimes a crowd of Mi'kmaw women and children gathered around to watch.

Relations were good with the Mi'kmaq, and every day the Habitation had visitors. Membertou called Poutrincourt his "great friend, brother, companion and equal." There was little competition for hunting or fishing

"Domiciliated Indians of North America," by G. Heriot (c. 1807). (NAC, C-12781)

rights or concern over property ownership. During that winter of 1607, Frenchmen would learn to survive by following the lead of their Mi'kmaw neighbours. Some of the colonists even moved into the Native community nearby. Lescarbot praised the local population for their lack of "vainglory, ambition, envy and avarice." His worst criticism of the Mi'kmaw people was that they were "destitute of all knowledge of God"; that is, they were not Christians. Lescarbot and Poutrincourt tried to convert some of them, with minor success.

In the spring, the colonists learned that de Monts's control of the territory where they lived had been revoked in France for political reasons. On July 17, 1607, Poutrincourt, Lescarbot, and all of their men abandoned Port Royal for the small French settlement of Canso, on the Atlantic side of the Strait of Canso between the Nova Scotia mainland and Cape Breton Island. They left Membertou in possession of the Habitation and gave the Mi'kmaq ten barrels of flour for the trouble of looking after it. Champlain was on board one of the ships that sailed around the coast of Nova Scotia on his way to Canso, and, along the way, he documented the course by making improved maps. In particular, he noted "a very sound bay of seven or eight leagues long, where there are no islands in the channel save at the end." This inviting "good safe bay" he would call "une baie fort saine"; it would eventually be called Halifax harbour.

Grim Reapers of the Sea

While the Europeans sniffed the coast of Newfoundland for fish and for handy shore stations, the Beothuk preferred to stay clear of the potential menace of the newcomers, and with good reason. As early as the 1500s, they did some minor trading with the few white men brave enough to leave their formidable sailing ships and come ashore on the Rock. But the island was big and sparsely populated, and it was easy enough to keep to themselves rather than mingle with the widely scattered Europeans.

An English merchant named John Guy, however, left a good impression on some Beothuk in Trinity Bay in 1610. He told them he'd come back the following spring and make some favourable deals. The Beothuk watched for him after the ice broke up the next year. Sure enough, he returned, and many gathered to greet him. A bit testy after a long sea voyage, John Guy didn't like the look of the welcoming committee. Lacking the good sense to query the intentions of the Beothuk, he had his men open fire on them. The Beothuk had no choice but to fight back with bows and arrows.

Although Guy bungled his attempts at good relations with the Beothuks — direct gunfire cools friendships quickly — he did succeed in establishing a colony at Cupids on Conception Bay in May of 1610. Along with thirty-nine settlers, he built wooden houses and a stockade complete with artillery. His was the second "permanent" English settlement in the New World, although, despite the influx of a couple more shipments of colonists, it didn't last long. The immigrants weren't prepared for the elements, and there just wasn't enough profit in anything ashore, no justification for the trading company back home to keep the place alive. A number of other half-hearted attempts to colonize and populate Newfoundland met the same fate. But the waters teemed with fish, and hundreds of English ships arrived each year to harvest tons and tons of the resource. Although they had little to fear, some greedy fish merchants tried to prevent settlement, thinking that a permanent local population might hoard some of the catch to feed themselves and thus cut into their profits.

As if the pirates in high places back in England were not bad enough, the other kind of pirates haunted the waters around Newfoundland. Those grim reapers of the sea would storm ashore at any settlement they could find to steal goods and commandeer men to work aboard their ships. Peter Easton was one of the pirates who set up his headquarters at Harbour Grace, and from this vantage point he had a free run at the Spanish and Basque ships. This certainly didn't bother the English — if anything, Queen Elizabeth encouraged such looting, even though it didn't always directly swell her purse because this scoundrel often kept the loot for himself and his cronies. Easton plundered the seas far and wide. Legend has it that, on one of his forays, he captured an Irish princess, Sheila Nagueira. Gilbert Pike, one of Easton's crewmen, fell in love with her. Easton performed a marriage ceremony, and Sheila and Gilbert settled into a quieter life ashore at Bristol's Hope.

As more fishing stations sprouted on the shoreline, the Beothuk moved on, in many cases moving inland, away from the riches provided by the sea. John Guy's attack was only the first of many episodes of slaughter. European diseases, coupled with malnutrition and starvation, also took a heavy toll. The Inuit of northern Labrador had been wary of Europeans almost from the start. They liked the novelty of the foreigner's goods, but they had watched Englishmen capture some of their neighbours to become slaves, or kidnap men and women to take back to show off in England as curiosities. They fought against the invaders to preserve the bays and the lands that were rightfully theirs.

The Knights of Nova Scotia

The French did not completely abandon Acadia, but when Poutrincourt tried to re-establish his trading post on the Bay of Fundy, he discovered that the English had already sent ships to Port Royal to demolish the empty fort. Then William Alexander, a friend of King James I of England, was granted a charter in 1621 to create something called "New Scotland" out of a portion of the wilderness along the northwest Atlantic coast; both men ignored the fact that the French had already claimed Acadia. Alexander had no intention of travelling there himself to oversee the land he would control. Instead, he cobbled together a party of settlers that included farmers, a minister, and a blacksmith. They set off from Scotland in June 1622, but in the fall they ran into a raging storm near Cape Breton. They backtracked and landed at what is now St. John's, Newfoundland, and many of them died there that winter.

The next ship followed in 1623, took on the ten dispirited survivors in Newfoundland, and pushed on to Nova Scotia. Those who later returned home to England boasted that they had found fertile land, beautiful rivers, virgin forests, and, of course, huge quantities of fish.

Sir William came up with a gimmick to raise the money he needed to populate the new land. He gave away 30,000 acres of land to each gentleman who could put up some hard cash and was willing to send his own settlers to occupy that foreign soil. Alexander ended up making lots of money, creating eighty-five "knight baronets" of Nova Scotia between 1625 and 1631. The newly knighted landlords were supposed to settle themselves in New Scotland on the land that they owned — or at least set foot on it — but they evaded this requirement by declaring a patch of soil in Edinburgh Castle yard as official territory of Nova Scotia. William Alexander the Younger and Lord Ochiltree were sent with a cargo of unenthusiastic colonists to build a new life at Baleine, not far from the future site of Louisbourg on Cape Breton Island. Ochiltree tried to make some profit by taxing the fish caught by the foreign vessels offshore, a deep insult to the French, who had already claimed Cape Breton. The French Navy responded by battering the tiny community at Baleine, taking the citizens prisoner, and eventually shipping them back to Scotland. By this time, William the Younger had moved his settlers to old Port Royal, and at first it looked as if they might establish a permanent community. In fact, their life was reasonably comfortable for a few years. But when the English and French decided to stop fighting and sign a treaty in 1629, Port Royal was supposed to revert to France. William Alexander was outraged. In 1632, another treaty was signed whereby the English again agreed to leave Acadia altogether. Neither treaty seems to have had much real impact on this side of the Atlantic.

Dividing Acadia

In 1632, the French king sent Isaac de Razilly to re-establish a stronger French presence in Acadia. He would replace Charles de La Tour, who was the somewhat ineffectual lieutenant governor living in Acadia at the

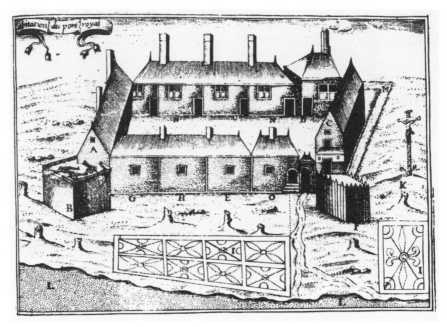

Champlain's drawing of the Habitation at Port Royal. (NLC, NL 8760)

time. De Razilly set off from France in a warship, prepared to chase off the Scottish settlers if they would not leave on their own. The French dropped off some new settlers at LaHave and went on to confront the English soldiers at Port Royal, who were working under the command of Captain Andrew Forrester. Forrester's men had only recently raided La Tour's fort on the St. John River at what is now Saint John, New Brunswick. Forrester surrendered Port Royal, and most residents were put on a French ship and sent back to Europe, although some of the Scots settlers stayed on to live comfortably with the French.

By 1635, Acadia was divided into two halves. When Razilly died, his cousin Charles d'Aulnay took over the eastern half of Acadia and built a new fort on the Annapolis Basin, now the site of Annapolis Royal. Rivalry flared with his countryman, Charles de La Tour, who was across the Bay of Fundy at what is now Saint John, and the two feuded for many years. At one point, d'Aulnay attacked the Cape Sable settlement loyal to La Tour and burned the family home to the ground. La Tour became friendly with New Englanders for purposes of trade, and d'Aulnay had an easy time convincing the French king that his rival was a traitor.

The COASTS *of* CANADA

The reconstructed Habitation at Port Royal. (BLAND, MU)

In 1645, d'Aulnay attacked La Tour's fort at the mouth of the St. John River. With her husband away, La Tour's wife, Françoise-Marie Jacquelin, was there to lead the defence of the community. D'Aulnay was humiliated when he realized he was fighting soldiers led by a woman. After he won the battle, he hanged a good many of La Tour's men while Madame La Tour watched, a rope around her own neck, although she herself was spared the death penalty. In the end, King Louis XIV of France declared d'Aulnay master all of Acadia.

D'Aulnay now had control of the entire region from the Atlantic Ocean to the St. Lawrence River. A greedy man, d'Aulnay created a monopoly for himself by eliminating both enemies and allies, but in 1650, an accident thwarted his ambitions: he fell out of a canoe and drowned. Ironically, to help pay off his enormous debts, d'Aulnay's widow, Jeanne Motin, agreed to marry Charles de La Tour, who was also widowed. She left France to live with her new husband near the St. John River fort that La Tour's late wife had once defended against her late husband.

At the same time, the English were determined to reassert their control of the region, and King James II sent Major Robert Sedgwick to vent English hostility against the French. The major arrived with three ships and 170 men to harass La Tour, but Sedgwick persuaded him to give up without fighting. The Frenchman travelled to England, where he succeeded in proving that he had a legitimate claim to the territory: he was the heir to the baronetcy that William Alexander had granted to his dead father. This stratagem forced the English to recognize that La Tour had the legal right to control at least part of Acadia, and he safely returned to live the rest of his life with his family at Cape Sable.

Other investors in Acadian land lost their ownership privileges, but many of the Acadians who were scattered throughout the region were allowed to stay. Many settled down and lost all interest in French or English political and military conflicts, having made Acadia their home.

To the north of Acadia, a handful of English merchants controlled Newfoundland for the most part, even though King Charles I announced in 1634 that the captain of the first ship to arrive there each spring would be the representative of English law and order. These "fishing admirals," as they were called, were well aware that the businessmen who ruled the island mangled civil law to suit their own needs, but if this worried the admirals at all, they usually turned a blind eye. As if the merchants and the elements didn't make life difficult enough for the seventeenth-century settlers, the fishing admirals often made it worse, with bull-headed and brutish governance. Many discouraged immigrants simply fled the island, and the population of many ports shrank.

The French and English each would have preferred a monopoly of the Northwest Atlantic fishing grounds; neither country was overly ambitious to send immigrants to Newfoundland, but both recognized the strategic importance of the island. In 1662, the French built a fort at Placentia, ruffling English feathers and raising the ire of fish merchants in London. Towards the end of the century, the English began to step up their harassment of the French outpost, and in November 1696, Pierre Le Moyne d'Iberville, along with some Mi'kmaw allies who were fed up with the bothersome English, attacked the town of Ferryland in revenge. They raised the ante by marching to St. John's to burn the city to the ground as best they could. They continued their rampage against other villages at Conception Bay and Trinity Bay, although some staunch Englishmen held their ground in a bloody fight at Carbonear Island. Having looted and burned, the French then turned their back on the territory they might have held. By the following spring, feisty (or ill-informed) English settlers rebuilt St. John's from the ground up.

As history reveals, a savage deed that succeeds once is usually repeated.

The French pillaged St. John's again in 1708, and both sides continued to glory in surprise attacks on each other's communities until the Treaty of Utrecht was signed in 1713. England now had a solid claim to the whole island, but the French would be allowed to catch fish and dry them ashore from Pointe Riche to Cape Bonavista.

Calamities Manmade and Natural

During Champlain's extensive career, he explored many uncharted bays, inlets and islands. His immediate impressions were not always accurate, however. At first, he believed Prince Edward Island to be part of the mainland. That was in 1610; in 1612 he had a better look and dubbed it Île St-Jean, claiming it for France. In divvying up territory in the New World, the Treaty of Utrecht gave clear title of the island to France, and the first permanent settlers, probably Acadians who had already been in the region, arrived. Seven years later, on a balmy August day, a shipload of new settlers docked; France had begun to consider the island a piece of real estate worth developing.

There were fish to be caught and crops to be grown in the red soil of the island, but no one became serious about profit and exploitation until 1731. In that year, four businessmen brought the French government a plan for a company to farm and fish Île St-Jean. On paper, it looked good, and Jean-Pierre de Roma was named to head up the project. He optimistically began building a town, but when he reported that he needed just a bit more capital to shore up the mini-empire, his partners back in Europe decided that they had poured in enough money already. As if the stingy backers weren't enough to discourage him, in 1738 de Roma faced an invasion of field mice that destroyed his grain stores. De Roma responded by writing a lengthy intellectual essay on the physiological makeup of those very mice, which did little to repair his financial losses. The mice, in the absence of sufficient predators on the island, fed on grains and grasses and created havoc for humans. They swarmed across fields and, on occasion, committed mass suicide by scrambling into rivers or into the Gulf of St. Lawrence; ships off the coast reported running into enormous floating islands of dead mice.

The island seemed to attract natural calamities of biblical proportions: in 1749, a plague of grasshoppers chewed up the grain fields. Island historian Lorne Callbeck reports that the Mi'kmaq blamed the crisis on a single man and had him executed.

Aside from nature's frenzied attacks of grasshoppers, mice, hailstorms, and winter tempests, islanders fished and farmed. When possible, the Mi'kmaq kept their distance from the foreigners. As usual, urban gentlemen, often ill-informed, sitting at remote polished tables, made sweeping decisions that dictated the fate of those living in such an isolated and seemingly insignificant place.

CHAPTER NINE

To Explore and Exploit

Reconstructing the Maps

MOST CANADIANS don't know much about Hudson Bay. The Bay —
the store that descends from the Hudson's Bay Company — is much more
familiar. The real body of water is an enormous inland sea of sorts, but its
shores are still sparsely populated, and to most Canadians it seems remote
and of little influence on our lives. Yet it contributes significantly to who
we are as Canadians, and it played an important part in how this country
was explored and settled.

Hudson Bay is 822,324 square kilometres in area, and, although it
stretches far to the north, its southern tip is around the same latitude as
Saskatoon and further south than Gander. The coastal area is, alas, a fairly
inhos-pitable place to those who are unprepared for the winters. But to
the early adventurers, this big inland sea seemed certain to open up into
some secret passageway to China.

In the wake of Henry Hudson's disastrous expeditions, Captain Jens
Munk, a Norwegian sailing for Denmark, led two ships into the bay in
1619 and progressed in relatively ice-free waters all the way to the mouth
of the Churchill River. Here the weather turned ugly, forcing him and his
men to tough out the winter. And a tough winter it was. Sixty-one men
died, and only Munk and two of his crew survived to endure a very under-
staffed voyage home to Denmark. Their horrific tale was enough to
convince the Danish to forget about the Northwest Passage altogether.
The merchants of London and Bristol, however, sent a few more expeditions to the bay, convinced there was money to be made, especially if they
could find the so-far hidden passage from Hudson Bay's west coast to the
promises of the Orient.

At the same time, other traders were having better luck exploring the

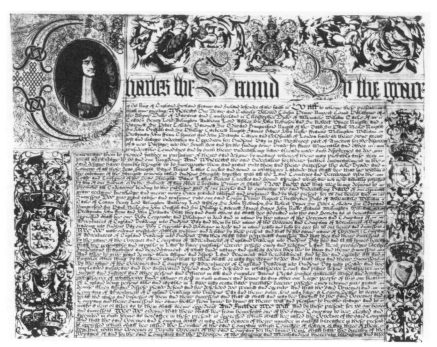

The first page of the Hudson's Bay Company Charter, granted on May 2, 1670.
(HUDSON'S BAY COMPANY CORPORATE COLLECTION)

continent by river and land far to the south of Hudson Bay. Two such French explorers, Pierre Radisson and his brother-in-law, Médard Chouart, Sieur des Groseilliers, learned from Native people around Lake Superior of a vast "northern sea" where there were great numbers of fur-bearing animals, perhaps the richest place in all the New World for furs. Radisson and Des Groseilliers were excited by the prospects, but their backers in France were not. Prince Rupert and seventeen other enterprising English merchants saw things differently. They backed the two *coureurs des bois* and gave them two ships, the *Nonsuch* and the *Eaglet*. The two ships sailed in 1668. The *Nonsuch* under the guidance of Radisson and Captain Zachariah Gillam and his crew reached the Rupert River. The *Eaglet*, with Des Groseilliers aboard was turned back to England after only a few days due to rough weather. In 1669, the *Nonsuch* returned to England laden down with pelts. In 1670, Hudson's Bay Company was formed, and a royal charter gave these lucky businessmen a monopoly over all trading business in every bit of land drained by a river flowing into Hudson Bay. As it turned out, this was an enormous piece of real estate to lord over. Nobody really knew what they were getting into, except for the fact that there was money to be made from this strange, distant piece of a continent that stood in the way of a sea route to China.

Although the French were now envious and saw another reason to spill blood over territorial claims, the 1713 Treaty of Utrecht finalized Britain's claim and the Hudson's Bay Company's control over the massive parcel of land and sea. A seventy-three-year-old former carpenter named James Knight became overseas governor and helped to drive off the French traders left in the bay area. While he was in Fort York (now known as York Factory), he learned from the Native people about deposits of copper — "lumps of it so big that three or 4 men cant lift it." He was pretty sure that where there was copper, there would be gold. Knight also conjectured that ships could be sailed out of Hudson Bay into the Strait of Anian and thus find themselves on the other side of the continent. He had little evidence for this theory, but it was what everybody wanted to hear.

English mapmakers had dutifully constructed maps showing the Strait of Anian connecting with Hudson Bay, but they were oblivious to the Rocky Mountains, the prairies, and all the rest of the topography that would wreck the fantasy. Back in England, Knight mounted a private expedition and returned to sail the westerly Ross Welcome Sound north and then west to . . . well, nowhere, as far as we know. Samuel Hearne would later find the remains of the expedition and tell the story of the unhappy results of James Knight's ill-informed optimism.

The Hudson's Bay Company was discouraged as much by the loss of their investment as they were by the deaths of Knight and his men. "Let's forget the Northwest Passage and stick to making money where we know for sure money can be made" was more or less the war cry of the Hudson's Bay traders now.

Dobbs the Dream Merchant

An Irish parliamentarian, Arthur Dobbs, became enamoured with the old familiar lure of the Northwest Passage. He was sure it was possible to sail from Hudson Bay right on down to California. "By making a few Settlements there," he blustered, "we should engross all their Commerce

and open a New Market for our Manufactures vastly Advantageous to us."
He was certain that, thanks to this quick route, settlers in California
would buy up English teapots at an alarming rate. He was equally certain
that finding that elusive passage would solve all of England's and Ireland's ills. It would enable traders to bring in more furs and thus "increase
our Navigation and Employ all our Poor and by civilizing those Countrys
make Numberless Nations happy." Solve economic worries at home and
save the world from unhappiness all at once — he had it all figured out.

A capable politician and a formidable dream merchant, Dobbs found
an ally in Christopher Middleton, a Hudson's Bay Company captain who
had actually spent some time in the north. With his smooth talk and grand
visions, Dobbs convinced the British government to send a naval expedition off to look for the Northwest Passage, with Middleton in charge.

The warship *Furnace* would be accompanied by a coal carrier with
a familiar name, the *Discovery*. Willing sailors for the venture were hard
to find, so the navy resorted to impressment. Men were hauled off the
streets and out of city pubs and told they were now in the navy and headed
for Hudson Bay. For good reason, armed guards had to be stationed
around the ships at night to keep men from deserting. Middleton led his
sorry crew straight to the Churchill River, hoping to hunker down for the
winter at Prince of Wales Fort, which, unfortunately, turned out to be in
bad repair: "Nothing but a Heap of rubbish," Captain Middleton said.
They men fixed things up as best they could, but by the middle of winter,
they suffered the familiar round of human misery, including near-star-
vation, scurvy, frostbite, and its frequent consequence, amputation.

In June of the next year, 1742, Middleton roused his weakened crew
and forged north through thick ice. He sailed into a dead-end inlet that
he hoped was the long-sought passage, but the ice closed in, and they
were locked tight until August. Buoyed by what appeared to be good luck,
Middleton sailed onward until his faith was shattered at the place he
named Repulse Bay: "Thus Hopes of a Passage this Way were all over."

It was a struggle to sail home, with bad health and broken spirits all
around. More sailors had to be impressed into service in the Orkney
Islands in order to bring the ships back to southern England. Middleton
tried to persuade Dobbs that there was too much ice to the north and nothing but solid land to the west and south. In the region he had scouted,
he said, "Undoubtedly there is no hope of a Passage."

Arthur Dobbs was not a man who dealt in reality; instead, he maintained his faith in his own propaganda. An indefatigable spin doctor, Dobbs argued to anyone who would listen that Middleton had actually found the Northwest Passage. When Middleton refused to go along with the lie, Dobbs demanded an inquiry into Middleton's journey and his supposed holding back of "the truth." The lowly captain was incompetent, Dobbs argued, and he persuaded (or bribed) some of the crewmen to back him. Middleton lashed back; Dobbs's efforts, he said, were, "the effect of Ignorance or something worse." Something worse was more likely the truth. By the end of the public wrangling, however, Middleton was humiliated. Dobbs was still conjuring and still trying to outwit the Hudson's Bay Company to explore and exploit the North. He went on to write a book explicating his theories about the territory and waters of the North. He claimed that ice blocked Hudson Strait for only a short time each year and that the climate in the region would allow inland settlement. With his North West Committee, he raised money from the ill-informed and sent off two ships, the *Dobbs Galley* and the *California*, to Hudson Bay. A candle nearly set the *Galley* afire, and ice jammed the way to the west, but the ships did make it to harbour at Fort York. Only seven men died that winter.

Explorations the following summer came to naught, but Henry Ellis, a passenger aboard the *Dobbs Galley*, like other true believers in the Northwest Passage, saw Hudson Bay as a "kind of Labyrinth." He wrote, "The Tide is a Kind of clue," and if only they could study the wanderings of that tide, they could find the way out. Dobbs liked that kind of thinking. Based on such convoluted logic, he lobbied to get a charter for his company and government backing for more exploration and potential trade. In his efforts to win favour, he falsified documents, slandered anyone who opposed him and bribed witnesses.

Dobbs didn't get a decision on his request until 1749, when the committee decided to keep things pretty much as they had been with the Hudson's Bay Company and not to allow other entrepreneurs into the area. Finally, Dobbs wearied of promoting the impossible dream by whatever means necessary. In 1753, he was named governor of North Carolina, and he ended his days there, a long way south of Hudson Bay.

On into the 1760s, ships searched for the way north and west out of Hudson Bay, but time and time again, they failed. Most knowledgeable navigators had come to the conclusion that there was no such thing as the Northwest Passage.

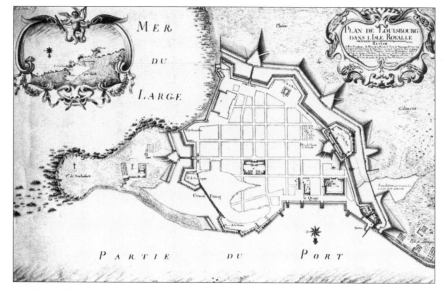

Plan of the fortress of Louisbourg. (NAC, C-21835)

CHAPTER TEN

Empires at War

The Great Fortress

TOWARDS THE MIDDLE of the eighteenth century, Britain as well as continental Europe seemed to favour misguided political leaders dazzled by illusions. The French invested liberally in a single outpost, heavily fortified, that they believed could somehow protect their interests on the entire northwest Atlantic coast. But it was a fortress with problems. Drunkenness was common in Louisbourg, and many soldiers moonlighted selling wine and liquor. The fines and punishments imposed to keep the men sober failed utterly.

Despite its unruly inhabitants, Louisbourg thrived as a trading port, shipping cod overseas and extending illicit trade with New England. Privateering, the "legitimate" hijacking of ships from other nations, was discouraged at first for fear that it would diminish the profits of the legitimate trade. Corruption in Louisbourg was rampant, however, even at the highest level. Money from privateering and other ethically questionable endeavours drained away from legitimate pursuits to line the pockets of the wealthy.

Even before the serious military conflicts began, Louisbourg had more than its share of difficulties. A ship arrived in 1732 bringing smallpox, which killed many townspeople. There was also a kind of famine, a severe shortage of food, that forced Louisbourg to rely on New England rather than France for basic sustenance to keep its people alive. Overcoming all hardships, the town grew, and, by 1737, Louisbourg had 1,500 civilians and over 600 military men. It was a burgeoning town of sailors, bureaucrats, tradespeople, fishermen, convicts, smugglers, servants, slaves, and soldiers. Nearby lived over 2,500 other colonists, and about 150 ships flying various flags made port that year.

Outright war with the British eventually broke out again, and by 1744 Governor Jean-Baptiste-Louis Le Prévost Duquesnel realized that Louisbourg would be in the thick of it. He wrote to a missionary, Abbé Jean-Louis Le Loutre, and told him to encourage the Mi'kmaq to make raids against English settlers. Duquesnel ordered soldiers under the command of François Du Pont Duvivier to attack and take over the closest English settlement, the small fishing village of Canso. Three hundred and fifty soldiers set off in seventeen fishing boats to attack Canso. When they arrived, the English troops had not even heard that England and France were officially at war. The town was easily conquered, and the French confiscated everything of value. English prisoners were shipped back to Louisbourg, where they were considered a nuisance because they consumed food that was still in short supply. Some were set free and some were traded for French prisoners. The liberated English soldiers returned to their own ranks with reports of extremely low morale among French troops.

Duquesnel sent Duvivier on a second expedition to attack Port Royal. With a mere thirty Frenchmen and a few hundred Mi'kmaq, Duvivier set off. The party arrived at what was by now called Fort Anne, and the Mi'kmaq were instructed to "harass" the garrison of English soldiers while the French waited for reinforcements. French backup never arrived, and the ill-planned assault was called off.

At sea, British privateers raided ships, sometimes pursuing French vessels all the way back to the shores of Cape Breton. The French navy began attacking New England merchant ships, some of which had been trading at Louisbourg. The French government actively promoted privateering, and privateers grew more daring and ambitious, attacking ships off the coast of New England. In Massachusetts, Governor William Shirley, who hated the French, argued that something had to be done about Louisbourg. He favoured a siege of the fort that would crush it and give British and Americans a monopoly on North Atlantic fish. Governor Shirley insisted that they should "attack and distress the enemy in their settlements, and annoy their Fishery and Commerce."

A first, Shirley hoped the English would do the job while his own people sat back and waited for the news. But there was popular support in Massachusetts for an all-out attack on Louisbourg, and in March of 1745, an invasion force set out from Boston with men from all over New England. William Pepperrell, a popular merchant with little military know-how, was in charge of 4,300 men in ninety ships, escorted northeast by a dozen privateers. They were hampered by snowstorms, and when they arrived in the supposedly ice-free port of Louisbourg, they were blocked by a frozen harbour. Pepperrell backtracked and took his men to Canso to practice for the eventual assault. While they waited for the ice to clear from the waters off Cape Breton, four British warships under the command of Peter Warren arrived to assist the New Englanders.

Louisbourg was most vulnerable to attack. The walls were weak and the morale of the soldiers even weaker, with everything in short supply except alcohol and attitude. Soldiers slept in dark, damp quarters with rats and mice, and there were not enough mattresses or blankets to go around. In May, when Pepperrell's troops began their assault, some people were on the verge of starvation. Five hundred and sixty French soldiers and 800 militiamen tried to defend the fort. The British and Americans came ashore and pillaged the nearby settlements, stealing the ample supplies of alcoholic beverages, and Pepperrell was appalled when many of his men became drunk and obnoxious. The siege was underway, nonetheless, and the attacking forces were able to use some of Louisbourg's own artillery from outside the fort to batter the walls. French military ships made as if to help, but first the *Renommé* turned back at the sight of British warships, and then the *Vigilant* was captured. All hope for saving Louisbourg was gone.

The New Englanders set up a position for their big guns at Lighthouse Point, after hauling the heavy artillery up the cliffs and dragging it over the rocky barrens. By pounding away at the French troops, they succeeded in making the harbour safe for British ships to fire directly on Louisbourg itself. Cannonballs smashed through the stone walls. Everyone inside, including young boys, tried to defend what was left, but after forty-nine days, the Americans marched into the middle of Louisbourg. Much to Pepperrell's chagrin, his men looted, rioted, and drank from the vast stores of liquor on hand. To trick incoming ships, French flags were left flying over the fort, and as French ships arrived, some loaded with gold and silver, they were easily taken. Commodore Warren rewarded each of his sailors with the equivalent of $1,000 from the new-found wealth. On July 4, 1745, the surviving citizens and military men of Louisbourg were put on ships and sent back to France.

The New Englanders' siege succeeded, but not without considerable loss. In one case, 400 men landed close to the fort in stormy weather and marched noisily to battle, alerting the French of their impending attack.

As a result, nearly 200 of them died in that assault alone. After the victory, the men badly wanted to go home to their families, but they were forced to stay on, nearly causing them to mutiny. Conditions were terrible at the ruined fortress, and they drank so much of the captured booze that many died from alcohol poisoning. By spring, nearly 1,000 had perished, and more died every day. Trying to live through the winter in what was left of Louisbourg took a greater toll than the battle itself.

Shipwrecks and Suicide

In 1746, to get revenge and regain control of Acadia, France dispatched sixty-five warships under the command of the Duc d'Anville to Chebucto Bay (Halifax harbour), where his men were supposed to encourage the Mi'kmaq to wage war against the British. The French also nursed the hope that the Acadians could be rallied to fight as well. On the trip across the Atlantic, however, the ships were hammered by storms, and the crews came down with scurvy. To make matters much worse, fevers broke out from smallpox, and many men died before they even reached Nova Scotia. Near Sable Island, more men lost their lives in shipwrecks. The damaged ships still afloat blundered on towards the coast, but before they arrived, one ship was struck by lightning.

By September, d'Anville's vessel, the *Northumberland*, made it to the harbour, where he hoped to meet other French military ships. Unfortunately, they had already arrived, waited for him, given up, and left for France. D'Anville went ashore along the Bedford Basin with his sick men and the few healthy stragglers of his own fleet, but his soldiers continued to die. When d'Anville himself died that month, his next in command, Vice-Admiral D'Estournel, tried to make the best of a terrible situation. Despite all the bad luck, he wanted vengeance against the English, but the majority of his men wanted only to return home to France. His honour damaged by his soldiers' lack of confidence, D'Estournel committed suicide by impaling himself on his sword.

A new leader named Jacques-Pierre de Taffanel, Marquis de La Jonquière, who had been appointed governor of what was left of New France, went looking for help from Acadian farmers and local Mi'kmaq. In the process, the Mi'kmaq were given the clothing of dead soldiers, and, as a result, smallpox spread through their communities, killing large numbers.

Six thousand men had left France in an attempt to recapture Louisbourg and bring back French control, but when the dregs of the fleet sailed out of Chebucto Bay on October 13, 1746, only 600 men were alive, and almost half of them were critically ill. Two ships stayed behind and sailed to the Annapolis Basin to capture the port, but when they discovered that it was still substantially defended by the British, they, too, returned to France. Other French soldiers travelled to the Minas Basin area to muster support from the Acadians, but they met with little success.

The English maintained control of Louisbourg until 1748, when the Treaty of Aix-la-Chapelle gave it back to France. New Englanders were outraged by this decision, since so many of them had died, apparently for no reason at all. Under the French, Louisbourg flourished between 1750 and 1755, mostly because of the resumption of illegal trade with New England. Despite hard feelings, businessmen on both sides continued to profit. The French repaired the fortress, shoring up the collapsing walls and replenishing their supplies, readying themselves for whatever conflict might come next.

Meanwhile, in remote pockets of Nova Scotia, Acadian families lived and prospered, particularly around the Minas Basin. There, generations of farmers had created a system of dykes to keep back the high tides, thus creating rich farm and pasture land. The first dykes had been built around 1640, and by 1710 the Acadians were working almost all the marshlands bordering the north end of the Bay of Fundy. They also learned from the Mi'kmaq how to build weirs. Making use of the dramatic receding tides, they easily caught an abundant supply of fish. For the most part, the Mi'kmaq and the Acadians lived together in harmony. They preferred not to associate with either the quarrelsome English or the French military establishment.

By 1749, there were 11,000 French-speaking people in Nova Scotia and only 2,000 English. In that year, the London *Gazette* ran advertisements encouraging English citizens to move to Nova Scotia and settle into a new life there, but in reality, it was a place that appealed to few. George Montagu Dunk, Earl of Halifax, head of the Board of Trade and Plantations, improved upon the settlement scheme by sending paupers and unemployed soldiers off to those distant shores. Land would be given

"Micmac Encampment by a River," artist unknown (c. 1800). (NAC, C-114481)

away free to every military officer who wanted to go, to skilled craftsmen such as carpenters and bricklayers, and to other professionals. Rations were promised for one year, as well as civil government and military protection.

A Harbour Full of Fish and a Headstrong Leader

Lord Edward Cornwallis was appointed governor in chief of Nova Scotia, and on May 14, 1749, Cornwallis set sail aboard the *Sphinx* with thirteen ships following him. The ships arrived on the further shore in June. The party included many single men as well as 1,174 families with 440 children; 420 servants; and 38 doctors and surgeons. Almost everyone survived the crossing, thanks to the invention of shipboard ventilation plus a good stock of food and medical supplies. Apparently, Cornwallis started out the venture as a man with a cool head and a pleasant demeanour, but as Thomas Raddall notes in *Halifax, Warden of the North*, "Later on his voice acquired a rasp, and so did his pen, as troubles mounted and the harsh winters of the new colony destroyed his health."

The good news upon their arrival was that the harbour was full of fish at that time of year, but the bad news was that the shoreline looked forbidding and uncivilized. The first government was military and civilian, with Cornwallis in charge. Joseph Goreham was on hand to deal with the Mi'kmaq, whom the English considered dangerous; Mi'kmaq historian Dan Paul considers Goreham and his "rangers" as "some of the most bloodthirsty individuals ever assembled."

Along the shores of the harbour, some settlers found the skeletal remains of Duc d'Anville's men — in tattered French uniforms and still holding rusty muskets. Everyone was nervous about the possibility of attack from the Mi'kmaq, whom they so poorly understood, and troops under the command of Paul Mascarene were brought in to ensure further protection. Cornwallis was frustrated to realize that in a very short time the population of his new town had diminished by almost 1,000 people, some immigrants having left for New England with the hope of finding a safer and more comfortable environment. In a letter to the Board of Trade, Cornwallis complained that many of his citizens were afflicted with "veneral [sic] disorders, some even incurables." He punished the sick and lazy by insisting that they leave, further diminishing the population of Halifax.

The first winter ashore, people lived in temporary shelters of logs and branches, yet in the December 1749 issue of *Gentleman's Magazine*, published in London, a writer asserted of Halifax, "There are already about 400 habitable houses within the fortifications and not less than 200 without." Nearly 240 people died that first winter before a hospital was established the following March to help minister to those souls still alive. Back in London, the authorities decided that Halifax was proving more expensive than it was worth.

Goreham's Rangers stepped up the terrorization of the Mi'kmaq whose homeland they had invaded. Cornwallis tried some diplomacy by welcoming three chiefs and nine warriors onto the *Beaufort*, anchored in the harbour. He told the chiefs that His Majesty wanted friendship with the Native people, and the chiefs signed a document of mutual trust that they may or may not have understood. Within a few months, however, the English and the Mi'kmaq would be very much at war; the treaty did little good.

A Mi'kmaq family looking across the harbour from Dartmouth at the expanding city of Halifax. (NAC, C-102863)

The newly minted Halifax became a hard-drinking town, residents had to rely on uncertain food shipments from faraway England for their sustenance, and the death toll from cold, malnutrition, and disease continued to rise. Raddall suggests that the epidemic of typhus was somewhat useful in getting rid of "the unclean, the drunken, the shiftless, the physical dregs."

In the summer of 1750, 795 more settlers arrived on three ships, and, by that fall, Halifax's population had grown to 3,200. Unfortunately, some of the new arrivals on ships including the *Anne* and the *Alderney* were also sick or dying. From August 1750, to March 17, 1751, about forty-two people per month died. Some of the immigrants, like those arriving on the *Alderney*, tried to establish homes on the Dartmouth side of the harbour. Here more conflicts arose with the Mi'kmaq, leading to violence, murder, and scalping — an atrocity, incidentally, that North American Natives are now thought to have learned from the European invaders.

CHAPTER ELEVEN

Reshaping the Atlantic Shores

The Boozy Seaport

BY 1752, HALIFAX BRIMMED with orphans, the destitute, and the sick. Sir Edward Cornwallis reported to the Board of Trade that there were far too few healthy, hard-working people in the city. He thought highly of the ambitious Germans and the Swiss, however, who were among the immigrants who came in 1751. More arrived in 1752, so that, by the end of the year, the population of the town had grown to 5,250 people, at least 2,000 of whom were soldiers. St. Paul's Church had been established in 1750. Here the Mi'kmaq and the Hessian soldiers were allowed to hold services in their own language in the off-peak Sunday hours. Catholics, however, were given no such privilege.

Halifax attracted an odd assortment of settlers and entrepreneurs. Joshua Mauger, for example, became wealthy in the West Indian slave trade. He even ran some of his ships with slave labour, and he had also helped himself to profits in the pillaging of Louisbourg in 1745. Mauger opened a fishing station on McNab's Island in Halifax harbour, and built warehouses for his goods on the docks in Halifax. He traded with the Mi'kmaq and sold food to His Majesty's fleet at great personal gain. Cornwallis disliked Mauger's profiteering, but, because of the man's wealth and power, he could do nothing to curb the greedy businessman.

Halifax was becoming more civilized; there were now hotels, schools, an "academy," a fairly well equipped hospital, and a vestige of upper-class British lifestyle. Canada's first newspaper, the *Halifax Gazette*, published by Bartholomew Green and John Bushell in 1752, featured news mostly cribbed from old English newspapers. On the other hand, Halifax in many ways remained a barbaric place. Mauger sold slaves — men, women, and children — at public auctions for English currency, and the bounty for a

Mi'kmaw scalp rose to thirty pounds as the English continued their efforts to wipe out the Nova Scotia Natives.

Rocks and tree stumps still obstructed the Halifax streets, which were muddy in the spring and fall, dusty through the summer, and strewn at all seasons with human waste and garbage. It was a smelly harbour town of inhumanity and disease, and those who couldn't tolerate it moved into the wilderness or south to New England. Each year on Guy Fawkes Day, Haligonians took to the streets, drinking heavily and brandishing effigies of the Catholic instigator of the Gunpowder Plot. Fights broke out until blood ran in the gutters with the sewage. The military supplied the only legal authority.

The soldiers garrisoned at Halifax lived in wooden barracks beyond the city slums near Citadel Hill, but near the military establishment were the shanties that housed pimps and prostitutes. Another community of the same ilk existed down by the harbour on Water Street, a boozy place that catered to sailors, soldiers, and anyone else willing to pay the price of admission.

More ships full of immigrants began to arrive: the *Speedwell*, the *Gale*, the *Pearl*, and the *Murdoch* each carried as many as 300 "Foreign Protestants," most of them German, who hoped to settle into a new life and escape poverty and persecution. Cornwallis and his associates were pleased to see these hard-working newcomers, preferable by far to the riffraff that had been coming from England.

A man named John Dick was in charge of bringing foreign settlers to Nova Scotia around this time. He gathered hopeful immigrants from war-torn Europe and sent them to these remote and indifferent shores on ships like the *Ann*. Those who couldn't afford the price of the passage would be obliged to pay the bill with their labour after they arrived. Anyone who tried to run off or refused to work for Mr. Dick could be sent to prison. Eventually, Dick made a deal with the Board of Trade, which paid him for each new immigrant he could deliver.

The crossing on Dick's ships was hell. The *Ann* was overcrowded and unventilated, and when the sorry passengers arrived in Halifax, Cornwallis noted, they were "very sickly and many dead. They were, in general, old miserable wretches and complain much of their passages not being paid as the Swiss were." When Governor Peregrine Thomas Hopson took

"The Town and Harbour of Halifax," from an engraving by R. Short (c. 1761).
(NAC, C-0054)

over from Cornwallis in 1752, he heard complaints about John Dick and the inhuman conditions aboard the ships, as well as the unsuitability of many of the settlers — some were too old or sick, and too many of them were Catholics. Many of the better-heeled immigrants who had paid for their passage felt cheated when they arrived because the land on which they were to live was not immediately available, nor were the promised supplies. Eventually, Dick lost his job, his monopoly on human freight and what was to all intents and purposes his slave trade.

The Foreign Protestants were unhappy in Halifax performing their obligatory civil duties — carving roads out of the wilderness and building military housing. Hopson decided to send many of them to what he considered a safe peninsula of some 6,000 acres to start a village that would be called Lunenburg. Colonel Charles Lawrence organized the project, moved the immigrants to the site, and then proceeded to build blockhouses, palisades, and a wharf. Rations were low, and some people headed off into the wilderness to fend for themselves. The Foreign Protestants hoped to be left alone, but Lawrence tried to rule Lunenburg with his troops. In 1753, the Lunenburg populace staged an armed rebellion against the British. It was quelled, but obviously some of their demands would have to be met.

These settlers were farmers and not traders, and they refused to be slaves to the British. Most were from inland Europe and not skilled at fishing, but a company from New York came in to set up fishing stations nearby, and eventually Lunenburg became an important fishing port. It was also a significant source of firewood for Halifax; the wood was shipped in small boats along the coast to the harbour city. In 1757, French privateers began to raid the shipments and steal the cargo to take it to Louisbourg. It would seem like a lot of trouble to transport mere firewood all the way along the coast to Cape Breton, but privateers stole just about anything they could get their hands on. To a degree, the piracy was intended more to anger the British than to provide fuel for French hearths.

By 1758, the Mi'kmaq and the English were at war in Lunenburg. In 1752, the English had coerced the Mi'kmaq into signing a peace treaty that allowed for settlement there, and now the Mi'kmaq were angry that their land had been stolen and that English soldiers had killed so many of their people. In retaliation, they killed at least thirty-two settlers from the new settlement and took others prisoner. Mi'kmaw leaders made some effort to establish a peace, but the English remained determined to hunt down and kill any Mi'kmaw men and women who were in the Lunenburg area. Most families eventually moved deeper into the interior to live in the forests, and by 1760, the members of the German community were permitted to get on with their farming and peacefully raise their families in the New World.

Acadian Exile

By the middle of the eighteenth century, more than 400 French ships were fishing the waters off Nova Scotia, employing more than 14,000 men. Louisbourg was the headquarters for the naval fleet, whose job it was to protect those fishing boats. The conflicts between the French and English over in Europe and in America to the south led to further armed clashes in Nova Scotia. In May of 1755, a French fleet with more than 4,000 men left France for Louisbourg, preparing to fight the English if necessary.

Charles Lawrence, now governor of Nova Scotia, realized that, with only 3,000 soldiers, his city was not well protected. Meanwhile, British Admiral Edward Boscawen encountered French ships off the coast of Newfoundland. He captured two of them, the *Alcide* and the *Lys*, and led them to Halifax with 1,200 prisoners of war to be jailed on George's Island. On board the ships, the English found, not only a war chest worth £30,000, but also 500 scalping knives that the French intended to distribute to the Mi'kmaq. Even though the English had themselves promoted the scalping of Native people, they were shocked to discover that the French were planning to scalp English soldiers and settlers.

With increased hostility between the French and English, privateering also increased again as Halifax prepared for full-scale war. Joshua Mauger's ships sailed off to sea to capture unwary vessels and plunder them for profit. The *Mosquito* captured a Dutch merchant ship loaded with French supplies, and Mauger's men proceeded to torture the Dutch sailors. One unlucky victim was tortured with thumbscrews while being danced around the deck as another crewman played the fiddle. At least fifteen privateering ships called Halifax their home port and brought ashore all manner of merchandise, which was auctioned off to the highest bidder. In this way, St. Paul's Church received a Spanish organ destined for a Catholic church somewhere to the south. When Lawrence received the military reinforcements he needed, Halifax became a boom town, over-run with 3,000 new soldiers and several thousand seamen preparing to do battle with the French. Prosperity, markets filled with stolen goods, and ever-flowing liquor made Halifax a lively place indeed.

Inevitably, the Acadians were caught up in the political and military struggle. Charles Lawrence saw the threat of the French all around him. The Mi'kmaq seemed to be loyal to the French, and the threat of the heavily militarized fortress of Louisbourg loomed large in his mind. Lawrence felt that Halifax was in a vulnerable position. With over 10,000 Acadians under his jurisdiction, Lawrence also feared that they would take part in some kind of attack against the English military.

With the support of nearly 2,500 troops from New England, the British attacked Fort Beauséjour, on the Tantramar Marsh at the head of the Bay of Fundy. Inside, they found 380 Acadians, some of whom had been coerced into fighting the British. This prompted Lawrence to become even more paranoid about these "traitors from within." Acadians who refused to swear the oath of allegiance to the British were imprisoned on George's Island, and others who came to Halifax to strike some kind of peace accord were also jailed when they, too, failed to sign the oath of allegiance. As always, most Acadians wanted to be left alone; they did not want to have to fight for or against anyone, French or English. Unfortunately, Governor Lawrence's superiors in England were demanding that he and his council order the deportation of families from Chignecto,

"Exile of the Acadians from Grand Pré," by Alfred Sandham, 1850. (NAC, C-24549)

Pisiquid, Beauséjour, Fort Anne and Grand Pré. Colonel John Winslow, who was in command at Grand Pré, directed his men to remove everyone from their homes. Four hundred men and boys were forced to gather in the church under armed guard to await the arrival of the ships that would take them and their families away. Before the vessels came, though, twenty-four men escaped. Winslow decreed that if they did not return immediately the entire village would be burned. All the men returned except two, who were shot by their pursuers.

Soon, everyone was herded onto ships, and by December of 1755, over 2,200 Acadians had been exiled from their homes around Grand Pré. The British soldiers burned the barns and houses to discourage the people from ever returning. Many families were separated, and a total of 6,000 souls were scattered to other parts of the Americas. Of the Acadian families who remained in the region, some were imprisoned, while others es-caped to remote areas. Many of the exiles longed to come home, and in the ensuing years they endured unimaginable hardships to find a way back to the rich farmland they had created, generation after generation, with their dykes.

Cabbages and Cannonballs

Empire building was the motivation for the Seven Years' War between England and France, which lasted from 1756 to 1763. Soldiers drilling for battle in Halifax were ordered to grow cabbages in the thin soil to ward off scurvy. Admiral Francis Holbourne, along with eleven warships, set sail from England to form a blockade of Louisbourg as John Campbell, Lord Loudon began to move his troops in that same direction for a fight. When the English captured the French ship *La Parole*, however, they found, hidden in among the fish, letters addressed to the French government reporting twenty-two warships at anchor in Louisbourg and enough French troops to outnumber the English. Loudon, not realizing that the letters were fake, decided to back down from the fight. Instead, he returned to Halifax, where his men started a smallpox epidemic that killed 700 citizens that winter.

In the spring of 1758, the English regrouped for the assault on Louisbourg, with General Jeffrey Amherst in charge of 12,000 men and Admiral Boscawen commanding over forty ships, all prepared to attack the fortress by the end of May. Boscawen dreaded sailing into Louisbourg, where he believed his ships would encounter "the dismal prospect of floating islands of ice sufficient to terrifie the most daring seamen."

Most Haligonians were not anxious to get involved in any kind of war; they preferred to let the British redcoats, their blue-jacketed New England counterparts, and the ruthless American Rangers perform the dirty deeds. Once all the troops and ships had gathered in Halifax, General James Wolfe realized that the men were ill-prepared for battle, poorly attired and unhealthy from having survived on a diet consisting mostly of salt meat and rum. Nonetheless, the siege would go ahead.

The British navy sailed into Gabarus Bay on June 2, 1758, with a thick fog and high waves making for a difficult landing. Inside the fortress, Governor Augustin de Boschenry de Drucour had 8,000 men and 800 guns with which to defend his position. Even his wife shot at the British troops, who pounded the walls with mortar fire and tried to kill civilians as well as soldiers. English cannonballs fell on everything inside the fortress, including the hospital. Drucour implored Amherst to allow a safe zone inside where the sick and wounded would be protected from the shelling. As a sign of goodwill, Drucour sent Amherst two bottles of champagne and some butter. Amherst, in return, sent Drucour's wife a couple of slightly rotten pineapples. But champagne and pineapples were not enough to stop the siege; it continued for seven weeks. Giant holes gaped in the walls, fires raged through Louisbourg. Finally, their town in smoking ruins, the French admitted defeat.

When Louisbourg fell, French control of Cape Breton and Île St-Jean came to an end. While Boston and Halifax celebrated with parades and bonfires, the British continued their assault on the Acadians. In Port LaJoie, farmers begged the 500 soldiers for permission to stay on their homesteads, but their pleas were denied. Some were put on warships and sent to Louisbourg as prisoners; others were sent back to France. The *Violet*, one of the ships carrying refugees back across the Atlantic, sank with all aboard. When the *Duke of William* was sinking, a priest gave the last rites to 300 Acadians who were about to drown; then he jumped into an English life-boat. All told, at least 700 French and Acadians died in such disasters.

A Dream Reduced to Rubble

In 1759, the British defeated the French on the Plains of Abraham at Quebec. Nevertheless, through 1760, British artillery went on attacking Louisbourg, though the battle had been over for quite a while. For many months this war without an enemy continued, smashing Louisbourg into rubble so that the French could never ever use it again as a stronghold. British and American soldiers then returned to Halifax, where they slept in tents through a cold winter; many died from disease and drinking.

The first General Assembly of Nova Scotia opened in October of 1758, a lighthouse was built that year on Sambro Island, and a dockyard began to take shape in Halifax harbour. With the war over, more immigrants began to arrive in Halifax, which was still so primitive that the newspapers advertised public slave auctions. Soldiers and sailors outnumbered civilians; excessive drinking and indulgence gained the city a reputation as one of the "most wicked" in all of North America.

After the fall of Louisbourg and Quebec City, the French still ruled Montreal. In a desperate attempt to hold onto what was left of its tattered empire, France sent six naval vessels under the command of the unlucky Captain François Chenard de La Giraudais. The ships were barely out of Bordeaux when they were hammered by the British navy. The three that

"A view of Louisbourg . . . when that City was besieged in 1758," by Captain Thomas Ince of the 35th Regiment, showing the British fleet in the background and the French fleet in Louisbourg harbour, to the right. (NAC, C-005907)

made it to the Gulf of St. Lawrence were turned back by more British forces waiting for them in the St. Lawrence River.

In his flagship *Machault*, La Giraudais entered the Bay of Chaleur and tried to hide out in the Restigouche River, not far from Campbellton, until things cooled down. Unfortunately for La Giraudais, the British navy sent "Mad Jack" Byron, the father of the poet George Gordon, Lord Byron, to do what he could to distress the French. On June 22, 1761, Byron sailed into the bay with some heavy artillery — over seventy guns apiece on the *Fame* and the *Dorsetshire* — and opened fired on La Giraudais. When it became clear to the French leader that he had no chance of winning, he ordered his ships abandoned and scuttled. It was the final naval battle of the Seven Years' War and the end of the remnant of the French fleet in North America. The British, however, continued to fear another French invasion. Halifax prepared for war again in 1762, but nothing happened.

For the most part, Newfoundland was considered a unique but unwieldy parcel of rock, with a strategic location and some great fishing nearby, but not the trump card in any big European conflict. In 1763, when the Treaty of Paris ended the Seven Years' War, Newfoundland and Labrador were declared forever British, and France had to settle for a foothold on the tiny islands of St. Pierre and Miquelon, off the shore of Newfoundland. In fact, the Treaty of Paris gave Britain rights to all lands once held by the French in North America, with the exception of those two tiny islands. At that time, the territory of Nova Scotia included what is now New Brunswick and Île St-Jean, which had been renamed Prince Edward Island after one of the king's sons.

Land was one thing but fishing was something else. With territorial disputes more or less settled, battles over the commercial fishery in this stretch of the North Atlantic would continue in one form or another for the next 200 years. Not only that, but as part of the Treaty of Paris, George III issued a declaration of rights and freedoms for Native people in British North America. This proclamation remains an important component of modern land-claim debates and lawsuits. The treaty is often at the centre of individual and community disputes over fishing, hunting, tree-cutting, and other resource-based activities.

CHAPTER TWELVE

A Coastline of Traders

Charting the Pacific

AS EARLY AS 1640, the Spanish Admiral Bartolomeo de la Fuentes made the first documented European contact with the Haida, but stories handed down in Haida culture suggest that they had encountered other white visitors before him. Although considered a somewhat unreliable source, de la Fuentes reports that the Haida had sea-going canoes up to twenty metres in length. He describes their beautiful art of painted and carved wood, and he found the Haida to be wily and knowledgeable traders, interested in acquiring iron tools and weapons.

The Spanish were not alone in their interest in this coastline. Danish-born Vitus Bering proved himself to be such an exemplary soldier for Russia that the emperor sent him off to explore the coast of Siberia. In 1728, he sailed through the strait that now bears his name, proving once and for all that Asia and North America aren't attached to each other. He came back for a second look in 1741 and charted much of the coast of Alaska before succumbing to scurvy and dying, thus missing out on the opportunity to go back home and personally report what he had seen.

Juan Perez was a Spanish officer involved in gaining military control of California in 1769. By 1774, Spain wanted to extend its empire as far up the West Coast as possible, and therefore Perez sailed northward as far as Alaska. On his return voyage, he visited the Queen Charlotte Islands — the first European to have that honour. He traded along the way with the Haida and Nuu-chah-nulth people. At Nootka Sound, an adventurous local resident pilfered a set of silver spoons, which turned up four years later when Captain Cook's expedition undertook some swapping with the Nuu-chah-nulth.

Perez never officially claimed all the land he saw for Spain. Nonethe-

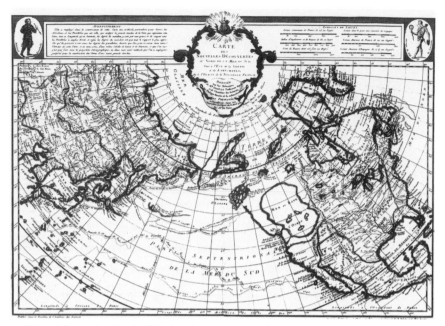

"New Discoveries North of the Southern Sea, East of Siberia and Kamchatka, and West of New France," by Philippe Buache and Joseph-Nicolas Delisle, 1750. Access to the Mer de l'Ouest, which covers most of British Columbia, is by the Strait of Anian. (NAC, NMC 21056)

less, despite the lack of flag-planting ceremonies and pompous speeches before the local citizenry, Spain considered these lands part of its domain because of this expedition. Perez was assigned to go north again to firm up the claim, but he died before his second journey.

Another Spanish expedition went north in 1775. Don Juan Francisco de la Bodega y Quadra, the Peruvian captain of one of the smaller ships, would prove to be an important player in the history of this coast. It was a rough and tumble voyage, however. In July, seven men from Quadra's ship, the *Sonora*, went ashore to look for drinking water and were killed by Native warriors. The coastal dwellers then tried to attack the ship itself, but their canoe was blasted apart by gunfire and six of their own died. Conflicts like this one and those that followed, often provoked by issues of resources and trade, created growing mistrust.

North to Nootka Sound

James Cook came to know both the East and the West coasts of Canada, first finding his way here as a British naval officer in the siege of Louisbourg in 1758. He later scouted around the Gaspé Peninsula and charted it as well as the path of the St. Lawrence River before taking on an even more difficult task: from 1763 to 1767, he mapped the knuckled coastline of Newfoundland. The following year, he set off from England to sail around the world on a scientific expedition that would take him to Tahiti, New Zealand, and Australia. Then, in 1772, he went to Antarctica, leading his crew further south than any European had ever navigated into some of the world's most dangerous waters.

Cook had great skill as a navigator and amazing luck in many things, but he would not survive his final journey. In the year the Americans declared their independence from England, he set out again to circumnavigate the globe, this time travelling eastward. While crossing the Pacific on his way to America, he happened upon the islands of Hawaii and took credit for their discovery.

After that, he sailed on to Nootka Sound, on the west coast of Vancouver Island. When his party caught some of the islanders stealing from the ships, Cook and his men took revenge by shooting the interlopers in the backsides with buckshot, a proper English response. An artist aboard ship, John Webber, sketched the life of the so-called Nootka people and brought sympathetic images of them back to Europe. These coast-dwellers used paints and grease to cover themselves, partly for decoration but also as protection from insects and the elements. This custom made for striking portraits.

Cook stayed in Nootka Sound for four weeks, repairing his ships, loading supplies, and trying to trade with the wily shore folk. When the ships were seaworthy again and the trading was over, Cook sailed north as far as Icy Cape in hopes of discovering the Pacific entrance to the everelusive Northwest Passage. After finding nothing but dead ends, he gave up and sailed back to the warmer shores of Hawaii, where he met his death in a fight with angry Hawaiians.

Whatever grief the British Admiralty felt over the loss of such a productive and feisty explorer was ameliorated by the news Cook's party brought back concerning the wealth of furs to be had on the West Coast of North America — pelts that could be traded at a significant profit in

"Captain James Cook," by Nathaniel Dance. (MMBC, 970.047.0001)

China, across the Pacific. The prospect of such gains was enough reason for England to lay claim to the territory that Cook had surveyed, despite any previous claims made by Spain or any other nation. As usual, the English simply ignored, not only their fellow Europeans, but also the obvious fact that this land was already occupied by people with their own customs, laws, politics, and government.

On April 15, 1785, James Hanna, another English captain, set off in the *Harman* from the Chinese port of Macao. When he arrived on Vancouver Island to trade with the Nuu-chah-nulth, he bungled the job and ended up with some serious hostility on his hands. Hanna punished their leader, Maquinna, by tying him in a chair with gunpowder beneath the seat and then igniting the powder, catapulting the poor man into the air and seriously burning his posterior. Maquinna had good reason to believe that his captors were sadistic, insane, or both.

Captain John Mares arrived at Nootka Sound in 1788 with his crew intending to establish a trading post. With him he brought seventy Chinese assistants, the first of the legion of Chinese workers to arrive on this shore. Mares not only built a fort but also constructed a forty-ton sloop christened the *North West America*. At first, his prospects looked good: the British seemed to have a monopoly on the lucrative trade. The Amer-

"Captain Juan Francisco de la Bodega y Quadra," by Julio Garcia Condoy, 1940.
(MMBC, 0473P)

icans, however, wanted in on the action, and so did the Spanish, who thought they had a prior claim to these lands.

Esteban José Martinez was sent north by the Viceroy of Mexico to regain what "rightfully" belonged to Spain. When he showed up in 1789, he announced that Mares had no right whatsoever to be trading with the Native people. Martinez built a more permanent fort and houses for his men, and, while Mares was away trading in China, he commandeered the *North West America* and many of the Chinese labourers. Indignant and outraged, Mares returned to England instead of to his trading post. With masterful exaggeration, he informed Parliament of the trouble with the Spanish. He lobbied for naval support, some sort of strategic military engagement in northern Pacific waters. The only problem with his plan was that Spain backed down from the fight even before it started. English traders, the Spanish agreed, could do business freely anywhere on the Pacific coast except where Spain had already established full control with settlements and forts. Nobody bothered to bring the Nuu-chah-nulth people into the bargaining, and so, as far as trader Mares was concerned, he could control Vancouver Island and anywhere else he wanted to dig in his heels.

Historians would dub this almost non-event the Nootka Sound Controversy. It appeared to be settled until February, 1790, when Mexico's new viceroy ordered Francisco de Eliza to sail three ships north to Nootka Sound.

Eliza brought on board as much Spanish influence as he could muster, and pretty soon a colonial capital of sorts had sprung up, complete with a governor's residence, a Catholic church, a small hospital, some farms, and the first cattle ever to munch on the salty green grasses of Vancouver Island.

"Ill-calculated and Unfit Vessels"

George Vancouver, a veteran of two Cook expeditions, arrived in the Pacific Northwest in April of 1792. His mission was to map the coastline from California to Alaska, do what he could to roust the Spanish from Vancouver Island, and try to claim the lands once and for all for his king, George III. Despite the fact that his former captain had been killed by the unruly Hawaiians, Vancouver favoured the climate of those tropical islands and retreated there each winter. On his northerly excursions, he succeeded in creating detailed charts of the British Columbia coast, an exercise that forced him to the sad conclusion that there was no Strait of Anian and no Northwest Passage, at least none south of Alaska.

When Vancouver encountered two Spanish ships, *Sutil* and *Mexicana*, he described them as "the most ill-calculated and unfit vessels that could possibly be imagined for such an expedition." Nonetheless, rather than saying that outright to any Spanish seamen or pushing the flag of England into anybody's face, Vancouver invited the Spanish to work with him to map the coastline in detail. He even became good friends with the Spanish captain, Bodega y Quadra. In fact, British and Spanish sailors took a liking to each other. Quadra invited them to his fort, where the limeys feasted on the luxury of fresh vegetables from the garden and five-course meals served on solid silver platters. Vancouver dubbed the territory "Vancouver and Quadra Island," although British mapmakers conveniently dropped "and Quadra" after a short time.

English-Spanish relations had certainly taken a weird twist, producing an eccentric hiatus in their conflicts. However, the parties never did work out a compromise on trading rights, which was really a bigger issue than who actually "owned" the land. Spanish influence on this part of the coast soon began to diminish anyway; a revolt in Mexico and other turmoil in the tattered Spanish empire kept military personnel busy enough without trying to hang onto outposts in the Pacific Northwest. It's uncommonly fortunate that no blood was spilled over this matter.

The first European settlement in British Columbia, founded at Nootka Sound by Don Esteban José Martinez in 1789 and abandoned in 1795. (NAC, C-027697)

Vancouver eventually returned to England, and, like all good British explorers, he took up his pen to write about his time abroad. Before he died in 1798, however, he garnered a bad reputation over the flogging of one of his officers. Flogger or not, he had proven himself to be an excellent navigator, and a city and an island still bear his name.

Rough Trade on the West Coast

The coastal peoples were traders by nature, and the arrival of these European traders was, in at least this one respect, part of a familiar pattern. Down through the centuries, they had welcomed the arrival of copper from Alaska and iron from Siberia, and myriad trade goods circulated back and forth among nearby and distant communities. Goods traded among the Aboriginals included blankets, cedar canoes, sea otter pelts, dried halibut and cod, deer and moose hides, tools, goat wool, sheep horns, obsidian, and amber. One of the most important export products was the grease of the oolichan fish from the Nass River. Europeans, however, were mostly interested in furs. They came ashore to do business, and in most cases, willing Native traders were more than happy to cut a deal for European goods.

Back in 1778, when James Cook arrived at Nootka Sound to refit his ship, he got along reasonably well with the locals. Furs, especially seal pelts, proved to be highly desirable, and more ships came to these waters to trade for this valuable commodity. The hottest deal for the English was to carry pelts west across the Pacific to China and trade them for spice, silk, and tea.

The Natives were shrewd business people who required the English to play according to their rules. They held ceremonies first, with feasts and dances that their guests neither enjoyed nor appreciated. Savvy observers, they knew when to hike their prices if they thought their customers were anxious enough. One trader, Captain Richard Cleveland, noted, "The Indians are sufficiently cunning to derive all possible advantage from competition." Like modern consumers hitting the malls for the best price on a new TV, Native traders went from ship to ship, spinning yarns about the fabulous prices already offered to up the ante. As Cleveland says, they were "well-versed in the tricks of the trade." Women, particularly Tsimshian women, often took charge of making deals and carefully examined the quality of the Europeans' offerings. More than one English captain noted with shock that women chastised and even beat their menfolk for making bad trades with the foreigners.

The English were both amused and fascinated by the trading acumen and methods of their counterparts. One captain named Bishop recorded a trading session that began with a ceremony of biscuits and wine, followed by a series of deals. An old blind man "conduct[ed] the whole of it . . . who would sell nothing, till the Goods had been put into his hands and his Assent given. It was a matter of astonishment to us, to see how readily he would find a Flaw in the Iron &c. and by feeling the Furs, the price they ought to fetch."

In exchange for their furs, the Natives received blankets and metal utensils and, in later years, commodities such as rum, tobacco, molasses, and guns. Some captains tried to capitalize on traditional coastal trading habits and brought abalone shells from Monterey, California, north to Vancouver Island, where they were in great demand.

Most trading between whites and coastal people began with some degree of decorum and friendliness that evolved into a fairly complex system of commerce. Occasionally, they even secured profitable future trading with marriage and business alliances. Even so, the Europeans had the upper hand, and the Natives always stood to lose more than they gained. Although the English did not inflict wholesale slaughter upon them, the traders brought tuberculosis, influenza, smallpox, and venereal diseases, and the effects were devastating. At least three tribes from the interior — the Tsetsaut, the Nicola, and the Pentlatch — disappeared from the face of the earth. Sometimes women became bargaining chips, but trading female slaves to the foreigners for prostitution often had the disastrous result of bringing venereal disease into communities. The generally peaceful situation went downhill in the last quarter of the eighteenth century. As George Woodcock suggests, this was a period of "mutual distrust punctuated by occasional and often sensational outbursts of violence."

Coastal chiefs, already wealthy, became richer as the result of trade with foreigners. Artists using imported metal tools became more adept at woodcarving. The introduction of horses failed to bring about any significant change in the lives of the coastal dwellers, but the acquisition of rifles and handguns had far-reaching effects. Firearms escalated and altered the nature of warfare between tribes. Sometimes American traders (known as Boston Men, since many were New Englanders) would do what they could to stir up trouble between communities in order to create more demand for the guns they had to sell.

Two Boston Men, Captain Kendrick and Captain Gray, were notorious for their dishonest and downright vicious methods of dealing with local people. Kendrick sailed from Nootka Sound to the Queen Charlotte Islands in 1789 to trade with the Haida. Not long after his arrival, someone stole some linen left drying on a line. Kendrick insisted it be returned, and some of it was. Nevertheless, Kendrick took advantage of this petty crime to exercise his own brutality. He and his men seized two chiefs, cut off their hair, painted their faces, and threatened to murder them unless their people turned over all their sea otter pelts at ridiculously low prices. To save their chiefs, the Haida made the deal, but they didn't forget what happened. When Kendrick returned after two years, warriors invaded his ship. After a fierce and bloody shipboard battle fought with guns and knives, Kendrick drove them off, blasted away at the village with his ship's guns, and sent his men ashore to kill any Haida they encountered.

In 1791, Captain Gray wintered at Clayoquot Sound, where he built a ship, the *Adventure*. Lacking respect for local custom, he mistreated a chief, and reports came back to him that warriors planned to take revenge by stealing his newly built sloop. True or not, Gray sent John Boit with weapons and men enough to massacre the people of the nearby village of Opitsaht. Other warriors retaliated by killing the shipwrecked crew from the *Argonaut*, a vessel that had foundered nearby.

Towards the end of the century, conflicts became more commonplace, and the climate became so emotionally charged that insults could escalate into open warfare. In 1794, Haida warriors, led by Chief Cumshewa, stormed the American ship *Resolution* and murdered all but one crew member. Nearly ten years later, at Nootka Sound, Captain Salter of the *Boston* insulted a chief in English, not realizing how well the chief understood the language. The chief did not let it slide. He performed a war dance on the deck of the ship and then had his warriors kill most of the crew. He took one prisoner ashore, John Rodgers Jewitt, who became a slave for two years. Jewitt was rescued when sailors from another ship lured the chief aboard and held him hostage until the white slave was set free. Jewitt capitalized on his bad luck by writing up his harrowing experiences and eventually publishing them in book form.

Alexander Mackenzie's River

The northwest Pacific coast was accessible by sea from England, but the journey around South America remained long, arduous, and indirect. Some men continued to dream of a shorter northerly route, if not by the Northwest Passage, then by way of a combination of sea, lakes, and rivers, or even by a direct overland trek from the Atlantic to the Pacific. Samuel Hearne was one such man. A London-born fur trader and explorer, he was employed by the Hudson's Bay Company to find a river route to the west. Hearne made two very difficult attempts, but in 1770 he employed a skilled Chipewyan guide named Matonabbee. Following a trail carved by migrating caribou, Matonabee and Hearne made it to the Coppermine River and followed it out to the Arctic Ocean. It was quite a feat, but it did not fulfill the dream.

Scottish-born Alexander Mackenzie was living in New York when he was sent off to school in Montreal to avoid the American Revolution. He became involved in the fur trading business and went west to a trading post on the Athabaska River, where he worked under a man named Peter Pond. Pond believed that Great Slave Lake emptied into the inlet in Alaska named for Captain Cook. The idea of a river "penetrating across the continent" inspired Mackenzie, and he dreamed of being the first white man to navigate this inland waterway.

Mackenzie did follow a great river, later named for him, but it led him to the Arctic Ocean, not the Pacific. In 1793, he gave up his explorations along the Peace River to hike west over the mountains. Eventually, he came to the Bella Coola River, which he followed to the Pacific. While he had not succeeded in finding a route to the farther shore that was easy enough for commercial passage, he had significantly helped to piece together an understanding of the vast geography of this northern territory. Like many English adventurers, he returned to England to write a book, and he became quite famous. He hoped to establish his own trading organization, tying together the North West Company and the Hudson's Bay Company, but he never succeeded.

"Ye Manner of Fishing for, Curing & Drying Cod at Newfoundland," an engraving inset on a map by Herman Moll, published in 1719. (NAC, C-003686)

CHAPTER THIRTEEN

North of the Revolution

A Near Rebellion

IN 1758, THE BRITISH took over the island that was once Île St-Jean, anglicized its name to the Island of St. John, and ordained it part of Nova Scotia. Six years later, a surveyor named Samuel Holland divided the island up into sixty-seven "sections" in three counties, while back home in London, interested parties petitioned the Lords of Trade for each of the properties. The arrangement looked nice and clean on paper, but almost no concern was given to the Mi'kmaq, the French, or even the English settlers who already lived on the island. Newcomers arrived, and as the population grew, people began to resent the fact that the political decisions governing their lives were made far away in Halifax. In 1769, the island became a separate colony, and an assembly was called, a very proper gathering of gentlemen. Rather than tackling important decisions that would affect the destiny of the island, they debated what to do about the doorkeeper to the chambers, Edward Ryan, who had "made use of insolent and unbecoming language relating to this House and very derogatory to the Dignity of it." After thorough discussion, the assembly concluded that Ryan would lose his sinecure and pay a fine of a full five shillings.

In 1764, as Holland was carving up the Island of St. John, the Nova Scotia government, thinking the colony too sparsely populated, changed its tune about the Acadians. It now decreed that they could return, and so the refugees began to make their way back to their homes, some enduring harrowing journeys in the lowest quarters aboard ships. Many New Englanders found Nova Scotia attractive enough that, with the incentive of free or cheap land, they moved north to take over the fertile farmland stolen from the Acadians who had made it so during more than a hundred years of intelligent cultivation. These settlers, known as Planters,

"Charlotte Town on the Island of St. John's, 1778." This watercolour by C. Randle is one of the earliest views of the city. (NAC, C-000277)

were fairly well off farmers from Massachusetts, Rhode Island, and Connecticut, some of them fleeing political and economic conflicts. Along the coast, as New Englanders increased their fishing on the Grand Banks, a few settled into towns such as Yarmouth, Barrington, Liverpool, and Chester.

Five hundred families from Scotland and Ulster sailed to Nova Scotia in 1764, looking for free land and a new life. Colonel Alexander McNutt saw a chance to profit from the wave of newcomers and proposed a scheme to the Board of Trade that, he said, would attract 8,000 immigrants. As it turned out, McNutt succeeded in bringing only 400 homesteaders to Truro and the Minas Basin area. Through the Philadelphia Company, McNutt continued to lure more settlers to northern shores, leasing a ship called the *Betsey* to sail hopeful Philadelphians to Pictou harbour and their new homes. Only forty passengers made the voyage. The brazen captain, who had no clear knowledge of how to get to their destination, hoped to sail to Halifax and ask for directions, but he got lost at sea. He was headed towards Newfoundland when the captain of another vessel pointed him back to the north shore of Nova Scotia.

Shopping around for other vulnerable and gullible human freight, McNutt commissioned the *Hector* to load up more immigrants, this time mostly Gaelic-speaking Highlanders from Loch Broom. Two hundred

desperate refugees from famine and immoderate landlords set sail on a ship not fit for ocean travel. Passengers could poke their fingers right through rotting boards that had been covered with a coat of fresh paint. They were lucky enough at first, with smooth sailing across the Atlantic until they neared North America, when they encountered heavy fog and storms that made almost everyone seasick. Winds drove the *Hector* back toward Scotland as their food rations diminished; according to reports, many were saved from starvation by a man named Hugh MacLeod, who had hoarded food scraps from the early days of the trip just in case of an emergency like this. The *Hector* arrived at Pictou on September 15, 1773, with passengers and crew who were seasick, weary, and starving, but they put a good face on things with a display of broadswords and bagpipes.

As they settled in, mutual fear developed between the Scots and the Mi'kmaq, and many of the newcomers were unwilling to ask for help from the Native people. Most of the Scots refused to move inland, away from the harbour, thinking they could sustain their families with fish and imported grain. Some of the settlers rebelled against the control of the Philadelphia Company, which kept basic food supplies locked away from anyone who could not pay. News went off to Halifax that a full-scale rebellion was underway, but Halifax wisely decided not to get involved.

Shipbuilders and Stationers

William Davidson had moved to the Miramichi region on the coast of what is now New Brunswick from Inverness, Scotland. He began to see the potential for profit in making masts from the local white pine. Not all wood was reliable for masting a ship, and shipbuilders were often willing to pay a good price for a commodity so important to the structural integrity of a vessel. In 1766, Davidson had twenty-five New Englanders working for him, preparing furs and fish to ship to Europe, but it soon became clear to him that there was more money in white pine. The American Revolutionary War made his operation vulnerable, but it also meant that the British would pay over £100 for a mast 100 feet tall or more. On peninsular Nova Scotia, few trees filled the bill, so Davidson nearly had the market cornered.

For a time, he tried building entire ships himself, but his first, the *Miramichi*, sank on her maiden voyage. He had much greater success with producing only the masts. Masts were bundled and floated down the St. John River to the Bay of Fundy. And from there, the British Navy would convey the precious cargo across the Atlantic. After the war, he began to export fish again, and he expanded his lumber operations. Because this increased business required workers, he helped to bring English settlers into a predominately French area. An aggressive entrepreneur, Davidson was a kind of forerunner for K.C. Irving, who would begin to build his fortune in this part of New Brunswick. Davidson died in a snowstorm at fifty years old while snowshoeing across the Miramichi River.

In 1768, the governor of Newfoundland, Hugh Palliser, sent Captain John Cartwright on a journey to try to re-establish contact — and possibly even assist — the destitute Beothuk. Along the Exploits River, he found abandoned camps but few living Beothuk. It seemed to him almost as if the Beothuk were disappearing, and indeed they were; the population had declined drastically.

Newfoundland had become a hostile place for the Beothuk because of immigration, but Labrador was a hard land for most people of European descent. Living ashore was attempted only in the summer by the whaling men and those who caught fish to dry them on the stony beaches. Trav-

"*The* Hector *arriving in Pictou Harbour, September 15, 1773," by J. Franklin Wright.* (SHF)

ellers from the relatively comfortable island of Newfoundland would come in the warmer months to fish the bays, but essentially they lived aboard their ships. If you stayed on, you'd become a *liveyer*. If you dared to stay only through the summer, you were a *stationer*, and if you preferred to fish and hightail it back to Newfoundland without even going ashore, you were known with good reason as a *floater*.

Governor Palliser encouraged a Moravian missionary named Jens Haven, who wanted to bring his Christian God to the Inuit of Labrador. Haven could speak Inuktitut, and he convinced the Inuit to allow his missions at Nain, Hopevale, Okak, and Makkovik. The church, as is often the case, was a mixed blessing for the Natives. The Moravians brought a certain amount of goodwill that smoothed over a century or so of hostility, but they also threatened the traditional way of life, and the European diseases they imported killed more souls than they saved. The effects of such diseases would continue for generations.

Golden Years for Privateers

By the outbreak of the American Revolution in 1775, Nova Scotia had 20,000 people living within its borders; nearly half of the population had originated in New England, so there were strong American ties. The Stamp Act of 1765 had enforced taxation on the colonists and made many Nova Scotians as disgruntled as the New Englanders. Angry protests led to the repeal of the Stamp Act in 1766, but the greedy English imposed a new tax on tea, a stinging insult to all colonists, that resulted in the infamous Boston Tea Party. American pamphlets of dissent began to find their way to Halifax, and a fair percentage of the population sympathized with the Americans; Nova Scotia was on the verge of joining the rebellion. In 1775, at Machias, Maine, a plan evolved to invade Nova Scotia with the assistance of its unhappy citizens. George Washington himself called it off, fearful that his army didn't have enough ammunition to attack such a highly militarized port as Halifax.

Within Nova Scotia, Jonathan Eddy and John Allan tried to get a home-grown revolution kick-started in January of 1776 and attempted to persuade Washington that Nova Scotia was ripe for rebellion. Their effort failed. Even though Eddy was able to take control of the Chignecto area, it turned out that there simply wasn't enough popular support. The rebels were up against the ruthless Joseph Goreham, whose men were still performing the dirty work of the king. They ran down the revolutionaries, chasing most of them into the woods.

In the spring of 1776, British troops pulled out of Boston along with Loyalist refugees, who headed north to their new home. They called it "Nova Scarcity," due to the fact that there seemed to be less of everything here compared to New England. There was no shortage of military personnel, however. Halifax was once again overrun with men in uniform, and it was the job of the civilians to cater to them. From 1778 to 1781, Scottish and Hessian troops were stationed in Halifax with the British. Whenever the navy arrived in town, press gangs swept through the streets, "recruiting" any and all men they could kidnap into service. The Halifax government approved of the press gangs' activities, arguing that they helped to rid the city of the poor, the homeless, and the criminals.

These were golden years for privateers on both sides. New England looters jumped British ships, stealing what they could, and raided coastal towns such as Chester, Liverpool, Charlottetown, and Annapolis Royal. Some grew brazen enough to sail right into the Northwest Arm of Halifax harbour. There was little difference between piracy and privateering, except that privateers carried licences from their own governments giving them the right to perform any violence necessary to rob the enemy or anyone aligned with the enemy. It was an adventurous, daring, macho, and bloodthirsty job, and the investors back home grew wealthy from the terror the privateers created. While they did not directly participate in the violence, the owners of the vessels kept half of all that was seized on land or sea, while the officers and crew split the other half. Stan Rogers's legendary song, "Barrett's Privateers," tells the story of a Nova Scotian ship that would "cruise the seas for American gold." Based on information Rogers found in the provincial archives, it tells the story of the *Antelope* and one poor fellow who goes in search of wealth and thrills. Captain Barrett is "smashed like a bowl of eggs," and, at the age of twenty-two, the young man returns to Halifax with both legs gone.

George Washington criticized New England privateers who took advantage of Nova Scotia and insisted that there should be no torture, but many, driven by greed and blood lust, ignored the rules. In November, 1775, the American schooners *Hancock* and *Franklin* sailed all the way to Charlottetown, where they kidnapped Governor Phillips Callbeck, looted his house, and threatened to kill him and his pregnant wife. Instead, they left with the stolen goods and some hostages. In some small communities, they stole everything, even stripping the citizens of their clothes. Liverpool was particularly hard hit by the *Benjamin* on one occasion, but the citizens didn't give up easily; the militia fought back and captured the captain.

Privateers would steal anything: money, ammunition, food, furniture, or tea. One Yankee captain, Amos Potter, was sailing the *Resolution* back to New England with a load of stolen dry goods. While passing Halifax harbour, he encountered an English naval ship, the crew of which did not recognize the *Resolution* as an enemy, and the captain invited Potter aboard for a drink. Potter intended to board and capture the ship, but his plan failed and he was trapped. His men sailed off and decided to attack Annapolis Royal for revenge. Here they kidnapped some Loyalists, got drunk, and accidentally shot their own ship's pilot before relenting and heading for home.

As the American Revolution heated up, many New Englanders considered the territory along the Bay of Fundy and the St. John River Valley a
northern extension of Massachusetts, whereas the British in Halifax considered all of it to be part of Nova Scotia. Each side hoped to hang onto
the territory through agreements with the Aboriginal people living there.
Yet the Massachusetts Bay Colony had waged war against them, destroying
many settlements, and the British military had been equally cruel, often
hiring Indian killers from Massachusetts.

Many Natives in the disputed territory had previously sided with the
French, and when the wars with France had ended, they had "buried the
hatchet," at least ceremonially. Ambroise Saint-Aubin and Pierre Tomah,
two Maliseet chiefs, made a deal with the rebel New Englanders involving
600 warriors who would fight against the British, and Maliseet warriors
aided John Allan in his attack on Fort Cumberland in 1777. The British
fended off Allan's men, but they now realized that the Maliseet would
continue to cause them problems.

Around Saint John harbour, pirates from Maine were harassing British
inhabitants, and the Maliseet were in conflict with the white settlements.
There were no garrisons left, and old Fort Frederick had been decimated
by the Yankees. At this point, there was a strong chance that all of modern
New Brunswick might have become part of rebel America. The British
sent the warship *Vulture* to the mouth of the St. John River and proceeded to establish Fort Howe, which included a blockhouse constructed
in Halifax, then taken apart and reassembled piece by piece at Saint John.
Cannons were installed, ready to pound rebels or Machias pirates, but
these "six pounders" never fired a shot.

It was Halifax businessmen and diplomat Michael Francklin who
travelled to the shores of Fundy to work out a deal with the Maliseet. He
could speak the language, and he showed some sympathy for the Mali-
seets' loyalty to the Catholic church by bringing along an Acadian priest.
In September of 1778, he signed a treaty with Pierre Tomah that ended
hostilities between his people and the British. Another treaty would be
signed the following year with the Mi'kmaq of the New Brunswick area.
While the wording suggested some friendship and goodwill, in truth the
treaties ensured that more territory would be opened up for the deluge
of Loyalists, who would push more and more Maliseet and Mi'kmaq from
the coast and from their traditional hunting and fishing grounds.

Life as a Shipwreck

Jacob Bailey arrived in Halifax in 1779, a refugee from the American Revolution expecting to see "lofty buildings rising in conspicuous glory." He also anticipated that the harbour would be filled with "a respectable part of the Royal Navy." Instead, to his great disappointment, he saw only scattered, primitive homes and a few battle-scarred military vessels. Bailey's ship was greeted by Mi'kmaw canoes whose passengers he described as "Copper faced Sons of Liberty." On the wharf, thrown into a rabble of ragged-looking men and women, Bailey apologized for his own appearance, shouting to the crowd, "I must entreat your candour and compassion to excuse the meanness and singularity of our dress."

The American war had brought new money, new people, and new growth to Halifax. The city even had a proper newspaper. John Howe, Sr. published his first edition of the *Halifax Journal* in 1781, the same year that Cornwallis surrendered at Yorktown and dispatched thousands of Loyalists to Nova Scotia. The more well-to-do immigrants built veritable mansions in Halifax, and the traditionally poor people of Halifax built shacks with the leftover lumber. Runaway Black slaves from New England and beyond began to arrive with the flood of white refugees, creating segregated Black communities in and around Halifax, Shelburne, Digby, and other parts of the colony.

Raids by American privateers — often assisted by the French navy — increased between 1781 and 1783 to the point that even poverty-stricken fishermen were held for ransom. In July of 1782, privateers arrived in Lunenburg to do the usual loot-and-plunder job, but a Mrs. Schwartz, out milking her cow, saw the scoundrels coming ashore and raised the alarm: "The Yankees are coming!" The town had little defence as the looters had their way, trashing the town and stealing what they could while giving away candy, knives, and trinkets to the kids who followed them around. They threatened to burn Lunenburg to the grounds unless the people signed a promissory note for 1,000 pounds. Three Lunenburg hostages were taken as insurance. Finally, in the spring of 1783, the raids let up, and coastal Nova Scotians could go back to worrying about the basics of life — feeding their families and getting by.

Sir Guy Carleton led more and more American expatriates north to Nova Scotia where they could remain British subjects. This mass migration made Nova Scotia's population jump from 17,000 to about

35,000. Rations were in short supply, and there was considerable unrest. At least 2,000 people moved on from Nova Scotia, finding it too primitive and lacking even the means of basic sustenance for their families. In 1789, many Nova Scotians faced starvation, finally forcing the government and citizens to come up with a plan to improve agriculture.

With the population growing along the shores of Fundy and the St. John River, it was decided in London in 1784 to make this area a colony separate from Nova Scotia. Originally it was to be named New Ireland, but instead, it became New Brunswick, named for the ruling House of Brunswick. The official seal showed a ship sailing past a small village and some pine trees, with the motto *spem reduxit* — hope restored — as inspiration for the transplanted Loyalists. Colonel Thomas Carleton would be the new governor. Aided by some of the Loyalist upper crust, he envisioned a "gentlemanlike" government and a thoroughly civilized society, one which, of course, would preserve the social order of the past: there would be no voting privileges for men without land or money, and certainly none for women, Aboriginals or Loyalist Blacks.

The new society wasn't to be as civil as ordained. Riots broke out during an election in Saint John, and troops from Fort Howe had to settle things. Even the borders were somewhat uncertain, as New Englanders still argued their claim to territory well east of the St. Croix River.

Benedict Arnold, the renowned American traitor, who had actually fought for both sides during the American Revolution, moved from London to Saint John in 1785. His ship foundered in the harbour upon its arrival, and he would have done well to accept that as a warning. Instead, he moved into town and, with his partner, Monson Hayt, built a warehouse, a wharf, and a store from the profits they made trading with the West Indies. Arnold, pompous and arrogant, was still considered a traitor by many on both sides of the revolution. Effigies of him were burned outside his house. When Hayt accused him of torching his own store for the insurance money, Arnold sued him for slander and won a mere twenty shillings for his pains. Only the lawyers were unhappy when Arnold decided to vacate the town that so despised him, and he wrote back to one of them, "I cannot help viewing your great city as a shipwreck from which I have escaped."

A Land of Loyalists

Around 1771, Hugh Montgomery approached the shore of St. John Island with his family from the Old World; when he had his first peek at his intended home, he disliked it intensely, finding it too wild and untamed. He fully intended to weigh anchor and tell the helmsman to take them on to someplace more civilized — Quebec, maybe — when his wife, fed up with too many days stuck aboard ship, had some crewmen launch a small boat and row her ashore. Once there, she refused to leave. Hugh Montgomery, realizing his wife's strength of will, relented, and they settled on the island after all. Lucy Maud Montgomery was one of their descendants.

When the government of Montgomery's island was not worrying about derogatory language in its house of assembly, it became concerned for the defences of the capital, Charlottetown. Governor Phillips Callbeck agreed that a fort should be erected in 1777. In 1785, a visitor noticed that parts of the fort and the structure that supported the guns looked severely charred. When he asked why, he learned that "the inhabitants set fire to the fort as it was a harbour for muskitos." Prince Edward Island was a place of both promise and poverty. In 1786, when a Black youth named Jupiter Wise was caught stealing rum, some called for the most severe of punishments, but instead, he was sent off to a kind of exile in the West Indies for seven years.

Settlement of Cape Breton Island was slow at first. A group of Halifax businessmen had set up a coal mining operation in Spanish Bay (later known as Sydney Harbour) in 1766, and some families had begun to settle into lives of farming and fishing in various parts of the island. But everyone in Cape Breton was ruled by the distant and seemingly uninformed Halifax government. In 1784, Cape Breton was granted independence of sorts. Major Joseph Frederick Wallet DesBarres became the first governor, and Spanish Bay became the capital of a colony of some 2,000 inhabitants. Loyalist refugees received land grants, but many found life in Cape Breton much less comfortable than what they were used to in New England. Independence lasted only until 1820, partly because the island's prosperity was never realized and the expected wave of Loyalist settlers never occurred.

Shelburne, on the other hand, grew rapidly with the influx of Loyalist immigrants. Here there was also a growing population of Blacks, many of them coerced into becoming indentured servants. Most were forced to live on the fringes of town by the sober white Loyalists, who feared that their dancing, singing, and convivial way of life would be a bad influence. In 1784, tensions between Black and white settlers erupted into a riot in which the homes of twenty Black families were wrecked. Many were driven out of the seaport into the segregated inland community of Birchtown, where the soil was thin and the land barren. Shelburne grew into a New England style town and prospered by sending out men on whaling ships, but that was an industry doomed to falter. Shelburne aspired to become the major centre of trade along the entire Nova Scotia coast, and some expected it to be larger and wealthier than Halifax. However, there were too many sellers and not enough buyers, and a spate of hard winters, fires, and smallpox epidemics set back the lofty plans. By 1788, the population had diminished to 300, and already 360 houses stood empty.

Shelburne proved not to be the promised land for either the white or the Black settlers, many of whom had fought with the British army against the American revolutionaries. Three thousand Black Loyalists had come to Nova Scotia, but instead of the promised freedom they found indentured servitude and a hard life. Many began preparing to move again.

In 1790, the Sierra Leone Company was granted a licence to set up a government in part of West Africa. John Clarkson, a recruitment officer with the company, encouraged Black Nova Scotians to seek yet another new home. Thomas Peters, a former North Carolina slave and a Loyalist soldier, was among those who felt cheated, and he persuaded many Blacks from Shelburne and Birchtown to head for Africa. In January of 1792, more than 1,000 left Nova Scotia, and within a few years, nearly a third of the Black population had moved off to Sierra Leone, returning to their ancestral continent.

White Loyalists who still held slaves in Nova Scotia continued to assert their "property" rights, while those Blacks who stayed on fought for their freedom through the courts. The buying, selling, and ownership of slaves would not be completely eradicated until the abolition of slavery within the British Empire in 1833.

CHAPTER FOURTEEN

The Sea of Merchants and Marauders

The Spoils of Privateer's Wharf

AFTER THEY LOST THE WAR on American soil, the British used their naval might to keep the Yankees out of the lucrative markets in its colonies in the West Indies. Thus trade for aggressive entrepreneurs like Benedict Arnold flourished. The British reconsidered in 1791 and began to permit American trade in the Caribbean, but this change quickly took the proverbial wind out of the sails of the British North American fish merchants. To stimulate their sagging West Indian sales, Nova Scotia and New Brunswick shippers were offered cash premiums on their cargoes, and, to counter the American success in the fish trade, England imposed an embargo on any shipment of salted fish coming to their Caribbean ports from a non-British port.

President Thomas Jefferson countered with his own embargo to keep American ships out of British ports, especially those along the coast to the north in need of direct Yankee trade. Both sides realized, however, that they required each other's goods. English industry had come to depend on American raw materials, and the Americans needed British clothing and manufactured goods. New Englanders consistently broke the law and traded north anyway, right up to the passage of the British Free Ports Act in 1807; this act insured safe passage to American vessels in and out of the ports of Saint John, St. Andrews, Shelburne, and Halifax.

Halifax's postwar slump probably bottomed out in 1788. Soon after that, however, King George III sent his son Prince William to Halifax, and he brought along wealth, decadence, and new European fashions, including layered waistcoats, oversize hats, and low-cut bodices. As if this disruption wasn't enough for John Wentworth, who became the new governor in 1792, tensions with the French began to mount again. Halifax would return to full military status, the fleet would be in port, and press gangs would resume their work of "enlisting" men from the taverns as fodder for war.

Another of George III's sons, Prince Edward, the father of the future Queen Victoria, came to Halifax as a result of squabbles with his father. He wasn't as lecherous or raucous as his brother William, but he liked playing military games, sometimes of a vicious nature. Sure that the French would soon attack Halifax, Prince Edward began investing heavily in building up the city, with a fortress at the Citadel as well as new public buildings, roads, and barracks for the military men. In order to create the fort, he had his workers chop some fifteen feet off the top of Citadel Hill and dig bunkers into the ground. Fortunately for him, much of the construction was made possible by the arrival of the Maroons, former slaves from Jamaica who had been causing the English government of that island great grief.

The British had taken advantage of the Maroons ever since booting the Spanish out of Jamaica, and the Maroons had armed themselves to fight back against British persecution. The colonial government figured it could salvage some kind of peace by cutting a deal with the Maroons, promising them liberty as well as free land if they would move to Nova Scotia. In July of 1796, the *Dover*, the *Mary*, and the *Ann* arrived in the north with 568 Maroons aboard. The Halifax authorities feared them at first, but soon they began to see an advantage, and a deal was struck. The new immigrants could move into tents and barracks, where they would receive regular soldier's wages to work on Prince Edward's fort.

Later that year, however, the Jamaicans were coerced into moving to Preston, where they would build the governor's summer home. Their first winter there was said to be one of the worst in the recorded history of Nova Scotia. Naturally, the Maroons were not happy; they wanted to go home and escape a climate they were not prepared for and a government with little compassion for them. As time went by, they filed grievances with the government in London, but they did not get the response they hoped for, and they continued to work as cheap labour on roads, forts, and buildings, their labour partially subsidized by the colonial government in Jamaica. Some landowners tried to buy them from the government for ten pounds each, but the former Jamaicans insisted that they were not slaves and could not be sold. Governor Wentworth tried to convert many of them to Christianity, and he insisted that they give up polygamy, despite the fact that he had himself fathered several children by Maroon women. In 1800, most of the Maroons followed in the footsteps of the Black Loyalists and departed for Sierra Leone.

Meanwhile, Prince Edward, enamoured with endless construction projects, had his men build a star-shaped fort on George's Island and stretch a chain across the Northwest Arm to keep out unwanted ships. French prisoners of war shipped to Halifax were incarcerated on Melville Island or left on prison ships near Dartmouth and in Bedford Basin. While the Halifax underclass remained impoverished, the new generation of socialites, merchants, and bureaucrats led lives of ease and decadence. Relative prosperity reigned until Prince Edward returned to England in 1800.

Privateers plied the waters right up to the end of the century. The ship *Charles Mary Wentworth*, named for the son of Governor Wentworth and built by Simeon Perkins in Liverpool, was, like other privateer vessels, a goldmine. In 1798, it overtook a Spanish ship loaded with cotton and cocoa, and Perkins sold the vessel and goods in Halifax for £9,000. Another entrepreneur, Enos Collins, made big money on the harvest of "legitimately" stolen goods. As a merchant, he invested his money on the Halifax waterfront, and when he died, he was among the richest men in North America. Some of Collins's buildings, now called Privateer's Wharf, still stand on the edge of Halifax harbour.

The French vessel *La Tribune* was captured by British sailors in 1797, and, en route to Halifax, they ran aground on the rocky ledges called Thrum Cap. Captain Scory Barker sent for help, but he refused to allow his crew or passengers to take refuge on the barge that arrived. The winds increased and so did the size of the waves. As night fell, the storm grew worse, but the captain still refused to abandon ship. Finally, it was too late: the ship lifted free of the ledge and began drifting towards the rocks of Herring Cove. Not far from shore, in the middle of the night, *La Tribune* sank to the bottom. While many drowned, others clung to the rigging that stood above the water. In the morning, only about twelve survivors remained. Thirteen-year-old Joe Shortt, a fisherman's apprentice without a family who was said to be "weak in the head," began to row his skiff against the raging seas to help the survivors. Eventually, other Herring Cove men, inspired by the boy's lone act of courage, put to sea in larger boats to save the dozen survivors of a ship that had carried 250.

Nicknamed "Joe Cracker," Joe Shortt became a celebrity and was praised by the visiting Duke of York. The Duke asked him what he wanted in return for his good deed, and Joe replied that he wanted a pair of corduroy pants. The Duke responded by giving the young man a job as a midshipman on one of His Majesty's flagships. Joe hated the job, was homesick all the time, and eventually found his way back to Herring Cove after enduring more than his fair share of British naval life.

The Doughnut Dollar and the Forests of Gold

St. John Island received its present name, Prince Edward Island, in February of 1799 because of postal confusion. Mail addressed to people living on the Island of St. John kept getting misdirected to St. John's, Newfoundland, or to Saint John, New Brunswick, or to the nether parts of Labrador. A new name might mean that a letter would get to the right address.

In the early part of the nineteenth century, Prince Edward Island had its share of criminals, whom it punished by shackling them into stocks for public ridicule or by whipping them; thirty-nine lashes was the standard penalty for stealing an axe. Some unlucky miscreants were branded with hot irons with a letter indicating the nature of their offense.

Governor Charles Douglass Smith appointed his teenage son, Henry, to the position of Naval Officer and Provost Marshall of Prince Edward Island. Some thought the governor's son a wee bit green for the job and not always even tempered. At one sitting of the assembly, he grew restless and smashed a pane of glass. When asked for an explanation, he replied, "I ups with my fist and smashed it through the window." Although he caused some grief to his father and fellow islanders once in a while, he was generally tolerated, as was the sometimes whimsical government itself.

Around the same time, Henry's dad was experimenting with currency for his island. Many people still bartered, but others were using Spanish silver dollars, so Smith collected as many of the coins as he could get his hands on and hired a man to punch a fairly large circular hole in them, one by one. Smith's ingenious plan was for islanders to use the small centre piece as a shilling and the doughnut dollar that was left as a five-shilling coin. A wily Charlottetown merchant named George Birnie weighed the little shillings, however, and discovered that they contained two shillings' worth of silver. It wasn't too hard for an entrepreneurial shopkeeper to calculate the profit in that, so he collected all the Spanish Prince Edward Island shillings he could to send them off to England for a handsome profit. Sadly for him, it was a double-or-nothing game — the ship of shillings sank. Birnie lost his profit, and Prince Edward Island lost a serviceable coin.

Thomas Carlyle, famous for his book *Sartor Resartus*, sailed to Prince Edward Island in 1816 to teach at a schoolhouse in Kirkcaldy. Here he fell in love with Margaret Gordon, but their romance was quashed by a busybody aunt. Carlyle never quite got over his bad experience on the island or the loss of his sweetheart, and later he wrote, "She married some rich insignificant Aberdeen, Mr. Something, who afterwards got into parliament and thence out to Nova Scotia."

By 1800, New Brunswick had no real cities; the population lived mostly in scattered villages. Loyalists held the reigns of power over the Acadians, and reserves consisting mostly of unwanted land were set aside for the Mi'kmaq and Maliseet of the colony. The population of New Brunswick would grow from a mere 15,000 in 1803 to a quarter of a million by 1860. Saint John, able to profit from the Napoleonic Wars and from the British demand for timber, would become the third-largest city in British North America.

As in Nova Scotia, slavery was unpopular but accepted in New Brunswick up to 1800, although there was opposition from some of the more enlightened citizens. The Quakers of Beaver Harbour, for instance, posted a sign near the docks saying "No Slave Masters Admitted." In 1800, however, a slave woman named Nancy Morton presented her case against slavery to four Supreme Court judges, three of whom owned slaves themselves. Morton lost her court battle with a tie vote, but one of the judges, as a result, set his own slaves free. Many slaves were able to change their terms of service by becoming indentured servants — not a big step forward, except for the fact that their servitude had a time limit. By 1822, there were virtually no slaves left in New Brunswick, and in 1834 emancipation was decreed, although full voting rights were not given to Black men who met the other qualifications until the 1840s.

The forest had been the engine of the New Brunswick economy since the English had settled there, but prosperity hit a peak around 1807,

"In the Stocks at Charlottetown, P.E.I.," by R. Harris, June 17, 1876. (NLC)

when a treaty between France and Russia closed the Baltic Sea to Britain. Napoleon had shut Britain out of Europe and cut off its timber supply from the north just when England needed wood to replenish and increase its military and mercantile fleet. The white pine and other lumber from New Brunswick forests was now in great demand. Farmers left their fields and fishermen abandoned their boats with gold-rush fervour to hack away at the forests. In 1807, 27,430 tons of timber were shipped to Britain, and that amount more than tripled by 1815. Although woodsmen did not have the megadeath capabilities of their late-twentieth-century counterparts, they succeeded in drastically reducing the forested land in Charlotte County and in the St. John River Valley. Eventually, almost all the stands of tall trees were plundered throughout the colony, forcing Britain to look elsewhere in Canada for the valuable commodity.

Grass Growing on the Wharves

British and American ships had more than a few scuffles at sea during the early part of the nineteenth century. These and other irritations led to a declaration of war on June 18, 1812. Halifax once again heated up as a home base for British warships. It was a city of 10,000 now, mostly loyal British citizens anxious to see the upstart Yankees defeated. Nova Scotia was far from most of the battles, which took place to the west and south, but the city achieved some glory when the American warship *Chesapeake* was towed into the harbour, captured by the man-of-war *Shannon*. Privateers were back in action as well. One of the most famous, the American ship *Young Teazer*, eluded the British along the South Shore until sailors on board accidentally set off the gunpowder kegs and blew themselves to kingdom come.

When war broke out, it appeared that New Brunswick would be right in the thick of it, located as it was along the U.S. border. But no such thing occurred. New Englanders who had been trading with the north for many years had no great desire to do battle with their neighbours. American ships were still allowed into port in Saint John and continued to trade, despite the conflicts at sea. People living on both sides of the St. Croix River stayed on good terms and swore they would not fight each other. On one occasion, the garrison in Fredericton sent a fresh supply of gunpowder to St. Stephen. Not needing it, they generously loaned it to their neighbours in Calais, Maine, to help them celebrate the Fourth of July.

As in Nova Scotia, though, greedy shipowners procured letters of marque and became privateers in the cause of politics and profit. John Harris, captain of the *Dart*, brought eleven captured ships into Saint John harbour. His tiny ship had a daring crew, but they eventually became too cocky, capturing a much larger American brig right in Boston harbour under the noses of the American navy before their own ship was captured by an American privateer. About one-third of all the American ships captured by the British during the war were taken by privateers, who did so much damage to the fishing and shipping industries that Nova Scotia historian Phyllis Blakely reports, "Grass grew on many of the wharves of New England."

During the 1814 invasion of the United States, British warships upped the ante for land as well as vessels. They stormed Eastport and Moose Island, Maine, and then took control of the coast as far down as the mouth

Inuit in front of their skin tent (tupiq), Okak, Labrador, 1896. (MUNL)

of the Penobscot River. British ships sailed from Halifax in 1814 to the coastal community of Castine, took over the port, and began to collect customs money from ships coming ashore. (Incongruously, in 1818 this money helped get higher education off the ground, funding Dalhousie College back in Nova Scotia.) In spite of these inroads into American territory, however, at the end of the war, Britain agreed to go back to the old pre-1812 boundary.

Homes for Refugees

As a result of the War of 1812, 1,200 Black men, women and children came north to Halifax from the Chesapeake Bay area, and, like their predecessors, they ended up living in poverty. The Treaty of Ghent, signed in 1814, provoked Americans to demand the return of their property, including the slaves who had escaped north, but the British refused to recognize these people as "property." Life in Nova Scotia was miserable for these immigrants, with smallpox taking a terrible toll even as the Americans kept arguing that the British should send them back into slavery. Finally, the Russian czar stepped in as an arbiter and resolved the matter. Britain agreed to pay the equivalent of a million dollars in compensation, and in return, the Americans gave up their claims to about 3,000 former slaves, who were permitted to stay in Nova Scotia.

The *Regulus* sailed into Saint John in 1815 with 371 refugees on board. Most were escaped slaves from Maryland who had been removed to Bermuda during the war. The Loyalists in charge of immigration had little concern for these stranded souls and did almost nothing to help them. After much petitioning, the refugees received permission to live on land in the Loch Lomond area, near the city, but they would not be granted title until they could purchase their "licence of occupation" by paying for surveying and prove themselves worthy by means of "sincerity and exertion." While food, clothing, and housing were readily available to white immigrants, very little of anything was offered to the Blacks. The scanty soil around Loch Lomond was nealry impossible to till, and the immigrants were completely unprepared to survive in a harsh, cold climate. Held back by Loyalist bureaucrats, who feared that if the Black Marylanders owned their land, they might also have the right to vote, these unfortunate newcomers got off to a rocky start

In the early part of the nineteenth century, many immigrants from the British Isles found their way to Cape Breton. In 1820, the first Scottish Highlanders began to arrive, fleeing the Highland clearances, and by 1850, at least 25,000 had crossed the Atlantic to settle there. Among them was the Reverend Norman McLeod. With a large assembly of followers, the zealous clergyman tried to establish a Christian colony in what he thought was the Promised Land. He was headed for Pictou, but bad weather forced the ship ashore at St. Ann's in Cape Breton, and it was here that he settled his flock. They farmed and built small boats and, eventually, larger ships. McLeod's son went sailing around the world in one of those ships and found what he thought was a better place for his father's colony. Nervous about the inroads of modern civilization on Cape Breton, the clergyman decided that he and his people should move on, continuing their search for the earthly paradise on the other side of the world. His men built another ship, and they sailed as far as they could. First they tried Australia, and when that proved unsatisfactory, they ended up in New Zealand, the final stop on their long odyssey.

A Beothuk birch bark canoe, by David Preston Smith. (GNL)

The Innu who lived in southern Labrador had enjoyed trading with the Europeans for over 100 years, but by the early nineteenth century, they had grown dependent upon the very trade that had disrupted their way of life. When the fur trade declined, the Innu fell into poverty and, like displaced coastal Natives elsewhere, moved further inland in an at-tempt to resume their traditional fishing and hunting lifestyle as best they could.

In Newfoundland, a Native woman named Demasduit was captured in 1819 in an attack against a small Beothuk camp; her husband and child were killed. The governor of the day insisted upon returning her to her own people on the grounds of compassion, but his concern was too late. No more Beothuk could be found, and Demasduit died of tuberculosis aboard an English ship in 1820. Soon after that, more genuine concern for the welfare of the Native people grew. William Cormack, an explorer, had founded a society to save the diminished culture, but he could find only burial grounds and deserted encampments. It came to his attention that a woman working as a servant in the home of John Peyton, Jr. might be the very last of the Beothuk. Her name was Shanawdithit, and Cormack brought her to St. John's. On June 6, 1829, she, too, died of tuberculosis, and with her death, the Beothuk became extinct.

CHAPTER FIFTEEN

The Beauty of Icebergs

Chasing Whales West of Greenland

INTEREST IN THE ARCTIC revived in 1815, when Britain was no longer at war. The British navy had too many men in its employ, and it was top heavy, with one officer for every three and a half seamen. The Arctic seemed like a fine place to send more than a few good men. Most explorers and entrepreneurs had given up on the idea of a northern route to China; other trade routes were well established by now. But why not try to solve this riddle for the sake of knowledge itself?

John Barrow, Second Secretary to the Admiralty, believed that arctic exploration was worth the men and the price tag "for its primary object, that of the advancement of science, for its own sake, without selfish or interested views." Now here was a curious notion. No selfish motives at all? Well, there was a little bit of envy of the Russians. They had a profitable world trade in northern furs, they were heading east into Alaska, and wouldn't it be a pity if they found the Northwest Passage and took the glory? Barrow admitted that it would be "mortifying" if an upstart navy like that of the Russians succeeded in an endeavour "which was so happily commenced by Englishmen," the sixteenth- and seventeenth- century explorers who had frozen and starved to death. Barrow would later write *The Mutiny on the Bounty*; clearly, well before his literary career flowered, he had a way of mingling fact with fiction.

British and Dutch ships were already at work in the north killing whales, and navigators suggested that there was less pack ice now than in the old days. Whalers were chasing whales west from Greenland — another reason to assert British military presence in the Arctic. Barrow himself had spent a couple of months working on a whaling ship in the North Atlantic, and stories of the far north had captured his imagination.

Icebergs in Otto Fiord, northwestern Ellesmere Island. (GSC)

He believed the popular notion that the top of the world was ice-free. If you could get past an ice barrier of sorts, you would find smooth sailing across the North Pole.

Barrow sent one expedition east towards Spitsbergen and another to the west of Greenland. John Ross, a Scot, led the merchant ships *Isabella* and *Alexander* north and west, taking with him ninety men, including an astronomer, an Inuit interpreter, and a fiddler who joined the crew when they stopped off in the Shetland Islands. The year was 1818. The ship had been refitted with iron plates in the bow, the cabins were heated, there was science aboard as well as music, and, if they met friendly Natives, they could speak the language. The voyage should have heralded a new, comfortable era of exploration.

John Ross fell in love with the beauty of icebergs: "While the white portions have the brilliancy of silver, their colours are as various and splendid as those of the rainbow." Icebergs were pretty enough, but some chunks of ice just got in the way. When the going got too difficult, Ross had lines attached to the ice ahead of his ship, and then his men would haul at those lines, coiled around capstans, to inch the ship through or over big sheets of the stubborn stuff. Ross took the same route plotted by Baffin and Bylot nearly 200 years ago; nothing much had changed in the Arctic during that passage of time.

While Ross had some respect for arctic ice, he could muster little regard for the Native peoples of the North. Generally, Europeans and Inuit misunderstood each other's culture. Ross thought the Inuit were "disgusting brutes." We may not know if the Inuit had similar epithets for the explorers who were so poorly prepared for the northern climate, but we do know that they were baffled about why shiploads of men would travel so far from home without women, and the concept of military hierarchy was alien to them as well. Some Inuit referred to the whites as "kabloona," a term inferring inferiority. All an Inuit had to do was look at the gear, the low quality food, and the reckless ambition of the whites to see that these were not men to be admired.

Warping the Ice

Ross became discouraged by bad weather and even by the ice, and eventually he asserted that there was no northern exit from Baffin Bay. He was optimistic, however, about Lancaster Sound. After more bad weather and poor visibility, though, he was pretty sure he saw a mountain range ahead and gave up on Lancaster Sound as well. The two ships headed for home, where a disappointed John Barrow lambasted Ross publicly for not being daring enough. Ross, he said "knows no more, in fact, than he might have known by staying home." He accused the explorer of spending good hard English cash on a joyride to the north.

Lancaster Sound actually turned out to be the entrance to a passage west, and Ross had made the wrong decision. But the expedition hadn't exactly been a pleasure cruise. Barrow railed publicly at Ross through the winter but, more sensibly, got on with the search by the following spring, when he sent off William Edward Parry, twenty-eight at the time, and Ross's former second in command. Parry led the *Griper* and the *Hecla* to search some more, this time with the latest in the way of convenience food: canned meats and vegetables, which were about to change arctic adventuring in a big way. Ross had taken canned foods, but not in such great quantity; Parry had enough to last a winter if need be.

Once again, the men had to work long hours, manually "warping" the ships over thick ice. But they encountered some open stretches of water and favourable winds, and they discovered that, sure enough, Lancaster Sound did lead somewhere after all. Parry sailed his ships all the way to

Sir John Franklin. (NAC, C-005150)

Melville Island before turning back. When it was time to settle in for the winter, his men had to saw a passage through solid ice to a relatively snug bay.

The men stayed on the ships and suffered through a cold dark winter. The shipboard heat was not enough to drive off frost inside the cabins, and tinned meat was no antidote to seemingly endless nights. Discipline was essential for maintaining order and sanity. Drunkenness was punishable by whipping. Parry had his men up each day before six a.m., and in the dead of winter they often went hiking along the shore. Only one man died. In June, they began sawing away at the ice to make a channel out of there, but it wasn't until August that they were actually sailing.

Parry explored further west in the brief time available. He climbed a hill and saw the most westerly lands yet seen by a European in the region, but by then it was time to escape before the ice thickened. Unlike Ross, Parry was treated like a hero back home. He was, after all, still optimistic that a westward route was possible, and Barrow told the world that Parry had "opened the door to the Northwest Passage."

While Parry was slugging it out with ice in the stubborn waterways of the north, John Franklin's assignment was to explore and map the shoreline of a fairly hefty parcel of the Arctic by land and canoe. His survey party, sent out in 1819, was so poorly prepared for the conditions that ten men lost their lives. Because of love conflicts involving a Native woman, scurvy, murders, starvation, and of course, cold, cold, cold, the survivors didn't make it back home until 1822. This desperate project should have been enough to discourage any Englishman from returning to the Arctic.

Edward Parry, however, was undaunted and already back exploring his favourite reaches of the north. He still couldn't find what he was looking for, but fuelled by Barrow's relentless enthusiasm for northern discovery, he wasn't ready to give up. Parry and Franklin both published books; the royal treatment they received as celebrities must have erased all their harsh memories of northern life, because both returned to the Arctic to search on. Parry left England in 1824, but the ice in Baffin Bay was worse than he expected. During his second season in the north, one of his ships was wrecked, and Parry was forced to admit defeat and return home.

John Franklin sailed to New York and then travelled to Lake Superior. From here, he trekked on to the Mackenzie River, his party, which consisted mostly of naval men, ably assisted by the more reliable Canadian voyageurs and knowledgeable Native guides. His aim was to meet a British ship, the *Blossom*, on the north coast of Alaska. Along the way, he explored vast sections of arctic coastline, encountered — or created — hostilities with the Native people, and endured predictable frustrations on land and afloat in mahogany boats: fog, ice, and violent, bitter storms. Despite these almost overwhelming obstacles, Franklin and his men came within a couple of hundred kilometres of their rendezvous point. Then, convinced that they were doomed to reach their destination without disaster, Franklin turned his party around to paddle and hike the long way back across the continent. Despite the cosmic absurdity of this venture, Franklin and his men actually charted the western section of the Northwest Passage.

A Matter of Despair

John Ross could forget neither the sting of Barrow's humiliating words nor the proof that the mountains he believed blocked Lancaster Sound did not exist. He convinced Felix Booth, who ran a gin distilling company, to put up £20,000 towards a steam-powered vessel with paddlewheels, an unlikely contraption for northerly waters. But, Ross argued, steam would keep the ship moving when the wind gave out, and the paddlewheels could be raised above ice when necessary. It was a creative dream for the ambitious Scots explorer, and even Edward Parry called it a "bold, public-spirited undertaking."

The *Victory* set to sea in May of 1829, but soon problems, big problems, plagued the boilers and engines. Replacement parts were unavailable, and a leaky boiler had to be repaired with a concoction of potatoes and dung. Men deserted, slipped off to nearby whaling vessels, and sailed home to safety lest they be trapped on a ship of bad luck.

By September, the *Victory* had made it as far as the shore of Lord Mayor Bay — a charmingly ludicrous moniker for a wilderness wintering place. The men stripped much of the engine and accompanying machinery out of the ship to create more room, and everyone thought it good riddance. Ross, like Parry, kept his crew disciplined and active and even started evening classes to upgrade their education. In January, they made friendly contact with some nearby Inuit, who taught Ross considerably more about the geography of the area and the waterway to the west. In the spring, he took some men on land excursions with sledges, exploring Boothia, Spence Bay, and King William Island.

The following summer was cold, and Ross failed to make more than a few kilometres of headway before giving up. He brooded through the winter. Night school would not be enough to keep the crew's spirits alive, and, he wrote, the north was a "dull, dreary, heart-sinking monotonous waste." In the spring, they took to sledges again to explore the land and ice, and on June 1, 1831, Ross and some of his men determined that they had arrived at the precise location of the Magnetic North Pole.

The joy of this victory faded during the next unkind summer, when they moved the ship only another half-dozen kilometres. The ice was "a torment, an evil, a matter of despair," Ross said. In the spring of 1832, he set up a series of supply caches north along the shoreline and set out on the arduous trek north, the only way out. After a month of hauling supplies and boats, the men reached Somerset Island and waited for open water, but it came so briefly in August that they did not have enough time to sail away from their land of exile. They were stranded for another interminable winter, but finally, the next August, the water opened up, and they set sail in their small craft to seek out whalers. Gaunt, starving, and some near death, they were rescued by the *Isabella* after four years of being trapped by arctic ice. Back in England, Ross became something of a hero. He had charted unknown territory and returned most of his crew, despite nearly impossible odds.

Blubber Ships

While explorers searched for the Northwest Passage to gain knowledge, personal fame, or national glory, others took on the dangers of the formidable Arctic purely for profit. The bowhead whale was a floating gold mine. It could grow as large as eighty or ninety tons, and it was slow and relatively easy to kill and process aboard ship. In its mouth was row after row of baleen, a plastic-like substance used by the whale to strain its food out of the sea water and by humans as hoops for skirts, stays for corsets and collars, buggy whips, and any number of desirable commodities. The oil from the bowhead's blubber lubricated machines and lighted lamps. Great profit could be made by slaughtering the beasts, and the English government paid a bounty on them to encourage anyone willing to venture into those dangerous waters.

In the early years of the nineteenth century, the Dutch were the primary whalers in Davis Strait, with over 100 ships there, but the English and Americans outstripped them, gleefully joining the slaughter until the population was decimated, never to recover.

Off the west coast of Melville Island, the Breaking-Up-Yard was one of the most hazardous stretches of water for explorers and whalers alike. Here, in the spring, ice islands smashed into each other in a nightmare battle that could splinter or crush any vessel within their dominion. Ice chunks the size of houses and small mountains crashed into each other or turned from horizontal to vertical and then slammed back down into the water, obliterating anything in the way. In 1830, nineteen ships sank in the horrific cacophony of the Breaking-Up Yard, twelve more were battered badly, and many more left the area without killing a whale.

Harpooned whales could sometimes drag their assailants for many miles away from the mother ship and leave men lost in fog and ice, but usually the fight ended with the defeated beast being towed back to the ship. A harpooner who had earned the honour hacked off its head, the blubber was chopped off with sharp spades, the baleen was harvested from the head, and the rest of the carcass was shoved back into the sea. Sawdust littered the decks, slippery with blood and blubber, to give some semblance of footing. It was a dangerous and gruesome business; nevertheless, stalwart vessels sailed and steamed north in a relentless procession each year when the ice permitted, and, if all went reasonably well, the owners profited greatly. The "blubber ships" killed over 8,500 whales between 1825 and 1835.

CHAPTER SIXTEEN

To Chart the Arctic Shores

The Great Western Ocean

WITH TWENTY-TWENTY HINDSIGHT, we wonder at the perseverance of those who kept plugging away to find a "direct" route to China around the top of North America. After several centuries, the enterprise remained futile and deadly. Curiosity, dreams of empire, the pursuit of wealth, and now scientific discovery still drove exploration, with a giant twist of cultural chauvinism and the desire to dominate any territory, hot or cold. The Hudson's Bay Company, which had a big stake in the region from early on, had more success with land routes than the northern mariners, who continually fought stubborn sea ice. The fur trade was still lucrative, but the English feared that the Russians might be moving north and east from their base at Kodiak Island.

In 1836, Governor George Simpson thought it was time for an accurate survey of the vast lands in the north, and he sent Peter Warren Dease and a party of men into the wilderness to improve the maps. Dease, along with the governor's young cousin, Thomas Simpson, who was bored with his job as a clerk, would pick up the work left undone by Franklin. They would try to chart the arctic coastline.

Dease and Simpson wisely chose a land and river passage to the north. They had many encounters with the Inuit of the north coast, most of them fairly pleasant, although Simpson reported that they had a habit of sneaking things away from the exploration party as if they were playing a game. Simpson called it "deceitful good-humour." Aside from that, the Inuit were cheerful and downright helpful.

Young Simpson and some of the men left Dease and the rest of the party behind and trekked as far as Point Barrow, on the north shore of western Alaska. This gave the egomaniacal Simpson occasion to claim,

"I, and I alone, have the well-earned honour of uniting the Arctic to the Great Western Ocean." In the spring of 1839, Dease and Simpson, still hiking and boating in the North, discovered a strait — which they called Simpson Strait — separating an island — which they called King William Island — from the mainland. Explorers had a hard time figuring out which chunks of land were islands and which were peninsulas. Peninsulas implied barriers, while islands suggested secret passages of water leading to that Great Western Ocean. Dease and Simpson had found just such a passage, and they took their boats further north to check out the land known as Boothia.

Simpson and the others returned south that year without solving this riddle, but in 1840, he went back to the north without taking a year off like everyone advised. Dease did take a break, and this suited the smug younger explorer well. Simpson said, "Fame I will have but it must be alone," and so far his search for fame was going well. Why give up? Even though the Hudson's Bay Company had approved his request to fund another journey, they were slow in coming up with the necessary cash. He hastily prepared to return to London to argue his case, but he didn't make it back across the continent. His prejudices against the "worthless half-breed population" led him into some kind of a gunfight, where Thomas Simpson lost his life, never having had a chance to savour his glories or receive his much-coveted adulation.

John Rae, described as "one of the best snow-shoe walkers in the service," had signed up with the Hudson's Bay Company in 1833 as a ship's surgeon. But he was more of a hiker than a sailor, good at trekking long distances in rotten weather, a great skill for any Arctic adventurer. In 1846, Governor Simpson sent him on a mission, departing from York Factory on Hudson Bay with eleven men in a couple of open boats. They had enough food for only four months; after that they would live off the land. Rae's orders had a familiar ring: find the Northwest Passage.

Rae and his men sailed north in the small craft to the head of Repulse Bay, where they constructed a stone house as a winter camp. The building was cursed by a poorly designed fireplace that would not draw properly unless they left the caribou-skin door open even in the dead of winter. The Inuit who visited probably had a few laughs over the white men who couldn't design a working chimney, but they also enjoyed watching the new visitors playing an arctic version of rugby when the weather allowed.

Unlike Simpson, Rae had acquired a true respect for North American Native people, at least to the extent that he was willing to ask for their expertise and gratefully accept their help in travelling into unknown territory. In the winter of 1847, just when everything was running low — fuel, food, and spirits — the thermometer at Rae's camp dipped down to minus forty-four degrees Celsius. Nonetheless, the men survived, and in April, Rae set off with dogsleds and Inuit guides across a sixty-kilometre-wide isthmus that led them to Committee Bay. He travelled north to Boothia and confirmed that John Ross had been right all along: there was no Northwest Passage in this neighbourhood. Rae's next investigation took him to the westerly side of the Melville Peninsula. It was near the end of May when he turned back, less than twenty kilometres from Fury and Hecla Strait. The water was open enough back in Repulse Bay to launch his boats and sail south, having helped to establish a cursory knowledge of the shape of the coast and the lay of the land on this northerly edge of the continent.

Lost Men in a Vast Wilderness

John Franklin had basked briefly in the glory of his early arctic explorations, but the military had soon put him back to work in 1830, commanding a warship in the balmy Mediterranean. After that, he became Governor of Tasmania (known then as Van Diemen's Land). After seven years, he returned to England, just as John Barrow was firing up enthusiasm for yet another attempt to find the Northwest Passage.

Franklin was not exactly at the top of the list to lead the trip, but Edward Parry thought Franklin was the man. Besides, Parry wrote to the Admiralty office, "If you don't let him go, the man will die of disappointment." Disappointment would have been the kinder form of demise.

In June of 1845, Franklin led the *Erebus* and the *Terror* away from the comforts of home and headed straight for the icy passage of Lancaster Sound. They got as far as the Wellington Channel and backtracked to winter at Beechey Island. During the next summer, Franklin tried a route into Peel Sound and south to King William Island, where the ships became stuck in the ice. It was time to hunker down for another long, dark winter.

All Franklin needed would have been one more season of navigation to finally reach the open waters to the west. Unfortunately, he died the following June, and F.R.M. Crozier took over. Optimism flagged, and the situation became worse when the next summer came and the ice didn't open up. Twenty-four men had died. Towards the end of April, 109 survivors said goodbye to the two big ships, and, hauling sleds, they began their trek south to civilization. Many died in the impossible hike across the island. A few of the hardiest souls crossed Simpson Strait and camped at what would later be dubbed Starvation Cove. But there were no rescuers in the vicinity to help them.

Nobody in England knew what had become of Franklin. Sixty-nine-year-old John Ross raised the alarm and volunteered to attempt a rescue personally; his offer was turned down. There was considerable debate over where to start looking for the poor lost expedition. In 1848, a three-pronged rescue attempt was launched. Captain Henry Kellet approached from the Bering Strait, John Rae and John Richardson led their men overland from the Mackenzie River, and James Clark Ross searched Somerset Island. All the search parties returned to England, having found nothing.

Futile as it was, the attempt seemed noble as well as ambitious, and now would-be rescuers considered all kinds of options. One idea, never acted upon, was to send crews of convicted criminals off into the wilds; if a few men died of cold or scurvy, it wouldn't be much of a loss. The task of finding lost men in such a vast wilderness seemed formidable but not impossible, and eventually, more than forty expeditions tried to solve the riddle of what happened to Franklin and his men.

By 1850, the plight of Franklin had lured a diverse group of hopeful rescuers. Amazingly, there was a strong (if irrational) generally held belief that the men were still alive, trapped in some kind of arctic ice prison. Soon, six separate expeditions set out in search of Franklin: Richard Collinson and Robert McClure sailed through the Bering Strait and proceeded east; Horatio Austin and William Penny led ships into the Arctic from the Atlantic side; Sir John Ross, the veteran arctic explorer who had sounded the alarm, finally set off himself under the auspices of the Hudson's Bay Company; and the Americans joined ranks with a search party headed by E.J. De Haven.

It's hard to say which expedition met the greatest challenges along the way, but McClure's journey encountered some of the most dramatic obstacles and ultimately received a fair chunk of the glory. In the summer of 1850, McClure and sixty-five unhappy men aboard the *Investigator* were cruising the Beaufort Sea. They avoided the ice packs as best they could and found open water near the mouth of the Mackenzie River, then sailed east towards Prince of Wales Strait. Having covered so much territory, McClure did not want to give up the gain, so he decided to allow his ship to simply become lodged in the drifting pack ice and see the winter through aboard ship rather than going ashore. The ice locked the ship in its grip but carried it back in the direction from which it had come. Monster icebergs periodically carved through the pack ice, as if driven by their own maniacal momentum, and threatened to collide with the *Investigator*. A Moravian missionary aboard recorded the monumental war with the ice: "great massive pieces of ice three and four times the size of the ship were pushed one on top of another and under continuing pressure forced into a towering heap which could then come tumbling down with a thundering roar. In the thick of the ice-revolution lay the ship."

Miraculously, through the fall, winter, and spring, the *Investigator* did not get smashed to bits or crushed. By the following September, it reached what would be called Mercy Bay, where the captain allowed his men to go ashore onto Banks Island. When the crew was rescued, the stalwart McClure had to be issued a direct order to give up his vessel, despite the fact that most of his crew were in terrible health and could not sail a ship anywhere.

Cold, Contamination and Cannibalism

All of the debates about where to find Franklin and how to rescue him and his party were moot. By the time the first rescue party sallied forth, all of Franklin's men were dead. Franklin was ill-equipped for his job in the Arctic and lacked the savvy to deal with conditions as he found them. His baggage included 1,200 books. He took tins of salt meat and lemon juice, but these proved insufficient to ward off scurvy. Like other English

Chief Trader Paddy Gibson, of the Hudson's Bay Company, looks over the remains of members of the Franklin expedition, which he discovered on King William Island in 1931. (PAM, 1987/363-F-75/27, N7339)

explorers, he was pitifully slow to learn from the people already living in the North. The use of dogs, for example, caught on among the English with fatal slowness. Leopold McClintock, in searching for Franklin, had his young crewmen haul sledges across the ice rather than rely on dogs, despite the advice of William Scoresby, a whaler who had spent time in the far north before the 1820s. Scoresby was not a navy man, and therefore his advice had been laughed at.

In general, the English did not take kindly to any information put forward by someone of the wrong class or ethnic group. Uncooked seal blubber or the stomach contents of wild animals may have helped keep Inuit people happy and healthy, but Sir William Edward Parry found such food "horrible and disgusting." John Ross had hinted that this diet might allow an Englishman to survive, but by this time his ideas had fallen out of favour. Learning lessons from the Native population seemed absurd to the English mind. A doctor on one of the ships searching for Franklin admitted his prejudice by labelling the inhabitants of the Canadian north "the most filthy race" on the planet. And so Franklin and dozens of

The mummified remains of John Torrington, exhumed in 1984 on King William Island by University of Alberta anthropologists. (OWEN BEATTIE)

his fallen brethren who explored the far reaches of the north died, aware of but unheeding the knowledge they needed to survive.

Franklin's 1845-1846 winter camp on Beechey Island was found first, but not a trace of the men or their remains. This had prompted Lady Jane Franklin to raise enough money from friends and the public to send a search team of her own in 1851. The rescue of Franklin became a very popular cause indeed, and the admiralty did not give up altogether, either. Finding Franklin outstripped finding the Northwest Passage in terms of national pride and public prestige. Besides, at that point, the admiralty had also recently lost track of McClure, Collinson, and all their men; no one had heard from them since their departure. For a time, it seemed there would be an unending parade of searchers looking for searchers looking for lost explorers.

Sir Edward Belcher headed up the most ambitious campaign. Notorious among his men as a spiteful, ill-tempered, and venomous leader,

Belcher led a well-appointed expedition and made it to Beechey Island, but there he lost his supply ship, the *Breadalbane*. By the time he returned to England in 1854, he had abandoned four ships in total and learned nothing new of Franklin's fate. Nonetheless, he had performed the good deed of rescuing McClure, and McClure had won the admiralty "prize": he was declared the first to officially traverse the Northwest Passage in his harrowing drift journey from west to east.

There was money and, of course, fame to be had for discovering the truth about, if not the survivors of, Franklin's expedition. John Rae won the hefty sum of £10,000. After his first unsuccessful foray, he had given up the search. In 1853, when he set out from Hudson Bay, he was back on the job of seeking a navigable Northwest Passage. Instead, he was led to the Franklin camp by Inuit people who told him stories and carried artifacts from the crew who had died at Starvation Cove.

Rae had a look at the corpses himself and concluded, "Our wretched Countrymen had been driven to the last dread alternative, as a means of sustaining life." He was talking about cannibalism. Back in England, this news did not go over well. Naturally, the public turned against Rae, certain that Englishmen could never be that barbaric. Charles Dickens, a writer who of course had never been to the Arctic, published his theory that the Inuit had probably murdered the weary travellers. The public liked that much better. Rae was criticized for not studying the evidence of the tragedy more thoroughly but instead racing home to claim the veneration. The Admiralty ultimately didn't condemn Rae but gave him the reward for finding the remains of the Franklin crew. Better to try and close the Franklin chapter as quickly as possible, they thought. A war was in progress in the Crimea, and it was time to put an end to losing men and ships way off in the Arctic ice.

Franklin's wife was among those who did not wish to believe the evidence, and she sent out yet another expedition, with Leopold McClintock in charge. McClintock found more remains and skeletons of the men whose bones had been chewed upon by wild animals. McClintock also found a record left by the Franklin party. Written in May of 1847, the document simply stated, "All well," but before a year had passed, someone had scrawled a sad postscript that Franklin was one of two dozen men who had died.

American explorers Charles Francis Hall and Fredrick Schwatka collected more evidence in the late nineteenth century, and Canadian researchers took up the cause in the 1930s and again in the 1980s. Modern studies show that scurvy took the heaviest toll on the men. Lead in the tinned food and other forms of food contamination may also have led to deaths. In 1984 and 1986, University of Alberta researchers went so far as to exhume three of Franklin's buried crewmen from the permafrost to determine the true cause of death. Tainted food, scurvy, and pneumonia proved to be deadly allies against the beleaguered nineteenth century Englishmen. Modern studies also reveal that, in their desperation to survive, the men had indeed turned to cannibalism.

The SS Beaver *aground off Prospect Point, near Vancouver, 1888.* (MMBC, 4634P)

CHAPTER SEVENTEEN

Pacific Potential

Fighting, Furs, and Dangerous Inlets

FUR TRADING WAS what attracted European entrepreneurs and settlers to British Columbia well into the nineteenth century. Wild animals diminished in number, especially the sea otter, but the notion persevered that this was a place of limitless resources, and few spoke of conservation. The Hudson's Bay Company was the big player in the region. Furs meant money, money meant power, and no one wielded that power more vigorously than the "Little Emperor," Sir George Simpson, the governor of the Hudson's Bay Company from 1821 to 1860.

The rival Pacific Fur Company, owned by the New York businessman John Jacob Astor, had sent the *Tonquin* to the mouth of the Columbia River in 1811, equipped with men and supplies to build Fort Astoria. From this base, the *Tonquin*, under Captain Thorn, had sailed to Clayoquot Sound on Vancouver Island to undertake trade with Chief Wickanninish. Captain Thorn didn't know that an American sealing captain had "borrowed" twelve of the chief's men and then traded them off far to the south along the coast of California, relegating them to slavery or death. Hence Chief Wickanninish bore a stinging grievance against anyone from the sealer's "tribe," and that included Captain Thorn.

Thorn learned too late of Chief Wickanninish's plans for retribution. As he attempted to head his ship safely to sea, Wickanninish's warriors attacked and killed all who fought back or tried to escape in lifeboats. Before they succeeded in killing all the crew, however, one sailor lit a slow-burning fuse. It ignited the gunpowder magazine, blew up the ship, and killed most of the Native warriors.

By 1821, the North West Company had bought out Astor's Pacific Fur Company and merged with the Hudson's Bay Company, and George Simpson undertook to reduce redundancies. He wanted a leaner, meaner, more profitable business, and he didn't mind stepping on toes or throwing his financial and political weight around. He worried that the Americans posed a threat to business if not territorial rights, and therefore he kept a keen eye on potential competition from traders in the New Caledonia and Columbia districts.

John McLoughlin, a big, grey-haired Scot called "the white-headed eagle" by some Native people, would later earn the epithet "the father of Oregon." He came into the fold of the Hudson's Bay Company when it absorbed the North West Company, and Simpson appointed him superintendent of trade on the west side of the Rockies. In 1824, Simpson took a quick but dangerous trip west from the company station at York Factory to ensure that business reforms proceeded according to plan. McLoughlin, who took the safer route by way of the Athabaska River, joined him. The trade in pelts was still good, but Simpson had to admit that the Americans were firmly entrenched in what should have been his domain. Soon he urged his men to harvest every fur-bearing wild creature they could before abandoning territory to American traders and settlers. Fort George, to the south, was abandoned, and Fort Vancouver was established at the confluence of the Columbia and Willamette rivers. Two years later, James Douglas established Fort Connolly, north of the fifty-sixth parallel, to solidify land claims in that region. McLoughlin worked closely with James Douglas, the future governor of the colony of British Columbia, who became administrator of Fort Vancouver in 1830.

At Fort Vancouver, Simpson discovered that McLoughlin and his men were having serious problems with Aboriginals. As their resentment against the English grew, they became increasingly hostile, and with good reason. Douglas had made many enemies, having created his share of conflict with Native people in the region, and he found Fort Vancouver a place of convenient personal safety. As well as providing a refuge for Douglas, the fort also sheltered Jedediah Smith, an American trader whose men had experienced a bloody clash with the Umqua people. Despite this and other turmoil, however, Simpson was pleased to see the settlement more self-reliant than it had been earlier. The staff was reduced — some men had been fired, others had died of diseases, and some had been killed in conflicts with Natives. This was an excellent thing from Simpson's standpoint: it meant fewer mouths to feed, less pressure on the company purse for wages, and a more efficient operation all around. His men grew their own wheat, oats, peas, barley, and potatoes, and they had 150 head of cattle.

Simpson realized that the fur trade was changing due to the whimsy of European fashion. Beaver fur was yielding its glamour to silk, which was being used for men's hats and women's apparel. Fishing, logging, and farming might provide a more sustainable future if the market for fur continued to go downhill. After all, British Columbia had so much of nearly everything to offer, and no commodity should be overlooked.

Diversification meant that Simpson needed to strengthen his position along the coast. He sent Captain Hanwell sailing off in the *William and Ann* with a small contingent to perform yet another survey of the coast. Hanwell didn't like taking his ship into what he considered some of the more dangerous inlets, so his information on the current state of coastal affairs was somewhat incomplete, but he did determine that the Nuu-chah-nulth people (known to the English as Nootka) could find almost no fur-bearing animals to trap and thus had no furs to trade. Business had been good — too good for a while — but now that resource had been tapped out. The mouth of the Nass River seemed a suitable place for a trading fort, but ships doing business anywhere along the coast would need to be geared up for fighting as well as shipping.

"Fifty-four Forty or Fight"

The Boston traders still had a fair stake in coastal trade. Simpson and McLoughlin found this annoying enough to consider dramatic measures to flush them out of the competition. The Hudson's Bay Company would begin a two-pronged trading plan sure to work: they would trade both booze and guns to Native people, like their American counterparts, and they'd match or beat the prices set by American traders.

Fort Simpson was built on the Nass River in 1831, and Fort Mc-Loughlin on Milbanke Sound and Fort Nisqually on Puget Sound in 1833. In 1836, the Hudson's Bay Company became even more nervous about Americans elbowing into their trade territory, and the company imported more ships for coastal trade, including a twin-engine wood-burning steamship, the *Beaver*. Native people were highly impressed by this ship that could sail without wind. It was expensive, burning as much as two cords of wood a day, but it could travel quickly and steam farther north with relative ease. It could also navigate the tricky channels and powerful, shifting tidal currents more readily than the traditional sailing vessels. Both, however, had to contend with fog and rain, hidden reefs, and islands with high cliffs hungry to bring white traders to their deaths.

Booze, guns, steam, and high prices for furs gave the Hudson's Bay Company the edge Simpson was looking for, and the company also forged a deal with Russia to supply the Russian outposts along the lower Alaskan coast. To squeeze the Boston Men even harder, the Hudson's Bay Company decided to increase its farming and cattle raising ventures to supply the Russians as well as themselves and to firm up territorial rights.

Simpson and McLoughlin didn't always agree on the best methods for further development of the region. McLoughlin was less paranoid about the Americans than his boss, and on another junket to Fort Vancouver, Simpson found McLoughlin hosting some Americans under the command of Charles Wilkes. Wilkes wanted Washington to lay claim to all lands from the Mexican border to 54°40' latitude. Simpson didn't like the sound of this Yankee expansionism in the slightest. He decided to do his own survey of the coast again, this time with James Douglas. On this excursion, he saw some very habitable shoreline on Vancouver Island that he thought could bear the imprint of English civilization, and he visited the Russian governor to the north to firm up good will and business alliances. This trip also persuaded him to bring a halt to the liquor trade along the coast, however lucrative, now that the Boston traders were out of the picture.

Despite his fear of Americans, Simpson continued to try to keep his operation lean and efficient, and by the 1840s he had closed down smaller coastal forts, leaving Fort Simpson as the central trading post. The diminished role of Fort Vancouver did not sit well with McLoughlin. McLoughlin had also suffered a personal tragedy when his son, John, was murdered to the north in Russian territory in a drunken dispute. Simpson had arrived in Sitka soon after the incident, and, upon hearing the details, had decided that the murderer acted in self defence. The issue was turned over to Russian authorities, who did nothing. When news of this reached McLoughlin, he felt outraged and betrayed by his colleague.

And so McLoughlin's sympathy for his American counterparts grew, and American settlements increased in the Willamette Valley near Fort

Vancouver, side by side with the French Canadian farming families that Simpson was bringing in to counter the American influence. In 1842, 140 American settlers arrived with an agent of "Indian Affairs." McLoughlin obliged them with seed and farming equipment. By 1843, there were 300 settlers. Sixty-five of them signed a petition to the U.S. Senate requesting that the territory of New Caledonia be annexed to the United States, and later that year, the settlers decided to adopt the laws of the state of Iowa. By the fall, a swarm of 900 Americans moved in. The next year, a whopping 1,400 more arrived, and the men began to organize their own militia.

By now the British were alarmed enough to send one warship, the HMS *Modeste*, and a pair of secret agents, Lt. Mervin Vavasour and Lt. Henry James Warre, to study the situation. But the evidence was quite clear: all the territory south and east of Vancouver was so well occupied by the Americans that it would have to be abandoned. But the Americans wouldn't be allowed to have it all. The forty-ninth parallel would be far enough. In an ironic twist of history, Simpson's reluctance to increase employment and encourage serious permanent settlements in the region left the area wide open for the Americans, who seized the opportunity to settle people on fertile soil and so lay legitimate claim to it. Simpson's obsession with efficiency may have ultimately cost Canada a fair chunk of North America's West Coast.

By now, though, it was too late to worry about establishing more loyal British farms; warships would have to do instead. A flotilla of the British navy filed into Juan de Fuca Strait, having sailed north from the navy's western hemisphere headquarters in Chile, ready to stem the Yankee tide.

The war cry of the American politicians had the ring of a modern high school pep rally: "Fifty-four forty or fight!" the hawks shouted at the doves in Congress. But British and American representatives avoided war by sitting down at a table and parcelling up the land in something akin to a gentlemanly manner. Plenty of ordinary American citizens, eager to pick up rifles and take another crack at the English, were sorely disappointed when the line was drawn at the forty-ninth parallel, far short of the northerly 54°40'. The Americans now owned the fertile valley along much of the Columbia River, but Vancouver Island and the north mainland were maintained as part of the British Empire. However, as George Woodcock notes, all this wheeling and dealing created a treaty "that ignored the native peoples, still the most numerous population in the region."

Old Squaretoes

James Douglas, a man notorious for his stubborn nature and nicknamed "Old Squaretoes," wielded considerable power in the British Northwest. He liked the look of a rocky shoreline near the southern tip of Vancouver Island and declared that here should rise yet another outpost: Fort Camosun, later redubbed Fort Albert, then Fort Victoria, and eventually Victoria, the seaport that would become the capital city of British Columbia.

Douglas moved men from forts McLoughlin and Durham to the new location, but workers from the Songhee nation built most of the fort. Native people were also employed to clear land to grow wheat and raise cattle. There was little left in the way of fur trading, but now meat and grain could be sold at a fair profit to American whalers as well as to the Russians and, of course, to the Royal Navy. Salmon was still plentiful on the island as well as on the mainland, the prospects were good for a timber industry, and coal had been discovered on Vancouver Island as well.

Intimations of prosperity convinced the British government to pay a bit more attention to the Northwest, and in 1849, Douglas was told to move his primary base of operations to the flourishing Fort Victoria. He gladly loaded up his official stash of £100,000 in paper currency, gold, and furs and moved to the island, where he was pleased to discover men from his company living in their own well-appointed log cabins. He was more than gratified to see that something rather civilized, or at least something rather British, had already been carved out of the wilderness here.

In that same year, Vancouver Island was declared a British colony, but it would be "rented" to the Hudson's Bay Company for seven shillings a year if the company was simply willing to continue doing business and promote further settlement. Richard Blanshard was named the first governor, but Douglas remained the power behind the figurehead. Blanshard didn't last long. Bad health and a crisis over a mining labour dispute, as well as the murder of three sailors by Kwakiutl men, discouraged him to the point that he retreated to England. As he sailed away, he left a legislative council in charge, with James Douglas at its head.

At first, the young colony had no police force and no justice system except for Hudson's Bay Company cops — "bluejackets" hired to keep some semblance of order. For the most part, Native people were left

Sir James Douglas, September 15, 1877.
(NLC)

alone, unless some conflict arose between them and white settlers. Douglas brought in his brother-in-law, David Cameron, from Demerara to act as the colony's first judge, despite the fact that he had no real experience at such a job.

Douglas's company gave away free land and free supplies with a generous hand to new settlers who would create farms. Captain Edward Edwards Langford knew a good thing when he saw it. He moved his wife and five daughters to the island, where he threw extravagant parties and graciously allowed the host governing body to pick up the tab as part of his food allowance. By the time Langford's allowance was trimmed, he had become something of a political enemy to those in power, thanks to his social connections.

Back in London, the colonial administration feared that riffraff would be attracted to the colony of Vancouver Island, and, like Oregon, it would fill up with rabble. They agreed that Edward Gibbon Wakefield had sound ideas for bringing the right kind of settlers to the island. Wakefield's plan was to sell Vancouver Island land at one pound per acre to British gentry, who would then agree to resettle their own labourers on it. Each landowner had to buy at least twenty acres and bring in five men or three married couples per 100 acres. As well as attracting the right kind of landowners, this neat little plan would establish the English class system wholesale. Although few English gentleman rushed to join it and sail off to such a faraway homestead, most in the colonial government agreed that it would keep out the trash — the speculators and the poor.

Between 1834 and 1859, trading mixed with the British military presence had firmly entrenched a string of coastal forts: Vancouver, Nisqually, Langley, Victoria, Rupert, McLoughlin, Simpson, Stikine, and Taku.

In 1851, word leaked to the outside world about gold in Haida Gwaii, the Queen Charlotte Islands. Wild stories circulated about Haida making bullets of gold to shoot crows, and this news prompted outsiders to believe in a mother-lode of gold waiting for anyone willing to look for it. There was, in fact, a small pocket of the valuable mineral on the shoreline near what would become Gold Harbour, on land owned by the Haida. The Hudson's Bay Company sent the *Una* to dig up what they felt was "rightfully" theirs, but the Haida weren't about to give it up without a fight.

To complicate matters, Americans arrived from San Francisco to try to cash in, provoking the government to send in the HMS *Thetis* to assert British rule and chase out any Yanks who might want to annex the island to their own country. Haida Chief Edenshaw soon made a deal with the British and turned over the available gold, which was loaded onto the *Una*. Sailing south with the ill-gotten gain, the *Una* ran afoul of rocks and weather near Neah Bay. Displeased to discover more white traders in the region, the local Maka people set fire to the ship where it was stuck, and it sank with the gold aboard, returning it, if not to Haida Gwaii, at least to the sea which the Haida revered.

Deep Insults, Disease, and Homegrown Anarchy

By the early 1850s, the Royal Navy was docking a substantial number of ships at Esquimalt Harbour, near Victoria, and taking on coal for its steamships at Nanaimo, further up the east coast of Vancouver Island. In spite of the Crimean War pitting them against one another in Europe, the British and Russians on the northwest coast of North America remained on relatively good terms and successfully avoided infecting the region with battles fought in distant lands.

The English continued to have a difficult time understanding the Haida, and tensions grew wherever the English went. In 1861, some Haida raided the ship *Laurel*, seeking revenge for a bottle of diluted whisky the captain had sold them. Deeply insulted by this bad trade, Haida warriors carried off goods from the ship, eventually raising the ire of the military, who fetched a gunboat to defend English property. In the bloody skirmish, the English ended up killing a Haida chief.

Foreign diseases almost always attacked West Coast people who encountered Europeans. When a ship carrying smallpox arrived in Victoria, one well-meaning governor insisted that visiting Haida leaders — in town to discuss a dispute over land — be warned to leave. Unfortunately, the Haida negotiators interpreted the order as some kind of scam to swindle them out of more land. They refused to go, so the military forced them out, their canoes towed north by a steamship. But the infection had already set in, and before they reached Haida Gwaii, most of the Haida were dead or dying from the disease.

A kind of homegrown anarchy prevailed in many of the white communities of British Columbia. Governor Douglas tried to license the saloons, and charge a duty on cut timber; his citizens didn't like either of those rules. When Reverend Robert Staines, a schoolteacher, spoke up on behalf of the settlers, Douglas promptly fired him, and Staines set off for England to put the grievances before the London Committee. He never made it, dying in a shipwreck off Cape Flattery. Islanders, however, continued to present petitions and complaints about government interference in their lives, and eventually they succeeded in achieving some small semblance of representation.

In order to vote, you had to be male, of English descent, and own at least twenty acres of land. That left out most of the truly independent landowners, who could not afford plots that large. In 1856, the forty people on Vancouver Island eligible to vote elected seven representatives, who met occasionally in a smoked-filled room in the fort. It was a government of sorts, but it had almost no power; the Hudson's Bay Company ran the show and intended to keep on running it. The assembly tried to extend the right to vote to the smaller landowners, but the bigwigs in London handily fended off this move towards democracy until 1859.

By then, other factors had already created a shift in West Coast demographics. In 1858, nearly 30,000 Americans arrived in the Fraser Valley on the mainland looking for gold, and indeed there was gold to be had near the Thompson River, on the sandbars of the lower Fraser east of

Quesnel, and at the western edge of the Caribou Mountains. Governor Douglas saw this gold rush as an intimidating invasion of unkempt, unruly, and ultimately democratic forces from a belligerent neighbour. He declared all lands in the vicinity of the Fraser River to be Crown property, and he insisted that anyone who wanted to dig a hole had to have a license — and pay a fee, of course. Many of the miners were veterans of the California gold rush of 1849, and their arrival shot to hell the colonial office's intention to make this territory a quiet, gentrified mock-up of rural England. The mainland was declared a colony unto itself, and Queen Victoria named it British Columbia, the old name of New Caledonia having been assumed by a French colony in the South Pacific. James Douglas had the honour of being governor of both Vancouver Island and British Columbia, and therefore he stepped down from his job as western boss of the Hudson's Bay Company. Choosing a capital caused dispute, of course. The first site, to be called Derby, was scrapped, much to the chagrin of land speculators, and instead, New Westminster was selected.

The unruly miners were particularly offended by British notions that they should be civil, pay taxes, and generally accept government control. In July of 1858, a miners' riot in Victoria had to be quelled by soldiers ushered in from the mainland. Not long after this, there were other outbreaks of violence. A detachment of Royal Engineers was sent over from England to exert control over the miners and also to help improve the new colony with roads and buildings.

While the mainland was populated predominately by restless California gold men, a curious mix of people made up Victoria's population of 5,000. The first Blacks to arrive came from California with a promise from the Vancouver Island government that they would not suffer the persecution they did in the States. They formed, with little or no pay, the Victoria Pioneer Rifle Corps and swore allegiance to the Queen. Although the colony was not without racism, the Black militiamen were treated with somewhat more respect than they had received in their previous home. The Chinese, most of whom had been imported as indentured labourers, did not fare as well. Treated like second-class citizens, to put it mildly, they lived in strictly segregated communities, maintained their traditional diet, dress, and religion, and performed menial work for white employers or established their own small businesses.

The Pig War

It was a Nova Scotian operating much in the manner of Joseph Howe who helped to stir up stronger democratic sentiment on Vancouver Island. Amor de Cosmos was born William Smith, but, with such a common name, he found he had trouble getting his mail while living in California during the gold rush. So he changed his name to something unforgettable, started receiving his correspondence, and procceded to get rich speculating in land as people poured into California hoping to strike gold. He moved north after things quieted down there and started a Victoria newspaper, the *British Colonist*, in 1858. After a couple of failed attempts, he managed to get himself elected to the small legislative assembly and pushed for ambitious reform: true democracy, the merger of the two colonies, and a further union with the other British North American colonies.

In 1859, the Americans and British had not fully settled their grief over the western border. Vague wording in the 1846 Oregon boundary treaty meant that both north and south claimed the San Juan Islands in Georgia Straight. The Hudson's Bay Company had established a sheep farm on the largest island, even though the United States had declared this place part of the newly-minted territory of Washington, and it kept some pigs there, as well as the sheep. Unsuccessful American miners wanting to become farmers on the San Juan Islands were annoyed by the British. One of those men claimed some land in the middle of a sheep farm, and when a British pig broke through an American fence, the Yank shot the pig. Anger was expressed over this indiscretion, the pig owner wanted a cash settlement for his dead pig, and so began the so-called Pig War of 1859. The accumulated bad feelings raised the potential for a heated military conflict.

The American general William S. Harney visited James Douglas over this pig and land problem, and then he wrote to his commander back in Washington, D.C., "The English can not colonize successfully so near our people; they are too exacting. This, with the pressing necessities of our commerce on this coast, will induce them to yield, eventually, Vancouver's Island to our government. It is as important to the Pacific States as Cuba is to the Atlantic." Harney convinced the Americans on the San Juans to sign a petition asking for military help for protection from the Native people, who may or may not have been the least bit hostile. British and American troops were sent in — 100 men from each side — to create a nervous stand-off between trigger-happy soldiers. Ownership of the islands remained in question until 1871, when an unlikely arbiter, Kaiser Wilhelm I of Germany, declared the Americans rightful owners. But that would be as far as the Americans would go in trying to push the forty-ninth parallel boundary north to fifty-four forty.

The Esquimalt Naval Base was opened in 1864, replacing the former Pacific British naval headquarters that had been far to the south in Valparaiso, Chile. Now Vancouver Island had a very significant military presence, and if fighting were to break out again on this coast, British Columbians would have a formidable force behind them, at least on the high seas.

CHAPTER EIGHTEEN

The Sea in Their Blood

Driven by the Winds

MARITIMERS AND NEWFOUNDLANDERS enjoyed what is known as the Golden Age of Sail more or less between 1830 and 1880. Ships were built in the big harbours and in tiny coves all around the region. In many cases, timber could be cut readily from nearby forests, the keel was laid on blocks near the water's edge, and ships were built from scratch, based on carved models created by local designer-artisans. Frames were moulded into shape with steam and fastened to the keel with hardwood pegs. Sometimes a handful of men could build an entire ship in a matter of months by cutting the trees, sawing the logs into boards, fitting everything perfectly into shape, and then "corking" (caulking) the seams with oakum to make the ship watertight. Then water from the sea would be pumped into the hull to check for leaks and swell the wood before the vessel itself floated upon the sea.

These amazingly sleek and finely crafted ships were built in small communities like Dorchester, New Brunswick, on the Bay of Fundy, and set off to sail around the world. Boys as young as twelve could sign onto a ship to begin a life's work at sea. Captains took their families along on some of the larger ships, and occasionally children grew up on board, travelling around the world several times. Captains understood the construction of their ships down to every minute detail and had skilled craftsman aboard who could replace or reconstruct anything that needed fixing. The captain might keep a "slop chest" to sell tobacco and clothing to his men while at sea and he would act as doctor as well, on occasion delivering his own wife's baby if necessary.

Shipboard life was harsh, and captains were all-powerful. Most captains were reasonable men, and some generous and kind, but others were cruel, even brutal. At sea, the captain's rules had to be obeyed, and they were enforced by the first mate with severe punishment if necessary. One sadistic Nova Scotian skipper hung six disobedient crewmen by their big toes and thumbs from the rigging. Rats and mice infested almost every ship, and cats used to control them lived their entire lives without ever setting foot on land. Despite enormous hardships, though, some captains were like the cats and spent almost all their days at sea. The life was addictive for those who loved it, and many found retirement to mundane life ashore a great disappointment.

Men went to sea for every reason imaginable: some for adventure, some to avoid punishment for crimes, and others to support a family back home. Cooks were chosen with care because the quality of the food could control shipboard attitude, and a bad cook meant an unhappy voyage. Shipboard meals consisted of salted pork or beef, potatoes and onions, dried fruit, soup, molasses, and even sometimes the luxury of fresh bread. However, if the voyage lasted longer than planned, men might end up eating nothing more than hardtack or half-rotten potatoes and cabbage, and morale suffered badly.

Benjamin Doane was a young Nova Scotian on the brig *Reindeer* when it set sail in 1843. He kept a detailed journal in which he noted that the captain drank freely from a ten-gallon keg of brandy and ate fine food at his table, while the men fared quite a bit worse. Doane wrote, "The only bread we had was hardtack which had been in the bread locker two voyages, and it was black and hard and full of great fat weevils nearly as big as centipedes." The meat was "rancid and rusty," but the cook boiled it and served it anyway.

When ships travelling around the world found the need to replace crew — due to death from injury or disease or maybe simple desertion — new men were recruited from any port on the route. Thus, crews ended up as a diverse mix of men of all ages, backgrounds, and races. If new crewmen were needed in a foreign port, a "crimp" enlisted them, preferably but not necessarily without physical coercion.

Keeping a ship afloat and on course was a round-the-clock business, and work was divided between "watches," usually of four hours each. Injuries and accidents were common, with danger all around. In 1789, Peter Carrol was swept overboard from the *County of Pictou* by a wave that

Shipbuilding in Dorchester, New Brunswick. (NAC, C-017565)

washed over deck during a squall. The current pulled him twenty-five metres away from the ship before another wave picked him up and tossed him back on deck, shaken and bruised but alive. Not all sailors were so fortunate.

Danger and adventure at sea were accompanied by hard, repetitious work and boredom. Sometimes singing helped to relieve the stress or the drudgery, and sailors sang songs old and new, songs of love, whimsy, or protest to lighten their spirits. Although sailing a ship required a tremendous amount of knowledge, so much seemed beyond explanation that superstition guided almost everyone on board, including the captain. It was bad luck to launch a ship on Friday, for example, or to name a ship for a fish; whistling brought on bad fortune, as did setting down a hatch cover the wrong way. Some predicted tomorrow's winds by observing a shooting star.

Frostbite, Malaria and Murder

Colin McKay wrote extensively about life aboard ships during the Golden Age of Sail. Men commonly endured frostbite, he says, and frozen sea spray could coat the rigging with rock-hard ice, sometimes unbalancing the ship and capsizing it. In warmer climes, hurricanes caused terror, and in foreign ports diseases like cholera or malaria could knock a good man down. At sea, almost anything could go wrong and lead to disaster. McKay reports that in one year thirty-one ships and more than 100 men who sailed out of Yarmouth were lost in disasters at sea. The shipping business was lucrative, however, for the owners of sailing ships. They sent fish, wood, and other resources from the Maritimes to foreign markets, and on the return voyages the ships brought back coffee, molasses, sugar, rum, and coconuts. Sometimes ships did not return home for years at a time, instead travelling from port to port carrying coal, flour, oil, mahogany, or anything else that made for profitable trade.

When emergencies occurred at sea, sailors might have to replace a ripped or lost sail and rig a new one in the middle of the night in a storm. Sometimes waves would pound against the sides of the ship, loosening the oakum that kept the vessel watertight, or the sea might even crack the boards in the hull, allowing seawater to rush into the hold. To keep their ship afloat, the crew might have to man the pumps for hours, days, or even weeks until they could make port.

Wind was a good thing to propel a sailing ship, but too much of it could kill, and no wind at all meant that a ship would stay put until the air began to move again. Many sailors were happy to leave the cold and ice of the northern sea behind, but a night near a tropical seaport might mean fleeing a hot, mosquito-infested cabin to tie a hammock in the rigging, only to be soaked by rain. In McKay's view, most Canadian sailors from the east and west coasts were "abstemious with the bottle and enjoyed a surprising immunity from tropical diseases." Perhaps he was simply implying that more men died from other catastrophes at sea than from drink or malaria.

Maritime sailors faced dangers other than disease and storms, some of them created by the men themselves. Far from the watchful eye of any of legal authorities, many crimes took place on the open seas. Perhaps one of the most infamous is what happened aboard the *Saladin*. In 1842, George Fielding sailed from Liverpool, Nova Scotia, as captain of the *Vitula*, headed for South America. Off the coast of Peru, he began to illegally load guano — dried bird droppings considered to be a valuable fertilizer — from an island. He intended to carry the smelly cargo back to Nova Scotia, where it would fetch a good price. Unfortunately, he was breaking Peruvian law. His ship was confiscated, and he and his son were thrown in jail.

They escaped and fled to Valparaiso, where Captain Sandy Mackenzie agreed to carry them back home to Nova Scotia at no charge. Mackenzie had the *Saladin* loaded with twenty tons of copper, thirteen 150-pound bars of silver, and other forms of cash when it left Valparaiso in February of 1844. Fielding and some of the other men on board decided to hijack the ship and steal the valuable cargo. They first murdered a crewman loyal to Captain Mackenzie, and next they killed the captain himself with an axe. Fielding declared himself captain, and all the conspirators declared loyalty to each other, promising to share the wealth and never tell a soul about the bloody deeds. They intended to sink the ship and leave with the loot, but on May 22, the indelicate navigators ran the *Saladin* aground near Country Harbour, Nova Scotia. When a local skipper came on board, he sensed something was wrong. The guilty men were arrested, taken to Halifax, and charged with piracy, which called for death by hanging in chains. For four of the conspirators, the charge was "reduced" to murder, punishable by a simpler death, public hanging. Nova Scotians travelled to Halifax from as far as ninety kilometres away to watch the *Saladin* pirates hanged for their gruesome deeds.

Shipwrecks Aplenty

At sea, something as seemingly benign as sand can prove to be a murderous enemy. Sable Island, situated about 100 kilometres off the coast of Nova Scotia, is not much more than a fairly substantial sandbar that just happens to rise above the waterline. A beautiful grassy island of beaches, dunes, and small ponds, over the centuries it has been the demonic site of unnumbered catastrophes. The best guess is that some 5,000 ships have been wrecked on or near Sable Island since the mid-eighteenth century, earning it the nickname "Graveyard of the Atlantic." Nearby, the Labrador Current collides with the Gulf Stream, and other powerful currents swirl around the island itself, sometimes trapping lifeboats or swimmers who can't make their way ashore. To complicate things for mariners, the island has no safe harbours. At the whim of storms and currents, the island has shifted in shape and size and thus to some degree in location over the centuries, but it has always remained a hazard to navigation.

The French ship *Legere* went down off Sable Island in June of 1746, the already wary captain having miscalculated the outer sand bars that surround it. What remained of the crew washed up on shore, and help did not arrive until the following June. In the 1800s, a lifesaving station was set up to help sorry souls caught in the predictable calamities. Edward Hodgson was in charge there in 1825, living with his family and prepared with a team of men to rescue whoever needed rescuing. And many did. In September of that year, the *Adelphi* went aground, and fourteen people had to be hauled from the hungry sea and then cared for. A schooner soon smashed into the sandbars, and eight more guests joined the Hodgson household. In January of the new year, another schooner, the *Brothers*, ran aground; three drowned, but the rescue workers saved the captain, six crew, and a baby. Then came the timber ship, *Elizabeth*, and a shipload of immigrants on the *Nassau*. Seven died in that wreck, but thirty-seven made it ashore. Next to run aground was the *Agamemnon*, but no one drowned in that incident.

The schooner *Guide* ran afoul of weather and waves off Sable Island in 1853. The able rescue crew bravely brought all of these lucky men ashore through gigantic waves. The story goes that the captain preferred to go down with his ship, and it would have been a Maritime form of courtesy to let him do so, except for the fact that Dorothea Lynde Dix, the renowned American do-gooder, was visiting the island at that time. She arrived at the scene on the beach, and when she heard about the stubborn captain, she gave orders to the lifesaving crew to return through the heavy surf and retrieve the fool against his will, if necessary by tying him up. The weary rescuers rowed into the waves once more and succeeded in bringing the reluctant and raving captain ashore. Dorothea Dix rewarded the Sable Island heroes by raising money for newer boats and better lifesaving equipment.

Even modern navigational improvements cannot prevent shipwrecks off Sable Island. But this bad-luck sandbar proved to be a lucky location for relaying radio signals from ships at sea to bases on land, particularly in wartime. Thomas Head Raddall, a wireless operator who arrived on Sable in 1921, immortalized the place in his brilliant feminist novel, *The Nymph and the Lamp*.

An Age of Invention and Vision

The shipbuilders on the Atlantic coast were inventive craftsmen, often creating whatever tools or items they needed for building ships, without concern for technology used elsewhere. Out of such an environment came John Patch of Yarmouth, Nova Scotia. In 1833 he experimented with a wooden version of the screw propeller, with which he made a boat cruise around Yarmouth harbour by continuously turning a hand crank. Captain Silas Kelly tried out his amazing gimmick in 1834. Mounted on the schooner *Royal George*, it allowed the ship to move about without wind. Patch went to Boston and Washington to register a patent, but he was turned away. It's likely that an employee of the patent office stole Patch's idea and sold it to the highest bidder, for Patch's design was first registered in England, but not in his name. The marine screw propeller went on to become one of the most important inventions of modern shipping, but John Patch did not profit from it. In 1858, when he was 77 years old, he lived in the Yarmouth poorhouse, crippled and broke, never having received credit or money for an invention that changed the world.

John Fraser, along with Alexander Munro, pioneered the use of a diver's helmet in North America. Off Cape Bear, Prince Edward Island, they salvaged the *Mallabar* in 1839 using the newfangled helmet, bringing up thirty-five sunken cannons along with tons of lead shot. In Pictou harbour, they demonstrated a remarkable new diving outfit that consisted of a large hood with windows, attached to a rubber suit. Air was pumped from a boat into the helmet to sustain the diver below. Munro stayed underwater for more than half an hour. From the harbour floor, he brought back an anchor and chain, and the crowd went wild.

The same year that John Patch was experimenting with the first screw propeller, James Audubon, another visionary of a different sort, travelled to Labrador looking for birds and animals he had not sketched before. He had mixed feelings about the place. "The country, so wild and grand, is of itself enough to interest anyone in its wonderful dreariness." The American religious leader Robert Lowell had more dramatic words for what he observed of Newfoundland a few years later: "A monstrous mass of rock and gravel, almost without soil, like a strange thing from the bottom of the deep, lifted up, suddenly, into sunshine and storm." Charles Dickens visited Halifax in 1842. His ship ran aground on a mudbank when it arrived, and his first impression was that it was "dark, foggy and damp, and there were bleak hills all around us." Once ashore, his attitude improved little as he described Halifax as "a curiosity of ugly dullness." He must have met some Haligonians who lifted his spirits, however, for he later reported to the British press that the city was also "cheerful, thriving and industrious."

Dickens had obviously remained sheltered from some of the harshest of the region's realities, particularly the plight of poverty-stricken immigrants. He did not, for example, have cause to visit Partridge Island, in Saint John harbour. Noteworthy as the home of the world's first steam-driven foghorn and the site of New Brunswick's first lighthouse, it was also an island of great misery and sadness, a quarantine station where ships would unload any human cargo thought to carry disease. During the 1830s, cholera had savaged the passengers of many immigrant ships, and countless died in transit or shortly after arriving. They were buried on Partridge Island.

The hospitals built on Partridge Island could not accommodate the wave of desperate, starving Irish immigrants in flight from the potato famine in their homeland. In 1847 alone, the famine sent 16,000 refugees in search of a better life in New Brunswick, and at least 2,000 died of disease or starvation en route. James Patrick Collins, a young doctor just starting out, joined Dr. George Harding in the formidable and heart-wrenching task of trying to deal with a typhus epidemic on Partridge Island in May of 1847. Twenty-five hundred immigrants needed their care. Many lived in tents, some remained on ships; all too many were already dying of the disease. Soon, both Collins and Dr. Harding's brother, William, had come down with the infection, and Collins died in his attempt to help the suffering.

Ambitious Endeavours

Although the coastal dwellers of nineteenth-century Canada saw their share of pain and suffering, this was also a time of optimism and progress. It's estimated that at least 6,000 wooden vessels were constructed in New Brunswick during the nineteenth century; by mid-century, shipbuilding was by far the biggest business in New Brunswick. The "Johnny Wood-boats," humble craft for hauling timber, had come into their own as early as 1783, but they evolved into versatile ships for transporting all kinds of freight. Sixty feet long and twenty wide, they were stable but slow, and eventually the sleeker, more efficient schooners replaced them.

The first big boom came in the 1820s, when ships were needed to carry timber to England. Whereas most American and British ships were made of hardwood, many New Brunswick vessels were made of softwood such as tamarack (or hackmatack) and spruce. These ships were more buoyant because they were so much lighter in weight, but they were also much more prone to rot. Many lasted only ten years, despite efforts to salt and pickle the wood for preservation.

Ships started out in the 300-ton range but became much larger for the long voyages to California and Australia. In the 1850s, Richard and William Wright of Saint John built two huge vessels, the *White Star* and the *Morning Light*, each weighing in at about 2,500 tons. The *Morning Light*, slightly larger, remained New Brunswick's biggest ship until it went down off the New Jersey coast in 1889.

More famous than the *Morning Light*, however, was the *Marco Polo*, built by James Smith in Saint John in 1851. Considerably lighter and smaller than the Wrights' ships, the *Marco Polo* was renowned as the fastest ship in the world after making a voyage from Liverpool to Australia and back in less than six months. Faster than many steamships of the time, the *Marco Polo* travelled as much as 311 nautical miles a day with the right winds. On one of several trips to Australia during a gold rush, Captain James Nichol "Bully" Forbes, living up to his nickname, had his entire crew arrested on false charges and held in jail to insure that they would show up for the return voyage and not run off in search of gold. When he was ready to leave, he had them released into his custody and sailed away. Despite travelling throughout the world many times, the *Marco Polo* met its fate not far from home, breaking up in a storm off Cavendish, Prince Edward Island, in 1883.

Joseph Salter started building ships from tamarack, spruce, and birch at a place known simply as "The Bend" — an elbow in the tidal Petitcodiac River. The Bend would be renamed Moncton in 1855, after General Robert Monckton, although somebody lost track of the "k" in the general's name, and the town officials decided to keep the incorrect spelling rather than do more paperwork. Moncton became a highly industrialized town, and Salter's shipbuilding yards remained strong, employing more than

"The Marco Polo," *attributed to James Guy Evans of Mobile, Alabama (c. 1851).*
(YCM)

1,000 men as tree cutters and tradesmen, including carpenters, mill-
wrights, blacksmiths, and shipbuilding specialists.

Salter had lived his share of adventurers at sea. He was well liked by
his men, and when they came looking for a shorter workday, he agreed, as
long as they promised not to spend their time boozing it up in the local
pubs. Moncton prospered, as did Salter, who sold his giant square-riggers
in all corners of the world. For several years, thanks to the Crimean War
and the Australian gold rush, he could build ships on speculation and
then find a willing buyer. Suddenly, though, Salter suffered a reverse of
fortune when one of his unsold ships sailed into Liverpool harbour and
remained unsold — there were no buyers. This had never happened before. Cash-poor all of a sudden, with this and other vessels unsold, Salter
couldn't pay the men who worked for him. The result was a full-scale
recession for Moncton. The Westmoreland Bank went bankrupt, and so
did the town paper. Joseph Salter stayed around and tried to breathe
some life back into his business empire, but eventually, in 1870, he gave up

and moved to Cape Breton. Moncton wouldn't bounce back until 1875, when the Intercolonial Railway opened its headquarters there.

Between 1830 and 1873, Prince Edward Island, too, was on a boat-building binge. Trees were cut all over the island and over 3,000 ships, averaging 200 tons each, were built for the local and world market. By the middle of the century, much of the island had become "civilized," the cleared land proved excellent for farming, and the population rose to over 60,000. Connection with the mainland dramatically improved when the steamship *Pocahontas* started shuttling mail and people back and forth from the island to Pictou, Nova Scotia. While the Northumberland Strait was generally kind to those passing back and forth, sometimes the waters off Prince Edward Island got blasted by raging storms, including a famous one that struck in early October 1851. A hundred ships at their moorings were bashed about for two days, while off the coast, sailors who couldn't make it ashore were hammered hard. That one storm caused more than eighty shipwrecks and killed 150 people at sea and on shore.

In 1853, a freak storm caught the *Fairy Queen*, the successor to the *Pocahontas*, and Captain Bulye had to lower the lifeboats. Nine of his crew and the captain himself made it into the boats and the lines were cut, setting them free. Left on board were four women and three men who would die and a shipload of mail that would be delivered to the fish. The captain argued that he never intended to leave anyone behind, but he would be remembered as a captain who refused to go down with his vessel.

Grand Manan Island, off the coast of New Brunswick, had always been a rich fishing ground for pollock, herring, cod, hake, and lobster. Britain confirmed its claim to the island in 1817, and by 1850, the thousand or so islanders had more than 120 boats to fish the nearby waters, which, unfortunately, were already over-fished. One forward-thinking naturalist, Moses Henry Perley, conducted a detailed study of the fish in New Brunswick waters, and the Fisheries Act, which was based on his recommendations, was passed. The act limited the herring season to three months each year to ensure that the children and grandchildren of Grand Manan Islanders would find herring to catch.

The plan worked well enough, and Grand Manan fishermen and their Bay of Fundy neighbours still caught plenty of herring to be processed. By 1884, sardine canning was hugely successful: Grand Manan shipped more than a million cases or 20,000 tons of sardines to the United States and the West Indies. At Seal Cove, the larger herring were strung on lines, hung up in smokehouses, and cured into kippers or bloaters. Smoked herring was in great demand in American taverns, where patrons washed down the salty snacks with more and more beer.

Along these parts of the Fundy shore, as well as fishing from boats, fishermen also used weirs to catch all manner of sea creatures. They erected open rings of stakes and attached nets to them, and each day at low tide, fishermen without boats could walk the sea floor or take horse carts out to sea and collect the bounty that the retreating tide had left behind.

Nova Scotian Frederic Gisborne was responsible for creating the first telegraph link to Charlottetown in 1852 by laying a submarine cable from New Brunswick to Prince Edward Island. His next challenge, undertaken in 1854, was to connect St. John's, Newfoundland, with the mainland by cable. This job included an arduous overland route through rugged terrain that took 600 men all summer to accomplish. In the first attempt to lay the undersea cable from Cape Ray, Newfoundland, to Cape Breton Island across the Cabot Strait, storms made the effort nearly impossible, and seventy-two kilometres of cable were lost on the ocean floor. It was a setback but not a defeat for Gisborne, and the link to Newfoundland was successfully in place by the following year. Gisborne went on to even more ambitious endeavours. He succeeded in laying the first transatlantic cable connecting Europe to North America, with the cable coming ashore at Heart's Content, Newfoundland.

England's Navigation Act had worked well for New Brunswick ports, giving them special treatment as colonial trade partners. When the Act was repealed in 1849, New Brunswick had to operate in a free market, without protection. At first the Americans, willing to take advantage of new trade options to the north, remained somewhat unwilling to open up their own ports. In 1854, however, a treaty was struck giving free passage to British colonial wood, fish, and farm goods in exchange for

American fishing rights in Maritime Canada. New Brunswick lost fish but gained a market for its wood. The ensuing boom for woodworkers, farmers, and manufacturers lasted until the end of the Civil War, when the Yankees tightened up the border again in revenge for British support of the South. Economically, this move was troublesome; politically, it consolidated the anti-American feelings of Nova Scotians and New Brunswickers and encouraged them to look more favourably upon a union of British North America.

Another change that caused New Brunswick to look more toward its British colonial neighbours than out to sea for its economic sustenance was the coming of railways. St. Andrews, on its southern tip, became the eastern terminus for the St. Andrews and Quebec Railway, linking the seacoast by rail to the interior of Canada. The plan, unfortunately, included taking a short, straight route across disputed lands in Maine. The tracks eventually had to be rerouted north to Woodstock, and by 1853, only forty kilometres of forest had been cleared. By 1862, tracks were laid, and the train could travel as far as Richmond Corner, but the owners had not cleared permission to extend the route right into Woodstock, on the St. John River. A traveller could leave St. Andrews-by-the-Sea and have a pleasant enough trip through beautiful countryside, only to be left off in a field in the middle of nowhere. The St. Andrews and Quebec Railway folded, and the town's hopes for eventually outstripping Saint John as the major port in New Brunswick were dashed. A Saint John to Shediac line was constructed to carry passengers from that city to the shores of the Northumberland Strait, but other plans to connect Saint John to major urban centres in New England or to Montreal would be overshadowed by the more viable Intercolonial Railway linking Halifax to the St. Lawrence.

"Fire at Saint John, N.B., June 20, 1887," a Notman Studio photograph of ships burned at the wharf. (NBM, X11831)

CHAPTER NINETEEN

The Tides of Change

Confederation Against Their Will

FEW MARITIMERS AND EVEN FEWER Newfoundlanders felt any great inclination to be absorbed into a larger country in the middle of the nineteenth century. The population of Nova Scotia was roughly 340,000 in 1861, with a healthy mix of English, Scots, Acadians, Irish, Germans, Blacks, and Mi'kmaq. The entire region was rural, and even a "big" city like Halifax had a population of only 25,000. Traditional strong trading links with England and the Caribbean kept sailing ships coming and going from St. John's, Halifax, Sydney, Saint John, and Charlottetown, as well as diverse smaller communities on almost every shore.

The wooden sailing ships that dominated world commerce would soon be superseded by coal-fired steamships at sea and railways on land. In 1861, in the midst of the American Civil War, the American Union Navy boarded a British ship, the *Trent,* and found two Confederate agents aboard. Britain saw this as a form of piracy, and tensions grew. W.H. Seward, the American Secretary of State, began to talk about a possible invasion of British North America, and Great Britain dispatched 14,000 troops to defend the colonies. The threat was mostly blustering on the part of a war-hungry politician, and no invasion ensued, but the noise had prompted increased concern about stronger political alliances and unification of the colonies.

A conference in Charlottetown in 1864 brought together the leaders of New Brunswick, Nova Scotia, and Prince Edward Island to consider a regional union, but delegates from Canada (now Ontario and Quebec) also showed up. Most people in Charlottetown paid little attention to John A. Macdonald, George Brown, George-Étienne Cartier, and the other prominent Canadians arriving in the harbour on the *Queen Victoria* that

September 1. The circus had arrived in town, which was certainly much more interesting. It also accounted for the fact that there weren't enough rooms available for the delegates to this seemingly mundane gathering. The Maritime leaders had planned to talk about forming their own union, but the Canadians had insinuated themselves into the talks and put forward a grander plan to unite all of the British American colonies. In the end, the Maritimers agreed to set aside their plan and to meet again with the Canadians in Quebec City to hammer out details of confederation.

In April of 1866, an unlikely army attempted to invade New Brunswick near the coast. Bernard Doran Killian had inspired soldiers of Irish descent who had seen the end of their service in the American Union Army to seek revenge on the British for the many generations of abuse that England had heaped on Ireland. The Fenians, as they were called, believed they could call on Irish Catholics everywhere to join the cause and overthrow British rule wherever it existed. The handiest point to strike would be the southeast corner of New Brunswick. About 1,000 Fenian raiders prepared to storm across the St. Croix River and, it was thought, march to Saint John and seize the banks there, if not the entire city. People in New Brunswick could scarcely believe their ears when they heard about this plan. The militia marched from Fredericton down through Charlotte County to fend off the invasion, and three British warships sailed from the Bay of Fundy into the mouth of the St. Croix River looking for a fight.

Shots were fired, and a few Fenians crossed into Canada to cause trouble, but the invasion bogged down immediately. The American military showed up on the Maine side to quell their former troops, who had to scuttle their plans to take control of Campobello Island. A customs house in Passamaquoddy Bay was burned down, but the general in charge of the American troops persuaded most of the Fenians to give it up and go home.

While the Fenian scare had little real effect on the citizens of the Maritimes, it had a powerful psychological impact, making many look far more favourably on the idea of confederation. If the Fenians were ready to invade, who might be next? Maybe there were other anti-British forces in the United States preparing to take revenge on the North American branch of the British Empire. Leonard Tilley, a strongly religious man who had once run a drugstore in Saint John, proved to be the New Brunswicker who would guide his colony into Confederation.

Two Nova Scotia political leaders, Charles Tupper and Joseph Howe, were at loggerheads about Confederation, with Tupper in favour and Howe bitterly opposed to the possibility. In the end, Tupper prevailed, and Nova Scotia joined the association even though the greater part of the population opposed it. Confederation ended Nova Scotia's political autonomy, and the colony that was once a powerful international trading centre soon found itself a mere province, a follower instead of an instigator of trade and industrial growth.

Ironically, even though Prince Edward Island had hosted the party that would lead to the formation of Canada, the island did not sign up as part of the Dominion of Canada when it was created in 1867. Like their counterparts in New Brunswick and Nova Scotia, Prince Edward Islanders wanted a railway, but the 80,000 or so inhabitants found the price tag, $5,000 per mile, a tad too rich for their blood. The Assembly considered heavy taxation but knew that would not garner popularity for anyone who wanted to hold onto his seat. Leaders went to Ottawa and cut a deal, and a good deal it was. By 1873, Prince Edward Island had joined Confederation. The new province would be represented by six members in Parliament. The federal government would take on the railway debt and give the provincial government $50 per resident, federal services for the people, and year-round steamer service to the mainland. However, providing this connection with the rest of the country proved onerous. To cross the Northumberland Strait in winter, the government had to use ice-breaking mail boats, which also carried passengers for a fare of $2. When the boats had to be dragged over the ice, even the paying passengers had to lend a hand. Despite complaints and disasters, this style of service prevailed until 1917, when a daily ferry that could transport motor vehicles replaced it.

Soon after Confederation, the island's population began to grow more slowly. Near the turn of the century, it began to drop, as many islanders went to work in the cities or fishing ports of New England.

Mail boats in Northumberland Strait, about 1899. (PAPEI, 2320/25-2)

The Dark Side

In *The Dark Side of Life in Victorian Halifax*, Judith Fingard documents the difficult lives of poor people in that city around the middle of the nineteenth century. Halifax was rife with orphaned children, squalor, prostitution, and drunkenness. Some of the most unfortunate citizens of this crime-riddled city were singled out for public chastisement, and the papers revelled in their misdeeds. Margaret Howard, the "wickedest woman in Halifax," first appeared in court in 1863, at the age of twenty, charged with drunkenness, and eventually she served more than fifty-two terms in jail, mostly for petty crimes. When R.H. Dana, the famed author of *Two Years Before the Mast,* visited Halifax, he described Barrack Street as "a nest of brothels and dance houses," and he saw women "broken down by disease and strong drink."

Women had very few rights anywhere in the region, but they probably suffered most acutely in port cities like Halifax and Saint John, due to the dependence of the local economy on men coming ashore from ships. In Halifax, society turned a blind eye to the abuse of women and children until Matthew Richey and John Naylor helped organize a movement to help them. Some women finding their way into the legitimate work force around this time taught in schools, but most worked in fish plants and at degrading, menial factory jobs. Often they worked in noisy, unhealthy circumstances, and it wasn't until 1906 that some protective limits were set; for instance, girls under sixteen could work no more than seventy-two hours a week. Women who tried to organize their co-workers and fight for better wages were almost invariably fired.

Throughout the region, the truly downtrodden lived in poorhouses, and in 1886 in Halifax, an old penitentiary housed the homeless, elderly, sick, and mentally ill. Orphans and children of the poor might be sent away as cheap labour to farmers in the Annapolis Valley, and everywhere illnesses such as diphtheria, whooping cough, and smallpox killed many children. During these hard times, small harbour communities that once thrived on shipbuilding, international commerce, and fishing now became more isolated, and some were abandoned as young people moved to Halifax, Montreal, or the Boston States (as people called all of New England) for a better life.

Many Maritimers resented Confederation, and some radicals argued for joining the United States, shifting alliances south instead of west. However, by 1869, even Joseph Howe was convinced that the union of provinces could never be reversed, and he became a minister in the federal cabinet. Ontario and Quebec outstripped the Maritimes in industrial growth for the last quarter of the nineteenth century, and prosperity in Canada shifted rapidly towards the west. There was little growth in farming, fishing, or shipping in the entire Atlantic region as the wealth generated by sailing ships disappeared. Looking to escape the flagging economy, many Maritimers and Newfoundlanders left for jobs in the Boston States and never returned home to live. Fish prices fluctuated wildly in the latter part of the century, so any job in the fisheries was an unreliable job. A depression swept through this part of Canada in the 1870s and 1880s, and money flowed out of the region. W.S. Fielding was elected premier of Nova Scotia in 1886 with another proposal for breaking away from the Dominion of Canada and forming a Maritime union, despite the fact that other premiers in the region were not excited by the idea.

Prince Edward Islanders shared in the economic woes of the region, but the problems that agitated the populace were a little different. In 1866, Father George-Antoine Bellecourt of Rustico (the priest who had baptized Louis Riel in Manitoba) started driving a steam-powered automobile that he had built himself. The citizens had never seen such a thing before, and some of them took up the cudgels. "The intelligent electors of this Province will not support this modern death producer," one critic railed. That same year, a fire wiped out four city blocks in Charlottetown, destroying 100 buildings and leaving thirty families homeless. But death almost took a holiday three years later after Prince Edward Island's final public execution. George Stewart Downie had killed a man over the love of a woman. He had some public support to spare his life but the law was still the law. When execution day came around, Downie read a poem, a really long poem that took him nearly half an hour, extending his tenure on the planet. Then when the trap door was sprung, the first rope broke. A second rope was rigged and this time the lover/poet's toes touched the ground and the rope had to be hoisted by a couple of stalwart men anxious to see the end of a bungled hanging.

Oscar Wilde probably remained aloof from the politics and the economic worries of the region when he travelled the Maritimes in 1882, but he met with less enthusiasm for his lectures than he had hoped. He complained, "It is a great fight in this commercial age to plead the cause of Art." Rudyard Kipling also travelled to these shores and wrote a well-received poem called "Song of the Cities," which praised Halifax for its "virgin ramparts" and hailed the city as "the Warden of the honour of the North."

Swept Away

Life on land for the unprivileged was fraught with woes and dangers, but off shore, nature was, as usual, unconcerned if its victims were well-bred or humble, wealthy or destitute. In 1873, the White Star liner *Atlantic* crashed on the rocks at Prospect, not far from Halifax. Five hundred and sixty people on board died in the storm that night as the steel hull was smashed by waves. Along the coast, women's bodies washed in still wearing expensive jewellery; some of it was carried off by scavengers before officials could retrieve the bodies.

The *Research*, built in Yarmouth in 1861, was a fine ship prepared to endure almost any extreme of North Atlantic weather, but sailing out of the Strait of Belle Isle in November 18, 1866, Captain George Washington Churchill and his crew confronted a terrifying storm that tore off the topmast sail and broke the rudder. Not wanting to be hindered by wet, freezing clothes, first mate Aaron Churchill was lowered over the side completely naked in order to affix a new rudder onto the ship; when he was dragged back up on deck, it was reported, he was "insensible," but nonetheless he recovered.

Unfortunately, that rudder was swept away, as were three more, and the ship was driven on by winds in a helpless state — right into January of the new year. The oakum came out of the seams and seawater gushed in continuously, but the ship, barely afloat, plodded on all the way to Greenock, Scotland. The newspapers in nearby Glasgow covered the story. Few would be surprised to learn that the men, all "greatly exhausted," tried more than once to convince the captain to give up the ship, but most were proud that he had not.

Even landlubbers occasionally felt the wrath of the sea. The Saxby Gale, one of the most famous storms ever to hit the Maritimes, arrived, as predicted by Lieutenant James Saxby of the British navy, in October of 1869. The storm ravaged both sides the Bay of Fundy, with hurricane force winds flooding roads and smashing ships along the New Brunswick shores. Two bridges were swept away on the St. Croix River. Houses were torn apart by winds and waves in the middle of the night, and families were swept out of their homes and lost in the raging waters.

Fundy tides reached a record high of seventeen metres. Most of the Fundy marshlands were flooded, and in the Tantramar Marsh, barns drifted away on the high tides. Near the border between New Brunswick and Nova Scotia, an old farmer named Steward was sleeping in his barn when he discovered it was afloat. The *Amherst Gazette* reports that he jumped onto a haystack floating by and sailed off into the crazy night. The haystack came aground the following day, whereupon Steward was rescued. In the town of Windsor, Nova Scotia, the streets were flooded, and at Grand Pré, the dykes gave way for the first time in centuries, drowning cattle and horses. Incredible stories abounded in the papers after the storm: some people sat on top of their barns to stay alive; one house was spun around on its foundation, and the occupants of another climbed onto a coffin and floated out a second-story window to safety. Men on ships in the Bay of Fundy faired much worse. Eleven men died on the barque *Genii* at New River, their captain ill prepared for the deluge, and a ship half loaded with lumber at the dock in St. Andrews was torn loose and smashed upon the rocks. Halifax, however, was spared and the *Chronicle-Herald* reported its disappointment: "The storm of Monday night was not a success in the city — did not come up to the expectations of the public."

Sailors and Salvagers

One of the most famous sea mysteries of all time began in Nova Scotia with the building of a ship called the *Amazon*, launched at Spencer's Island on the Fundy shore in 1861. After its first accident, the *Amazon* was renamed the *Mary Celeste* by the salvagers who took over as owners, and in 1872 they loaded the ship in New York with 1,700 barrels of alcohol. Captain Benjamin Spooner Briggs took along his wife and two-year-old daughter and set his course for Gibraltar. But along the way, something tragic occurred.

Halfway between the Azores and Portugal, another captain, David Morehouse spotted the *Mary Celeste* and could tell that something was wrong. He and his men boarded the ship and found not a soul aboard, even though the ship was sailing along and making good speed. The disappearance of the crew of the *Mary Celeste* drew worldwide attention, and several theories were put forward to explain what happened. Possibly the crew murdered the captain and his family, took over the ship, but then lost their nerve and fled in lifeboats. In 1929, an author proposed that the whole mysterious business was an elaborate hoax to collect insurance. Dr. Oliver W. Cobb had the most convincing theory, however. He suggested that the alcohol had warmed up, expanded, and pervaded the ship with fumes. Someone opened a hatch, and there was a violent explosion of gas but no fire. As everyone abandoned ship, the wind came up suddenly, and the lifeboat drifted far from the ship. The *Mary Celeste* sailed on unmanned for over 500 nautical miles, while the small boat sank with all hands.

Many ships from Canadian ports met disaster near home or far away, and often there would be legal proceedings, a "wreck court," to piece together the story and issue blame and/or award damages. One Captain Bain, whose ship had been lost at sea, said that his entire vessel had come apart at the seams, a sign of faulty workmanship, but he praised his men for their "stoic demeanour" and their "cheery defiance to the cold, the hunger, the thirst, and the menace of annihilation."

Newfoundland had more than its share of harrowing sea disasters in the last quarter of the nineteenth century. The 100-foot cargo schooner *Waterwitch* foundered at the ominous-sounding Horrid Gulch during a November blizzard in 1875. The ship was driven up onto the rocks at night. The captain and his son left it and clambered over the cold wet rocks as the waves beat over them. They mustered a rescue party and tied ropes around the remaining survivors, but only eight of the twenty-five survived the ugly night. The *Capulet, Arcadie, Florence,* and *Scotsman* were but four of the other ships that met disaster near or on the Newfoundland shoreline in the 1890s, all as a result of trying to navigate in dense fog. In 1901, there were as many as seven wrecks in six weeks near Trepassey during a summer when the fog ruled the coast without a break.

The *W.D. Lawrence* was one of the largest sailing ships ever built. Named for her builder, William Dawson Lawrence, she was conceived and built near the end of the Golden Age of Sail in the little town of Maitland, Nova Scotia. Critics scorned Lawrence for trying to create such a gigantic vessel, but he ignored them and set about his task, constructing his ship of pine and spruce. The *W.D. Lawrence* was launched in 1874, with 4,000 people watching. It weighed 2,459 tons and cost well over $100,000, a very expensive ship compared to others built in the region. Lawrence himself sailed his ship across the Atlantic, on to the Middle East, and back to France. A few years later, when he sold it to some Norwegians for $141,000, he had few detractors.

Unfortunately for the wooden ship crafters, steamships were taking to the seas, and a Nova Scotian was partly responsible for increasing their popularity. Halifax-born Samuel Cunard started a shipping business with his father in 1813 with a stolen sailing ship purchased from privateers. Soon father and son had forty ships at work, sealing, whaling, and hauling the mail to and from Newfoundland, Halifax, Boston and the Caribbean. Cunard made an important deal with the East India Company, and he impressed his friends back home when his ship, the *Countess of Harcourt*, sailed 6,000 chests of tea from China into Halifax harbour. Cunard had a vision of creating an "ocean railway," and he helped to form the company that built the *Royal William*, the first ship to cross the Atlantic powered entirely by steam. Steamships burned coal; much of that coal came from Nova Scotia mines; and Cunard steamships carried that coal as freight.

When Cunard decided to transport people as well as mail and coal aboard his ships, he faced formidable competition from the Shakespeare, Dramatic, and Blackball lines, but once again his venture proved successful. In 1859, Queen Victoria knighted Cunard for being so proficient at shipping people and commodities and at making piles of money. According to one biographer, Sir Samuel Cunard "remodelled the ocean navigation of the world."

Iron over Wood

The 1870s saw the decline of shipbuilding in New Brunswick as well as in Nova Scotia. Steamships and railways were the transport of the future. Clipper ships from New Brunswick could still deliver goods cheaply and fairly speedily, but it was only a matter of time before the new technology eclipsed them. In 1865, there were over twenty-five shipbuilding companies in Saint John alone, and in 1871 the city was ranked as the fourth-largest shipping port in the British Empire. Wooden sailing ships carried eighty-four percent of world trade in 1870, but unfortunately, by 1900, they carried only thirty-eight percent.

On "Black Wednesday," June 20, 1877, Saint John was delivered a deadly blow. A fire started near Market Square, a driving wind fed the flames, and the city of wooden buildings turned into an inferno. Saint John had seen fires before, but nothing on this scale; the fire raged for nine hours. It swept through the shipyards as well as downtown businesses and homes. Sixteen hundred houses were destroyed, leaving 15,000 people homeless. Merchants, their buildings aflame, ran to the banks to deposit their cash in fireproof boxes. Real estate worth $430 million went up in smoke.

It took five years to rebuild the city, but by then the decline of the shipbuilding industry was irreversible. Saint John tried to regain some of its former economic glory by competing with Halifax and Portland, Maine, as a large ice-free port, but it was a tough battle. While shipbuilding declined, New Brunswickers had argued about the best routes for the new railways. The "Lobster Act" of 1864 proposed building rail links in all directions to every coast and border, but it was an unprofitable idea, and, instead, British interests bankrolled the Intercolonial Railway, a single east-west line. Costing about $72,000 per mile, the Intercolonial linked Halifax to the North Shore of New Brunswick and to Moncton, but it did little for southern New Brunswick. It remained for the Canadian Pacific Railway to connect Saint John and Montreal as part of the Confederation package. In 1889, the completion of the CPR terminus gave Saint John an edge as the closest Atlantic port to Montreal, and in 1895, a grain elevator was installed, so wheat from Western Canada could be shipped to England through the port of Saint John. On into the twentieth century, Saint John would develop a dry dock and regain some of its shipbuilding glory — this time constructing iron ships, building and refitting thousands of vessels during World War II.

Although many blamed railways for the death of the shipbuilding industry and global trade by schooners, one man devised a plan to link rail and shipping to the advantage of both. Sea captains had dreamed about the possibility of somehow linking the Bay of Fundy to the Gulf of St. Lawrence across the Isthmus of Chignecto, which connects Nova Scotia and New Brunswick. Building a canal seemed like the logical way to achieve this. Almost twenty were planned between 1875 and 1886, but the price tag, estimated to be as much as $8 million, was always an impediment.

George Ketchum, a civil engineer from Woodstock, New Brunswick, worked out a plan for a rail line sixteen miles long; a train running over it would be capable of carrying up to six ships at a time across the isthmus. Ships would be floated over cradles on underwater tracks, lifted by hydraulic power and then hauled to the other side by steam engines at ten miles an hour. Ship owners would be charged a fee, but they'd save considerable money by not having to sail around Nova Scotia. When Ketchum finally got his project launched in 1888, the government of Canada was willing to ante up $1.5 million per year. It was 75% complete

The Chignecto Ship Railway, Cumberland County, Nova Scotia. (MMA, MP204.10.2)

by July of 1891 when the money dried up — despite the fact that the tracks were laid and the machinery manufactured. Another $1.5 million would have completed it but, instead, the Chignecto Ship Railway dream would turn to rust.

As iron replaced wood and steam replaced wind, the shipbuilding industry in the Maritimes and Newfoundland declined. But the Golden Age of Sail was not fully dead before one Nova Scotian named Joshua Slocum became the first man to sail around the world alone.

Joshua Slocum was born on the North Mountain of the Annapolis Valley in February of 1844 and grew up in the fishing community of Westport. He headed to sea at fourteen on a fishing schooner, travelled to many foreign ports, and eventually captained a number of diverse ships in various parts of the watery domain. In 1888, while sailing off the coast of South America on the *Aquidneck*, Slocum went aground. With his wife and two sons, he went ashore and into the jungle, where he built a new ship from raw materials and salvaged scrap. He sailed his family on the new *Libertade* to South Carolina, an adventure that he shared with the world by publishing a book about it. After that, he tried to settle down to the life of a landlubber in East Boston, but in 1892 he was given a battered sloop named the *Spray*. Slocum refitted it, and in 1895, he set out from Massachusetts intending to sail the *Spray* around the world single-handed. Many thought he was crazy, but, he said, "I had taken little advice from anyone for I had a right to my own opinions in matters pertaining to the sea." Slocum returned first to Nova Scotia to take on provisions, including his only timepiece, a watch with a smashed crystal, bought for a dollar. While crossing the Atlantic, the lonely skipper contracted food poisoning and began to hallucinate. Afterwards, he claimed that the ghost of Christopher Columbus guided him safely along while he was deathly ill. After touching down in Europe, he turned south and west. On the coast of Uruguay, he nearly drowned when his ship went aground on a reef.

Slocum sailed on through the Strait of Magellan, where the *Spray* was boarded by some Native people; they failed to overcome him because he had sprinkled tacks all over the deck to ward off intruders. Next he sailed over 2,300 nautical miles across the Pacific before touching land again. When queried about how this could be done single-handedly, he modestly claimed that the *Spray* could pretty much sail itself. In July of 1898, he sailed back into harbour at Fair Haven, Massachusetts, with no fanfare whatsoever. Slocum wrote another book and tried to settle down in Martha's Vineyard, but, ever restless, he set out once more in the *Spray* in 1909, never to be heard from again.

Nanaimo in 1859, showing the fort and coaling installations. (NAC, C-9561)

CHAPTER TWENTY

Opening the Coast

"Sixty Select Bundles of Crinoline"

THE HUDSON'S BAY COMPANY'S lease on Vancouver Island expired in May of 1859, and technically the territory returned to the control of the British government. James Douglas was, of course, still in charge as governor, and he maintained pretty tight control until he retired in 1864, even though the island government had an elected assembly and appointed council to offer up some advice.

Douglas was powerful, but he was not without detractors. Newspapermen like Amor de Cosmos attacked Douglas and what he referred to as the "Family-Company-Compact" that had a stranglehold on the people. He called for a more democratic government, one more open to, and lenient towards, entrepreneurs. De Cosmos may have befriended and advocated some aspects of democracy, but he was no friend to the Native people. In 1863, he called for severe punishment of any who might "trespass on white settlers." He argued that "a few lessons would enable them to form a correct estimation of their own inferiority." Another newspaperman on the mainland, John Robson, editor of the New Westminster *British Columbian*, felt strongly that the colonies should be completely independent of British rule.

Douglas was a law-and-order man, mistrustful of the rowdy gold miners, not terribly sympathetic to the large Native population, and still quite loyal to the British flag with its Old World notions of empire. He hired "gold commissioners" to keep a lid on mining operations, and he appointed travelling judges who, between 1858 and 1872, tried fifty-two murder cases, found thirty-eight men guilty, and hanged twenty-seven of them. Of those twenty-seven, only four were white; the rest were Native.

The miners may have been pesky, rowdy louts, but they were still big business. Miners needed transportation for their gold and for themselves. The Royal Engineers had a hard time cracking Rocky Mountain rocks to build roads, but that was their job. They opened a road from New Westminster to Burrard Inlet harbour, and Edgar Dewdney, a private contractor, forged a road east to allow access to the interior.

The Royal Navy kept watch over the Pacific. The Russians didn't seem to be much of a threat, but the Americans were still worth keeping an eye on. They had harassed and subdued the Native people to the south, and the white population there grew by leaps and bounds, doubling over a ten-year period in the second half of the century.

Ships occasionally foundered far away at sea or along the coast, and Her Majesty's navy tried to do the honourable thing. In 1859, for example, the gunboat *Forward* received a note by way of a Native messenger from a shipwrecked American, one Captain McLellan. The *Forward* found the members of the shipwrecked *Consort* and brought them to Nootka and then to Victoria, where they were treated with great generosity.

There was plenty of land to be doled out to anyone willing to settle. In 1860, the British Columbia government would allot up to 160 acres to anyone — including former Americans — willing to swear allegiance to the Queen. Settlers paid ten shillings per acre, and they had to agree to "improve" the land, that is, cut down the forests. This policy encouraged people to develop farms in the Fraser Valley, where the land was fertile and they could easily travel, ship their produce, and receive their supplies by water.

All three coasts of Canada have a long tradition of lawlessness among ships travelling the coastal waters. Looting vessels in distress, scavenging from shipwrecks, or even causing shipwrecks for the sake of salvage were fairly common practices along the West Coast. Native people, sailors, coastal settlers, government officials, insurance men, law enforcement officers, and military men all took part in the various shades of this illicit activity.

In accordance with the near-lawless laws of the sea, if a ship foundered, it was first-come-first-served for anyone who wanted what was left. The sea is always greedy enough about taking human life. Vancouver Islanders and mainland coast-dwellers cheerfully salvaged or scavenged whatever was left after the Pacific finished ravishing a ship. In December 1860, the *Nanette*, having travelled the seas for 16,000 miles, ran aground on Race Rocks, a mere eleven miles from its destination, Victoria, with a cargo valued at $165,000. At the time, Mate William McCulloch thought the enterprise would "prove a total loss, although some of the lighter goods may be picked up when she goes to pieces." Three days later, on December 26, the Hudson's Bay Company steamer *Otter* started to salvage the *Nanette* by cutting the rigging and hauling away casks of ale and gunpowder. ("Go for the beer and the explosives first, lads.") A schooner, the *Harriet*, showed up to harvest eight tons of cargo, much of it dry goods (well, wet dry goods) that the crew hung to dry at the wharf, which then looked like a billowy fantasy world as bolts of cloth blew in the breezes.

The *Harriet*'s captain reported that he saw nearly 100 men in small boats at the wreck, arguing and fighting over rights to cargo lifted from the hull of the unlucky ship. Special constables and at least fifty navy men tried to sort out the legitimate salvagers from the thieves, thin as the line may have been between them. Men from the ships *White Squall*, *Thames*, *Surprise*, and *Ino* all were caught with stolen goods. American customs inspectors snagged five ships with stolen booty, among them the *Rebecca*, which tried to sneak some of the swag into the United States without paying duty. The *Nanette* stayed together long enough to admit a lengthy parade of intruders; the rivals fought boozy battles and sustained injuries aplenty. Four men, a woman, and a child drowned in a canoe that capsized as they tried to spirit away stolen goods.

Issues related to gold and salvage rights were of paramount political and legal concern, but schools never topped anybody's list of priorities in the westerly colony. Four teaching nuns arrived from Quebec in 1858, and the Anglicans appeared soon afterwards. For the most part, volunteers provided educational services in Victoria and elsewhere, and they also staffed fire brigades, libraries, hospitals, theatres, and sometimes even churches.

Naturally, a great many men arrived to seek their fortunes, but not many women, so the Anglicans took it upon themselves to import young, single women. Sixty-two arrived in 1862 and another shipment of thirty-six in 1863. When the first batch came ashore in Victoria, shops closed, and men rowed out to greet the ship and get a look at what one observer called "sixty select bundles of crinoline." Another observer thought they seemed "a superior lot to the women usually met on emigrant vessels." Not all the imported women married. Some became entrepreneurs and opened up their own businesses to compete with the local establishments.

Loyalties Divided

Miners both responded to and fuelled the gold rush well into the 1860s, finding dust, flakes, and nuggets to line their pockets and maintain their enthusiasm. Two million dollars' worth of gold was found in 1860, and this rose to nearly four million by 1863 before levelling off at two million a year shortly after. The digging was temporarily good, but the limited resource would soon be reduced to spare change.

In a bureaucratic amalgamation, the two west coast colonies merged as the United Colony of British Columbia on November 16, 1866. It was decided that Victoria would no longer be a free port. Frederick Seymour, the governor, stayed in New Westminster, and soon the mainland politicians proved to have the upper hand.

After the gold rush, many miners took themselves off to the next potential bonanza. There was a growing and stable Chinese population, however, and the men worked in Nanaimo's coal pits or in the forest and lumber trade. Due to American tariffs on lumber from outside the country, much of the wood from British Columbia was sold to Latin America, New Zealand, and Australia instead of to the colony's nearest neighbour.

For those who stayed, the West Coast proved to be rich in resources and fertile soil. The mountainous terrain created transportation problems, and it was a constant challenge to build and maintain roads. Horses and mules were fairly reliable, but one entrepreneur believed that camels would be more dependable. He imported twenty-three "ships of the dessert" and put them to work, but settlers complained that the camels frightened their horses, and sometimes they blocked the roads because their hooves got stuck in potholes. When the camels were ordered off the roads, the owner simply set them free, and they roamed around this unsuitable land until they all died.

Communication with Europe was difficult, especially for a government fearful of its southern neighbour and generally enthusiastic about maintaining ties with London. Therefore, in 1864, politicians supported an ambitious plan to lay a telegraph cable north from Seattle, through

British Columbia and Alaska, under the Bering Strait, and across Siberia to link themselves with England. The Russian-American Telegraph was well underway when the first transatlantic cable came into service and rendered it obsolete. When the project was abandoned, however, it left behind a trail through the wilderness that proved useful for local communication and transportation.

Loyalties were divided and debates continued over the future of the colony. To remain a British colony, British Columbia would need even stronger ties to Britain, more political clout, and more money; finances were already strained to the limit. Joining the United States instead appealed to some. The miners and refugees from the American Civil War had already infiltrated the population to such an extent that they used a commingled currency of U.S. dollars and British pounds. With the end of the Civil War and the recovery of the American economy, removing the tariff wall could vastly improve British Columbia's economy by allowing freer north-south trade. So why not make the leap and merge with the States?

The other option was confederation with Canada West (Ontario), Canada East (Quebec) and the Maritime colonies. This compromise would have been more attractive if there hadn't been so many miles of nearly empty continent separating west from east.

The British North America Act was passed on March 29, 1867, and the very next day the Americans bought Alaska from Russia, boxing British Columbia in on top and bottom. A Nanaimo newspaper declared that the British connection was a "fast sinking ship" but that the Yanks offered a "gallant new craft, good and strong, close alongside, inviting us to safety and success." There was considerable popular support for the American option, and U.S. Secretary of State William Seward, who had just made the deal of the century by getting Alaska at a bargain-basement price, blathered, "Our population is destined to roll its restless waves to the icy barriers of the north." He saw no ice when he arrived in Victoria in August of 1869 to preach annexation; instead, he gathered petitions signed by quite a few Victoria merchants who hoped to become American without moving south.

Victoria's sagging economy seemed motive enough to move the capital from New Westminster to the island. There was not much gold in the vicinity and no manufacturing, and it was hoped that government jobs would help prop things up and cool the fever for union with the United States. The shift alienated more than a few mainlanders, though, who viewed Victorians as smug and old-fashioned. An island government, more than a little out of touch with life on the mainland, fostered divisions and communication difficulties that lasted well into the twentieth century.

Amor de Cosmos founded his Confederation League in 1868 to shore up support for joining Canada, particularly on the mainland. A new option was circulating as well: Henry Pering Pellew Crease thought British Columbia would make an excellent country all on its own. His dream did not come true.

In 1869, a Hudson's Bay Company miner named Robert Dunsmuir discovered coal on Vancouver Island, just north of Nanaimo at Wellington, and British naval men began ripping the valuable black rock from the earth. With the support of American investors, Dunsmuir and his son solidified control of the mine and built a railway. Dunsmuir became rich, but he didn't exactly share the wealth. He treated his workers poorly and used his own company store to exploit them. He refused to compensate injured men even when their injuries resulted from company negligence, and many men died from the dangerous working conditions.

Governor Anthony Musgrave was under pressure to resolve the problem of British Columbia's alliance and future allegiance; the legislature debated the issue in February and March of 1870. Many members feared that British Columbia would be overwhelmed and under-represented in the Canadian House of Commons and Senate. The eventual consensus was that if Canada wanted British Columbia badly enough, Canada would have to pay a fair-to-inflated price. Musgrave's terms were that the debt of $1.5 million be wiped out and that the per capita grant to British Columbia be based on a population of 60,000 instead of the actual 20,000. He also called for comfortable pensions for colonial administrators affected by Confederation.

And then there was the problem of the distance between British Columbia and the rest of Canada, a problem with one obvious solution: trains. In precise terms, Canada agreed "to secure the commencement simultaneously, within two years from the date of Union, of the construction of a railway from the Pacific towards the Rocky Mountains, and from such point as may be selected east of the Rocky Mountains, toward the Pacific to connect the seaboard of British Columbia with the railway system of Canada; and further, to secure such completion of such Railway within ten years." In May, three representatives presented these demands in Ottawa, with the further stipulation that the railway agreement include a link to Vancouver Island by ferry or bridges. In July 1871, British Columbia became part of Canada.

At first, Confederation changed day-to-day life for British Columbians very little, but after a while, business improved, with the value of exported wood, fish, coal, and other goods reaching three million dollars in 1871. Non-denominational public schools providing free education to all were established in 1872. An economic slump in 1873 slowed the progress of the railway, put pressure on Ottawa to help with unemployment, and, combined with ever-present racism, contributed to legislation in 1874 that took away the right to vote from any Native and Chinese men who met the other qualifications. The earlier three-way political split — for Canada, against Canada, or for British Columbian independence in whatever form that might take — persisted right through to the turn of the century, and Ottawa-bashing remained popular. Around 1875 and into 1876, much of the anger focussed on the stalled railway construction. Petitions were sent and secession threatened.

The Politics of Pacific

At sea, shipwrecks continued to take a toll. On November 4, 1875, the American vessel *Orpheus* rammed the steamship *Pacific* off Cape Flattery. Of the 250 passengers and crew, mostly from Victoria, only two survived. An editorial writer voiced the devastating impact on his community: "The catastrophe is so far-reaching that scarcely a household in Victoria but has lost one or more members, or must strike from its list of living friends a face and form that found ever a warm greeting within their circle." Few bodies were recovered, and all of Vancouver Island reviled Captain Sawyer of the *Orpheus*, who had not stayed on the scene to help rescue the victims. The *Orpheus* itself foundered the next day off Cape Beale as a result of damage from the crash.

In the middle of the 1800s, salmon were extremely plentiful, especially the highly marketable chinook. Alexander Ewen, a Scottish entrepreneur, established a cannery on the Fraser River, and in 1870 alone, he shipped 30,000 one-pound tins of salmon. The chinook were caught in the rivers with nets, which naturally caught every other kind of fish as well. The unwanted species were beaten to death and tossed back into the water. In May 1877, for example, something like 10,000 sockeye salmon, considered of no commercial value by Ewan's cannery, were killed and dumped, polluting the very river where they had once lived.

The sockeye, however, later turned out to be a very profitable fish, and the canners canned away; they fished and over-fished and dumped more dead fish into the rivers when they had killed more than they could sell. Of the fish that made it to the cans, over half the carcass was wasted and tossed back into the water. At the time, it was one of British Columbia's worst forms of water pollution. A few annoyed citizens wrote letters to the local papers complaining about the floating islands of dead fish stinking up the rivers and the towns.

In 1877, the first commercial canneries opened on the Skeena and Nass rivers. Sockeye were netted during spawning season just outside the factories, boiled, and packed into cans that were virtually handmade and soldered with lead. The workers were mostly Chinese and Natives, hired on a seasonal basis, paid very little, and made to toil in sometimes gruesome conditions. Over 50,000 cases of salmon were shipped off to England in 1877, and canned salmon soon became popular working-class fare.

Despite their low pay and nasty work, the salmon canners faced fewer life-threatening dangers than miners at the Dunsmuir and Sons mines near Nanaimo. It was also in 1877 that those miners went on strike. Dunsmuir had chopped their wages, and he threatened to close the mines altogether unless his provincial government would step in to pound some sense into the unruly men. After four months of unrest, the miners were forced back to work, receiving a 38% pay cut as punishment.

The Prime Minister of Canada had begun talking about a railway route through the Fraser Valley instead of the more northerly route chosen earlier, and controversy over how to link Vancouver Island to the rest of Canada continued unabated. A bridge seemed unlikely, and islanders aplenty felt miffed. Amor de Cosmos wasn't satisfied; now he fought, not for Confederation, but for separation. A new federal policy on the railway shored up the importance of this unifying thread of steel, and by 1880, an agreement with the Canadian Pacific Railway called for completion of the job by 1892. The auxiliary line promised for Vancouver Island got sidetracked, however, raising secessionist sentiment once again. The legis-lature had become somewhat more democratic: all adult white males could vote by 1876 — it was no longer necessary to own property. Premier John McCreight had formed a government after Confederation but lost out to Amor de Cosmos, who now held such strong anti-British views that he refused to conduct cabinet business until the Queen's representative, Lieutenant Governor Joseph Trutch, left the room.

The Chinese population was growing dramatically; 15,000 Chinese labourers were brought to British Columbia between 1881 and 1884 to work on the railway, undertaking the formidable tasks of blasting rock, constructing bridges, levelling hills, building railbed, and laying track. No one kept track of how many men were killed in the process of realizing this national dream. Meanwhile, the Native population declined drastically due to disease and loss of land and access to food. Under the guise of improving their lives, the government kept trying to transform them. The Kwakiutl and many of the other coastal peoples rejected change vigorously enough that the English considered them "difficult to civilize." In 1883, the Superintendent of Indian Affairs couldn't begin to fathom why the Kwakiutl desired to resist "the inroads of civilization," and he wondered out loud why they were downright "antagonistic towards the white race."

Dogs Barking on the Shore

Immigrant workers perished or were maimed at an alarming rate on the job of building the railway, but the press took more notice and offered more sympathy when white lives were in peril. In 1883, the *Grappler* sailed out of Victoria, loaded with passengers, cannery supplies, and gunpowder and headed towards disaster. A hundred souls were on board, including a considerable number of Chinese cannery workers. The ship caught fire, and sailors tried to quell the flames without telling the passengers that catastrophe was near. Communication broke down in an attempt to organize a bucket brigade, and chaos ruled as the ship continued to burn. The lifeboats could accommodate only twenty-two people. Crewman

John McCallister used a fishing skiff to save some of the desperate passengers, whereas his colleague, David Brown, chastised the panicked Chinese, who were trying to take their worldly possessions with them into the already overcrowded boats. Brown made it to a boat himself and sent its Chinese passengers back onto the sinking ship. McCallister landed his people ashore and returned to make a second rescue, rowing with improved oars — a broom and a bamboo cane. The ship eventually burned to the waterline and sank.

On the mainland, Vancouver's population reached 9,000, and on Vancouver Island, pressure for a railway on the east coast of the island eventually brought a subsidy from the federal government for a private line that would stretch from Nanaimo to Esquimalt. In 1886, the national railway was finished. The first train arrived in Port Moody on July 4, fulfilling the great Canadian vision. That same year, a hellish fire swept through Vancouver and destroyed much of the city, and as it began to recover from the catastrophe, the railway terminus was moved from Port Moody to Gastown.

Vancouver rebounded from the fire quickly, and Stanley Park was opened in 1888. The railway brought joy and profit: eastern goods could now find their way west, and lumber could be shipped east to the Prairies for building homes and businesses. But the railway also brought strife over monopoly and subsidy. The Canadian Pacific Railway had a financial stranglehold on most of the city, accounting for a quarter of its revenue and employing a tenth of the work force. It owned the opera house and the Hotel Vancouver, the British Columbia Sugar Refinery and the big ocean liners tying British Columbia to the Orient and Australia. In 1889, the CPR won the contract to provide mail service to Hong Kong and Japan. By 1891, the city's population had soared to 14,000.

The Anglo-British Columbia Packing Company had bought up eleven canneries, and, along with four other major companies, they shipped tons of fish back to England each year at substantial profit. When the worldwide recession of the mid-1890s capped British Columbia's volcanic economic growth, sixty percent of the province's people lived on the mainland, gold was still being mined (but nothing like in the days of the gold rush), and coal production had levelled off.

On the last day of December 1896, the *Janet Cowan*, which had sailed

A Chinese work gang on the Canadian Pacific Railway tracks in British Columbia, 1889. (GA, NA-3740-29)

all the way from Cape Town, South Africa, slammed into the rocks off of Carmanah Point after two days of trying to fend off a contrary wind. The ship was only eighty metres from shore, but monstrous pounding surf prevented an easy exodus from the jaws of the sea. A young English seaman, J. Chamberlain, attempted to swim a lifeline ashore, but he lost it as the waves churned him about. He made it to a rocky reef, where he held fast, and when the wind died down a bit, others safely joined him there. Unfortunately, however, the rising tide swallowed the reef. Another seaman swam a lifeline ashore, enabling twenty-nine sailors to follow him. But their troubles weren't over. The survivors found a remote cabin with a telegraph line, but the line was down. Three men put to sea in a boat to look for help, but they capsized and drowned. Another man broke a leg attempting to scavenge provisions from the ship. The captain died of exposure, and two others were injured when their tent caught fire. A tug from Seattle, the *Ryee*, eventually came to rescue the remaining survivors.

The Victoria *Colonist* called this disaster "a terrible tale of suffering . . . a coast tragedy without parallel."

In 1887, "C" Battery of the Royal Canadian Artillery came to Victoria to improve defences against whatever enemies might crop up, especially the worrisome neighbours south of the border. They shifted over to Esquimalt in 1890, but soon they were replaced by British artillerymen and engineers. After some wrangling over who should be paying to defend these shores, Canada or Britain, in gentlemanly fashion, they decided to split the cost.

The Union Steamship Company of British Columbia started up in 1889 to shuttle goods and people around the nearly 4,000 miles of northwest coastline. At first, all the ships had names beginning with the letter C. The 120-foot *Cassiar*, for example, known affectionately by travellers as "the logger's palace," had a saloon, smoking rooms, lounges, and electric lighting in the cabins for the comfort of its guests. Arrangements were fairly complicated: the company tried to keep women separate from men in the bars and Chinese and Native passengers separate from the whites in the sleeping quarters.

The ships carried mail and commercial goods and dropped off workers where they were needed for logging and canning. When a light was displayed from the end of a dock, even at a lonely, remote village, the ships picked up passengers. The ships also supported an embryonic tourism industry. Pamphlets — Aitken Tweedale wrote one called *Fin, Fur and Feather* — encouraged travellers "to enjoy to the full a visit to the Eighth Wonder of the World, the northern coast of British Columbia." To snake through the narrow passages in the fog, navigators used such reliable methods as judging their distance from land by bouncing the sound of a whistle off the mountains and calculating how long the echo took to travel back. Other standbys for reckoning included listening for dogs barking on shore or sniffing the air for the smell of nearby canneries. The first official weather service went into operation in Esquimalt in 1890 to keep an eye on storms that might wreak havoc on ships and those they served.

Gold, Copper and Coffin Ships

When the Klondike gold rush of 1898 attracted tens of thousands of people northward to search for riches, most of them had to travel through British Columbia. It proved to be good business for the Canadian Pacific Railway and a fantastic money grab for Vancouver. In the haste to move men north, all manner of unseaworthy vessels plied the coast. The steamship *Clara Nevada*, condemned after twenty-six years of use, was patched up and returned to service. Travelling south from Skagway with explosives illegally stashed on board, the ship caught fire, exploded, and sank, sending forty people to their deaths. Dubbed the "coffin ship" by the *Seattle Times*, the *Clara Nevada* was reported to be an "unsafe, ill-equipped craft with a drunken and blasphemous crew." The *Alpha* offered a free ride south to Victoria to the losers of the Klondike, a goodwill gesture to those who found no gold or quickly squandered their fortunes and to men suffering from hardships and over-consumption of booze in the goldfields. When the ship hit a reef in Baynes Sound, twenty eight were saved, but nine drowned.

Abe Heino raised hopes of instant wealth again in 1900 when he found copper on Moresby Island. Prospectors poured into the Queen Charlotte Islands from the Yukon, from the United States, and from England. Rather than wealth, most found a wild, inhospitable place, but, to encourage them to stay, the government issued mining licences anyway. The British Columbia Amalgamated Coal Company moved in and provided some dirty jobs breaking up the rocks of the islands for the big boss. The Haida residents, of course, suffered, with more and more white people throwing their weight around, and soon halibut and other species had been over-fished in the waters nearby. "Frontier life" in all its glory had found its way to Haida Gwaii, but it would be a while before any residents, old or new, had any say in provincial or federal politics.

At the turn of the century, James Dunsmuir became premier of British Columbia. He ran one of the most dangerous coal mines in the world, with death rates quadruple those of mines in other parts of the British Empire. He had more friends than enemies in high places, and he didn't give a rat's ass what the critics had to say about his mining operations. Power remained in the hands of a few. While Dunsmuir mixed coal with politics, the CPR extended its reach with "empress" class ships to Asia, "princess" ships plying the waters between Seattle and Alaska, and efficient, flat-bottomed stern-wheelers hauling over 200 tons of goods and a couple of hundred passengers per trip up inlets and rivers from the coast.

Parts of the province started to look pretty civilized, with farms on the Saanich Peninsula and in coastal island valleys. Settlements on the Gulf Islands and up the Fraser River boasted schools, churches, and post offices. Each year, British Columbia exported nearly $20 million worth of goods, including over a million cases of the ever-popular salmon. By 1900, Victoria had a population of 20,000. A year later the province of British Columbia did a head count of 2,000 Asians in their midst accounting for all but 200 of the total population of Asians in Canada.

CHAPTER TWENTY-ONE

Northern Conquests

"An Earthly Heaven or a Heavenly Earth"

ONCE THE ARCTIC whaling stations opened in the 1830s and 1840s, some whalers and their captains spent years in the north, rarely travelling south. The captain of the *Thomas*, for instance, spent over twenty years in the Arctic without returning to his home port. Many died performing their dangerous duties.

By the middle of the century, the Americans had established themselves as a major part of the whaling fleet. Sidney Buddington, first mate on an American whaler, spent a winter in an Inuit settlement with some other volunteers and fared quite well. He was able to get a jump on the whaling season and work with Inuit hunters to his company's advantage. Soon more Inuit were hired by the American whalers, and Inuit families started to settle in one place, giving up their nomadic ways in order to be part of the whaling economy. Unfortunately, this tempting new lifestyle had devastating results. Stations where whalers could spend the winter were created along Davis Strait, Baffin Island, and Hudson Bay. The Inuit there became dependent on the foreigners, changing their Native way of life dramatically. Many now lived in stone houses instead of in animal skin homes, and from the whaling men they contracted diseases virulent enough to wipe out many families.

Dangers were always plentiful for the white whalers as well. In July of 1866, the whaling ship *Diana* was one of several vessels trapped in ice at Pond Inlet, and, for the remainder of the summer, the ice did not let go. The ship drifted slowly with the ice pack as provisions diminished and nearly everything liquid froze. The ice carried the *Diana* into Frobisher Bay, and conditions got worse in November and December; winds and ice slammed the ship around until it began to come apart, splitting at the seams. The men pumped icy salt water back into the sea to keep their vessel afloat, while the captain died and scurvy set in among the crew. They burned their cargo of blubber to stay warm, or at least to keep from freezing to death. The ugly, desperate, interminable winter ended when the *Diana* was set free by the ice in March. Miraculously, with a much reduced crew, the *Diana* made it to the Shetland Islands. Eight men had died, three more would soon follow, and certainly there was no profit to show from the whales killed in the previous season.

Despite the horrors of arctic exploration, it never lost its glamour. Somebody was always trying to find something, to be the first. The Arctic would not be dismissed from the imagination. Men like Arthur Dobbs, who had never been to the Arctic, created elaborate fantasies about fertile valleys and comfortable living, and it wasn't difficult to dupe the public into thinking that any unknown territory could be a kind of earthly paradise.

Most men who had been to the Arctic knew it was a harsh and unfriendly place for those not prepared for it. But for many who survived their trips to the North, it remained a sublime region, full of wonder, beauty, and adrenalin-pumping dangers — glamorous dangers of menacing wild animals and gigantic travelling ice mountains that could crush a wood or iron ship to smithereens. All the mysteries and challenges of the Arctic continued to attract explorers well into the twentieth century. Enigmas remained about lost explorers, shifting magnetic poles, island topography, hidden wealth, and of course the North Pole itself, the very top of the planet.

Charles Francis Hall, toward the end of his checkered career as an explorer of the Canadian Arctic, said of the far north: "I love it dearly, its storms, its winds, it glaciers, its icebergs; and when I am among them, it seems as if I were in an earthly heaven or a heavenly earth." In 1858, Hall was a newspaper publisher in Cincinnati. He got the idea into his head that some members of the Franklin expedition were still alive and living among the Inuit, and that he should set off to find them. What were his qualifications? Mostly sheer guts and naive conviction, topped with a large helping of divine calling. God told him to do it, and he was ready to forge ahead.

Another American, the wealthy Henry Grinnell, who had previously donated a couple of ships to Lady Franklin's cause, liked Hall's enthusiasm for this wild goose chase and funded his first trip north on a whaling ship. Hall and his men were dropped off on Baffin Island with a nine-metre open boat, which was soon destroyed in a storm. He didn't come anywhere close to Franklin's place of demise, but nevertheless he stayed on for a couple of years and established a warm friendship with an Inuit named Ebierling and his wife, Tookoolito. He became a great admirer of the Inuit way of life, but he couldn't stop feeling that the whole lot of Native northerners should be converted to Christianity. Ebierling and Tookoolito travelled back to the States with Hall, and the newspaperman used them to help foster the cause of "protecting" and converting the Inuit. He hoped eventually to "plant among them, a colony of men and women having right-minded principles."

Unfortunately, he needed cash to pursue his efforts at exploration and "helping" the Inuit. The Civil War distracted public interest from the Arctic, but Hall took his Inuit companions on a lecture tour and raised some funds anyway. By 1864, he had returned to Hudson Bay with his friends, and he spent a troubled five years arguing with whalers and trying to convert Inuit who wanted neither his help nor his Christianity. His health deteriorated, and things just kept going wrong for him, but he heard more stories about white men living somewhere along the coastline, and he still believed he would find survivors of the Franklin disaster.

Hall finally made it to King William Island in 1869, where he collected a few artifacts that may have been left by Franklin. Lady Franklin herself travelled to Cincinnati to talk to Hall about yet another trip north, but Hall was tired of looking for Franklin and wanted to do something even more dramatic: to travel to "that spot which is directly under Polaris." He wanted to go to the North Pole. Hall had a wife and children, but he didn't like staying home; he'd been gone for most of the last ten years, either raising money or traipsing around the Arctic. Now that the Civil War was over, the government looked favourably upon northerly exploration. Hall was sent off again, this time aboard the sturdy *Polaris*, formerly the *Periwinkle*, which was no longer needed for combat support. Sidney Buddington was in command, and George Tyson was navigating.

They enjoyed smooth sailing right up to Ellesmere Island before an arctic blast drove the *Polaris* back to the shelter of a cove dubbed Thank God Harbour on the coast of Greenland. Here Hall died of arsenic poisoning, either from misuse of medication or from foul intent. In August of 1872, the *Polaris* could once again sail, and most of the men were happy to forget about the North Pole. They headed south, just in time to get trapped in a massive flow of ice. They stayed stuck in the ice until the middle of October, when a raging storm looked as if it would cause the ice to crush the ship into splinters. Nineteen of the crew got into boats and rowed away into the darkness. Then, around midnight, the wind shifted, and the ship, now clear of the ice, began drifting away from the men in the boats. The unlucky nineteen were led by George Tyson. Ten white men and nine Inuit men, women, and children, including Hall's friend Ebierling, landed upon an island of ice about half the size of a football field.

The Inuit taught the others how to hunt and fish and make the best of a bad situation. The *Polaris* ended up running aground, and those survivors would also have a tough time surviving, but the situation of the drifting crew on the ice island was desperate. The Inuit continued to hunt seal, and that sustained them through the dark months, and a long dark winter it was. But spring brought a new worry for the castaways: by March, the island was drifting south, melting and breaking up beneath them.

On April 17, Tyson wrote in his log, "The ice split right out under our tent!" The exclamation point was well earned — he had watched his meagre breakfast drop into the sea beneath him. Every day, winds and waves kept stealing the real estate out from under the *Polaris* survivors. One of the Inuit set off in his kayak into the icy expanse to find help; they were far enough south that they could hope to meet sealers on their yearly excursions. Captain Isaac Bartlett, of Newfoundland, was more than a little shocked to see a man in a kayak this far from anywhere. The brave Inuit led Captain Bartlett to the rest of the desperate lot, and Bartlett hauled them aboard. The ice island would not have lasted much longer.

Charles Francis Hall had not discovered much of anything for all his efforts, but he had fixed the notion of polar expedition in the public mind in North America and Europe. The romance of the north would not go away.

Depraved and Despicable

Whales were disappearing from some of the traditional feeding grounds, and ships were now venturing from the west into the more dangerous Beaufort Sea, where uncertain waters, treacherous reefs, storms, and unpredictable ice took a heavy toll on the ill-prepared. Twenty-seven whalers were wrecked in these waters off Icy Cape, Alaska, in 1871, and in 1876, fifteen more were bashed apart not far from Point Barrow. Despite the dangers, whale hunters persisted in their single-minded pursuit of the bowhead.

The youthful government of Canada didn't quite know what to do with the islands of the Arctic when Britain transferred control of them in 1880. But it did heed Sir John A. Macdonald's warning: "Americans would only be too glad of the opportunity, and would hoist the American flag and take possession" if Canada didn't jump in. Reluctantly, cautiously, Canada took over, uncertain what to do with this vast wilderness of snow and ice. Even after Canada had asserted its control over the arctic land mass and islands, there was little concern for the fate of the bowhead or any other kind of whale. In 1886, however, the visionary Commander A.R. Gordon recognized the damage and fought for a five-year hiatus from whale killing, lest extinction be around the corner. But his voice drowned in the sea of profit.

In 1870, Rupert's Land, the gigantic tract controlled by the Hudson's Bay Company, had been turned over to the Dominion of Canada. A relatively small parcel of it had been carved out to become the province Manitoba, and what was left over, still vast and thinly populated, had been renamed the Northwest Territories. By 1895, Canada got around to dividing the portion north of the sixtieth parallel into regions: Yukon, Mackenzie, Ungava, and Franklin. Captain William Wakeham took a whaler out of Halifax in 1897, under the auspices of the federal government, to survey ice conditions in the north. To let the American whalers know they were building stations on Canadian soil, Wakeham started planting the Union Jack, first at Baffin Island. The 140 or so Inuit who watched the ceremony were curious and amused, while the American whalers resented the threat of regulation by what they saw as a "foreign" (that is, non-American) government.

This 1903 photograph taken by A.P. Low shows Aivillik women with tattooed faces, Fullerton, Hudson Bay. (GSC, 2693)

Much further west, on Herschel Island, north of the Yukon coast, American whalers had established a port of operations and engaged in considerable international trade with the Inuit. In both the east and the west, the impact of continued contact with white Americans and Europeans was profound. The Inuit profited from access to guns, metal tools, boats, and money, but the positive influence of new technology was tragically and dramatically offset by the onslaught of disease. In Hudson Bay, for example, the entire population of the Saglermiut people on Southampton Island was killed by typhus brought in by a ship from Scotland. All along the northern coast, Inuit became sick and died from imported diseases including measles, smallpox, and pneumonia.

The animal population also became depleted as whale hunters came ashore to hunt meat or to buy it from Inuit, who could increase their caribou and musk ox kill exponentially with guns. Many Inuit became dependent on trading with the whalers and gave up their nomadic life entirely. When Reverend Isaac O. Stringer arrived at Pauline Cove, one of the whaling winter ports, in 1893, he discovered that the American whalers had settled into a wicked life of drinking, debauchery, and violence. This conglomeration of lustful, angry, and sometimes cutthroat whaling men had brought every imaginable sin to the north and embroiled many Natives in the deadly mix. The North West Mounted Police, too, had to contend with whalers who brought in large quantities of booze and abused Inuit girls and women near their coastal stations. Roald Amundsen, the Norwegian explorer, reported that the shore activities of the Americans were depraved and despicable.

To the Northern Pole

Swedish explorers had finally navigated the Northeast Passage above Russia in 1878-1879. Fridjof Nansen, a Norwegian, had explored the ice sheet of Greenland on skis in 1888 and undertaken a polar ice "drift" across far northerly reaches. Nansen had taken along a young man named Otto Sverdrup when he had skied across Greenland, and Sverdrup had captained Nansen's ship, the *Fram*, when it drifted across the polar north. These Scandinavians had a different style of exploring the north. Instead of trudging, they glided through the Arctic wastes, perhaps with a less showy heroism than their English predecessors, but more efficiently and with fewer hardships. Why fight the ice when you could just let it take you where you wanted to go?

While skiing and drifting sound a bit casual, Nansen and Sverdrup's trips were trying and dangerous. Sverdrup had barely returned from the great polar drift when a wealthy brewer and philanthropist asked him to go back to the Arctic again in the sturdy *Fram*. He left in 1898 to explore Ellesmere Island, and he spent four winters in the north mapping previously unknown territory. For land travel, sleds pulled by dog teams and, of course, skis kept the party mobile. They learned from the Inuit not to tame their dogs, but to tap their aggression for rapid travel. Nevertheless, they treated the dogs more like friends than like mere work animals. Sverdrup figured out, too, that it made sense to ski alongside the dogs, letting the animals haul survival gear but not the weight of the explorers.

In the summer of 1902, Sverdrup and his hardy troop of skiers arrived at the northwestern tip of Ellesmere Island, the last land mass before the Pole itself. From there they turned back and headed home to Oslo with a collection of rocks, animals, and fossils, as well as maps that would be of considerable use to the government of Canada when it decided to claim that region of the north.

Another Norwegian, Roald Amundsen, decided it was time to attempt "sailing" a ship through the Northwest Passage once again. More information was available now than in the days of the British ventures, and a good deal of glory might be gained by taking a ship all the way across the top of North America and coming home alive. In 1903, Amundsen sailed westward in a fairly small fishing boat, the *Gjoa*. He followed the traditional passage as far as Beechey Island, paid his respects to the place where Franklin's men had wintered, and then carried on. At the beginning of the first winter of this voyage, Amundsen was leery of the Inuit, but he soon discovered that they were friendly and willing to trade. He came to feel that he understood their culture during the next two years. He admired them and concluded that they would be much better off without any interference from anyone of European descent.

The next year, Amundsen took some of his men on sledges in search of the magnetic pole, only to discover that it wasn't where it was supposed to be. It had moved from where James Clark Ross had pinpointed it, and Amundsen's men never found the precise spot. It was an interesting bit of knowledge to take back home nonetheless: the north magnetic pole didn't stay put but "moved"; it had no fixed address.

By 1905, Amundsen had resumed his first plan: to traverse the Northwest Passage. The *Gjoa* slipped into the dangerous Simpson Passage and zigzagged its way between the jagged rocks on either side, finally emerging into the Queen Maud Gulf and then into what would be called Amundsen Gulf, which emptied into the Beaufort Sea. The *Gjoa* had proved the existence of the Northwest Passage once and for all.

Unfortunately, the ship got stuck in ice at King Point, along the coast of the Beaufort Sea. Amundsen travelled 8,000 kilometres by sled to telegraph news of his accomplishment back to Norway. He had no money with him, so he had to send the message collect. Then he returned to the *Gjoa*, and, like so many adventurers before him, he waited for summer to set his ship free of the ice.

Even though the Northwest Passage had finally been traversed, it would never become a quick route to China or an easy gateway to anywhere. Amundsen went on to explore Antarctica, and he arrived at the South

Pole in 1911. Still looking for adventure and glory, he led an air expedition over the North Pole in 1926. Two years later, Amundsen died in an air crash as he searched for a missing arctic explorer.

Robert Abram Bartlett of Brigus, Newfoundland, accompanied American explorer Robert E. Peary on several of his Arctic forays, but Peary was the driving force behind "discovering" the North Pole. Peary, a civil engineer serving in the navy, had conducted scientific investigations in Greenland, where he had collected meteorites that fascinated the American public. His fame garnered him enough support to fund a search for the North Pole, and in his 1898-1902 foray, he went as far as 84° north. In 1905-1906, another attempt brought him to 87° north, about 300 kilometres from his objective. Then, in 1908, he ventured north from Ellesmere along with Matthew Henson, who spoke Inuktitut fluently, and some Inuit guides. On April 6, 1909, he succeeded: he reached the North Pole. However, one of his colleagues from a previous trip, Dr. Frederick Cook, contested the claim and said that he himself had already reached the Pole. Although the dispute never was completely settled, Peary generally is considered to be the first person to set foot on the furthest northern piece of real estate on the planet. Of course, Peary had not achieved his great success alone. On several of his expeditions, he had been accompanied by his wife, Josephine, who had given birth to a daughter in the Arctic. He had the help of colleagues, most of them more loyal than Cook, and Inuit guides, whose people may have been traversing the area for centuries. One of the expedition members, Donald MacMillan, recalled, "Matthew Henson went to the Pole with Peary because he was a better man than any one of us." Henson's achievements were completely disregarded until the 1950s because he was Black.

Demise of the Bowhead

The Canadian government attempted to maintain the law and uphold some sort of morality in the northern territory that had, until recently, been without any rules and regulations except those imposed by the harsh environment itself. Something had to be done, if for no other reason than to assert Canadian sovereignty and prevent the Americans

Matthew Henson in furs aboard the SS Roosevelt, *1908-09.* (BC, AM1994.5.553).

The COASTS of CANADA

from having their way. In 1903, a mere two Mounties were dispatched to Herschel Island to collect duty on American goods and to keep an eye on the flood of imported liquor. They had a sod hut for headquarters and not much respect from the whalers.

A six-man squad of Mounties took ship with geologist A.P. Low to Fullerton Harbour in Hudson Bay to enforce law and order. J.D. Moodie, their commander, discovered that animals were being slaughtered at an alarming rate, and he curtailed the export of musk ox. Moodie also tried to explain to the baffled Inuit that he was now in charge and that they were living in Canada.

Conditions deteriorated for whalers fairly rapidly in the new century, and not just because the Mounties cramped their style ashore. A.P. Low saw the writing on the wall, but in 1903, when he assessed the future of whaling as "gloomy," few paid attention. In July of 1904, Prime Minister Wilfrid Laurier tried to awaken Parliament to the fact that foreigners were "cruising in those waters" of the eastern Arctic, and unless Canada did something to keep control over the region, "we may perhaps find ourselves later on in the face of serious complications." He sent a second ship, captained by Joseph-Elzéar Bernier, of Quebec, to keep an eye on things and plant a few more flags. Bernier really wanted to make the "polar drift" across the top of the world. Instead, he was assigned the job of patrolling the eastern Arctic; he made four voyages in all. By 1907, having traversed the Arctic thoroughly, he changed the status of the whale population from Low's "gloomy" to simply "exhausted." During his two summers on northern seas, Bernier saw one lonely bowhead. Only eight ships still hunted whales in the north, and they would soon give up the bloody job altogether due to lack of profit.

Meanwhile, back in Ottawa, a senator named Poirier proposed that the entire arctic region be chunked up like a pie, and all bordering nations — Canada, the United States, Russia, Norway, and Sweden — each get the slice to its north. Canada and Russia would obviously get the biggest slices. Captain Bernier liked the proposal, and in 1909 he installed a plaque on a barren hill near Winter Harbour (where his ship was stuck in the ice) boldly claiming to a few observers that Canada now owned all the islands from there to the Pole.

For the most part, however, the Arctic was not on the political agenda in Ottawa. The government called off the eastern Arctic patrols in 1911; they were costly and at best symbolic. By then, whaling was no longer profitable because there were so few bowheads to be found. In 1915, it was estimated that there were only six hundred of the great mammals left in the waters of the Arctic, and Canada belatedly decreed that whale hunting would henceforward be illegal.

Bowhead whale hunting would not become legal again until 1996, when Native hunters received a license to kill one whale per year. In Repulse Bay, thirteen hunters from various Inuit communities were allowed to hunt and kill a bowhead out of respect for their heritage. Although this event caused discomfort for many who watched it on TV in the comfort of their living rooms, it was a token recognition of a way of life and a culture that was dramatically altered and nearly destroyed by commercial whaling and the "progress" that followed.

CHAPTER TWENTY-TWO

Sea of Disasters

"The Ocean Strewn with Wreckage"

THE BOER WAR BROKE OUT in South Africa in 1899, and the next year 1,200 Canadian men, along with their horses, sailed from east coast ports to fight in defence of the empire. At the dawn of a new century, cities like Halifax continued to support military efforts and, as usual, profited from war. The pomp and circumstance that ushered men off to fight in Africa reflected dogged loyalty to old ideals, and sending men off to war was something Haligonians understood. Nonetheless, when the First World War brought the city back to economic life, the city's military role took a new and deadly twist.

Fortunately for most rural Maritimers, all wars were distant and non-threatening. If you weren't dirt poor or totally reliant on the whimsy of world fish prices, in fact, the region remained an idyllic place that often attracted outsiders seeking refuge from the newly hectic pace of the twentieth century. After 1885 Alexander Graham Bell divided his life between Washington, D.C., and Baddeck, Cape Breton. His telephone work was behind him, but at Baddeck he undertook the groundwork for many of his other great inventions. He experimented with photoelectric cells, the iron lung, the phonograph, steam-powered air-craft, and the desalination of seawater. He formed the Aerial Experiment Association and sent men aloft in "aerodromes." In February of 1909, he succeeded in sending a man into the sky in a heavier-than-air craft for the first time in the British Empire. Bell also developed hydrofoil boats that "flew" above the water's surface, some reaching speeds of 114 miles per hour. Bell always said he was happier at Baddeck than anywhere else in North America, and he died there on August 2, 1922.

Like Bell, Guglielmo Marconi, the inventor of the radio, found Cape

Breton a useful base for his operations. He sent the first successful wireless communication across the Atlantic from his station at Glace Bay with the whimsical message, "The patient waiter never loses." By 1907, he had established an ongoing communication service between Clifden, Ireland, and Port Morien, Cape Breton. The first wireless transatlantic voice message arrived at his Louisbourg station from Ireland in 1919.

Despite improvements to ship structure and navigation, ice remained a deadly danger off the coast of Newfoundland. On April 25, 1910, the *Normandy* was sailing towards Halifax with twenty-seven on board. No one saw the iceberg in the dense fog until it was too late. Everyone took to the two lifeboats, one of which was partially submerged, and waited for daylight. Fortunately, they could then see the shore of Tors Bay some fifteen miles away, and they rowed non-stop until they made it ashore.

Two years later, a millionaire named George Wright and a well-to-do woman named Hilda Slayter, both of Halifax, sailed out of Southampton, England, on the world's largest and supposedly safest ship. On April 14, 1912, the *Titanic*, as we all know, failed to recognize the right-of-way of a massive iceberg migrating south from Newfoundland and slammed into it. Two garbled telegraph messages went out from ships in the vicinity, and an operator on the mainland in Canada passed on what he thought was a happy end to a bad situation: "Titanic passengers safe, being towed to Halifax." The story went out across America and to Europe — the wrong story. The Halifax *Morning Chronicle* on April 15 went so far as to say that all the passengers were "safely taken off and on their way towards Halifax." The Intercolonial Railway and other rail lines prepared special trains ready to carry the *Titanic* passengers on the final leg of their journey to their destination. Extra immigration officials were sent to the city to deal with the overload of work.

The *Carpathia*, the first ship to arrive on the scene of the disaster, picked up the 705 survivors and shuttled the traumatized victims off to New York. The dead were left to float upon the sea until the steamship *Mackay-Bennett*, which had sailed out of Halifax, arrived to perform the gruesome task of picking them up. The crew, supplemented by ministers and undertakers, was mainly made up of Nova Scotians. They took twenty tons of ice to keep the bodies cold, and coffins — but not nearly enough for all the dead. Arminias Wiseman, a crewman on the *Mackay-Bennett*, described the scene when they arrived at their destination: "bodies bobbing up and down in the cold sea . . . as far as the eye can see, the ocean was strewn with wreckage."

Three hundred and six bodies were recovered. The *Mackay-Bennett* was joined by another Haligonian vessel, the *Minia*, carrying a fresh supply of embalming fluid, reserved for use on first class passengers only. These lucky ones were embalmed and placed in coffins. Second- and third-class travellers were packaged in canvas bags, while *Titanic* crewmen and steerage passengers were simply put on ice in the bow of the *Mackay-Bennett*. Once ashore in Halifax, the bodies were loaded into horse-drawn hearses and taken to the Mayflower Curling Rink, which served as a morgue. (Years later, this would be the location of the family court building, where my wife and I were married.) Some victims were shipped off to their hometowns. The remains of the world's wealthiest man, John Jacob Astor, for example, who had not taken to the lifeboats with his wife but gone down with the ship, travelled back to the United States in his private rail car. At least 150 victims, however, were buried in Halifax. Soon after the phenomenal success of James Cameron's film *Titanic* (partially filmed in and around Halifax), the city capitalized on its connection to the *Titanic* disaster. Tourism increased dramatically as visitors flocked to the graves of the *Titanic* dead, including that of the legendary J. Dawson, buried in Fairview Cemetery.

Dangerous Occupations

For Newfoundlanders, the generations-old occupation of seal hunting was a dangerous way to earn much-needed money to feed a family. There were few comforts aboard a sealing vessel, and when sealers arrived at their destination, they knew that nature was not going to make the work easy. In March of 1914, 150 men started walking across the ice near Funk Island, headed for a seal herd that was over eight miles away. The weather closed in and a blizzard ensued. Some men turned back and made it to shore, but others kept going and eventually became disoriented, lost in the storm. Seventy-eight died. The ship *Bonaventure* found the few lucky survivors huddled together on the ice. By then, however, frostbite had

"Hunting Seal," by Pierre-Narcisse Tetu, February 18, 1871. (NLC)

maimed many of the men for life. Perhaps the worst aspect of this tale is that such horrific events were not at all uncommon in the history of Newfoundland sealing.

Coal mining was on the increase, and there were industrial jobs to be had in Sydney, Halifax, and Saint John and in smaller towns. By 1901, 33,000 men and nearly 10,000 women were employed in heavy industry, usually at low pay and in miserable and unsafe working conditions. They began to form trade unions, and bloody conflicts broke out as a kind of class warfare between the wealthy owners and the lower-class workers.

Social reformers tried to rescue the poor, the drunk, and the abused, especially women and children. Women fought for and won new but limited rights. Halifax feminist Edith Archibald was a little ahead of the times when she told a crowd of followers in 1912, "Women of Nova Scotia! You stand today in the growing light of an early dawn of the most wondrous epoch that shall ever be."

A New Navy, a New War, and More Salt for the Sea

It was British naval power that enabled England to grab and hold North America, and even as its colonial holdings decreased to what is now Canada, the Royal Navy had the often-dirty job of keeping the coast free of enemy navies, pirates, and thieves while quelling any unruly Natives their guns could reach. When tensions mounted between Canada and the United States, the Royal Navy threatened or did actual battle with American ships. The Boer War had stirred up militant British-Canadian nationalism, although, in retrospect, it's hard to fully comprehend why a lad in Yarmouth or Ladysmith would feel a personal compulsion to uphold the monarchy a world away at the southern tip of Africa.

Military fervour waxed and waned, but after the Boer War ended in 1902, there remained a vocal and influential core of support. In 1905, Prime Minister Wilfrid Laurier bolstered the garrisons in Esquimalt and Halifax at the urging of the British; the men on shore were Canadian, but the ships were still British. For a time, Laurier deflected England's urging to build Canadian warships, feeling somewhat protected from European or Asian threat by the breadth of the Pacific and Atlantic and also aware of a certain lack of enthusiasm on the part of French Canadians. As global tensions grew, however, support for funding a full-fledged Can-adian navy increased. In 1909, the Canadian Defence League, backed by J.C. Eaton, was calling for every young Canadian man to undertake compulsory military training.

On May 4, 1910, the Naval Service Act created the Royal Canadian Navy, and soon four light cruisers and six destroyers were launched, despite the fact that many French Canadians saw the increased militarization as support for British imperialism. Laurier's compromise navy offended both the imperialists and the French Canadians and was a major factor in his defeat in 1911. The navy barely survived after that, and when Canada entered the fray of the Great War, she had only the warships *Rainbow* and *Niobe* to send to battle.

As before, enthusiasm for war revived Halifax. In 1914, when soldiers were sent to Glace Bay to protect the Marconi wireless station in case of attack, the *Halifax Herald* told its readers that Nova Scotia was about to be swept into a war of such immense proportions that the lives of everyone in the region would change forever. Unemployment in the cities of the Maritimes disappeared almost overnight as industry geared up for war. In 1916, a plant in Pictou County produced 300,000 rounds of ammunition a month, earning a healthy profit for its owner, Thomas Cantley.

Halifax harbour was mined, and nets had been stretched across the entrance to keep out submarines. Cunard steamships were converted to carry troops to the battlefields in France, and men poured through Halifax and other East Coast ports to become cannon fodder. Of those who returned home, many disembarked at the same piers as casualties of deadly new technologies. Prisoners of war arrived in Halifax to be confined in the stone fortress of the Citadel or on Melville Island in the Northwest Arm, among them the Russian revolutionary leader Leon Trotsky. Rumours abounded of German spies coming ashore and casually walking the streets, which led to paranoid fear of German families living throughout the region.

At sea, German U-boats became an ever-present danger to military ships, supply ships, and ships engaged in the ordinary to-and-fro of trade. By 1917, a convoy system was in place. Great numbers of vessels would anchor in Bedford Basin and then proceed out the harbour to be escorted across the Atlantic by Canadian and American warships.

During the war, schooners still sailed from Newfoundland with salted fish for Britain and other countries in Europe. Although they might seem of little importance as players in the war, they were often victimized by the German U-boats. On December 8, 1916, the *Duchess of Cornwall*, which had recently left its home port of Burgeo, on Newfoundland's south coast, was en route to Portugal with a load of fish when it was torpedoed and sunk. The crew of six spent two years in a prisoner-of-war camp before their release in 1918. Another Newfoundland schooner, the *Thomas*, was torpedoed off the coast near LaHave, Nova Scotia, in April of 1917. The small ship *Dictator*, captained by twenty-three-year-old Tom Fiander, was sailing back to Newfoundland with salt from Cadiz, Spain, when it was captured by a sub. The Germans sank the ship and took the men back to Europe as POWs; two died before the war was over.

Why any military force would go to such lengths to sink a cargo of salt and capture a handful of non-military sailors remains a mystery. The Burin schooner *Gladys J. Hollett* encountered somewhat less hostile (and more rational) submariners off the Nova Scotia coast in August of 1918. The Germans ordered the *Hollett*'s crew into small boats and sent them rowing back to the Sambro shore. They then shelled the schooner, but it didn't sink. Later, it was towed to Halifax, repaired, and given a five-year reprieve before being crushed in ice off Cape Race, Newfoundland.

"As the Earth Trembled"

Because of the heavy traffic, there were many minor mishaps in Halifax harbour, but none compared with what happened on December 5, 1917. The *Mont Blanc* was loaded with 200 tons of TNT, 2,300 tons of volatile picric acid, and thirty-five tons of benzol. The *Imo* was a Belgian relief ship, a tramp steamer serviceable enough to carry war supplies, and it was on its way out to sea through the Narrows when a series of mistakes drove it into the *Mont Blanc*. Historian Archibald MacMechan documented the events of that day. He wrote, "The *Imo* came with great violence against the starboard bow of the *Mont Blanc* and crushed the plating to a depth of ten feet." Sparks led to fire and dense smoke, and people ashore could see "flashes of fierce red flame." The crew of the damaged *Mont Blanc* abandoned ship and rowed in lifeboats for Dartmouth as the ship began to drift toward the Halifax side of the harbour. Men from other ships rushed to the *Mont Blanc* to try to put out the fire, but it was unstoppable. At 9:05 a.m., the largest man-made explosion ever to have occurred up to that date rocked Halifax and Dartmouth. The water in the harbour opened up, and a shock wave hammered through the very bedrock.

The Richmond area, in the north end of Halifax, took the worst beating. According to Hugh McLennan, "the ground rocked and reverberated, pavements split and houses swayed as the earth trembled." A wall of air from the explosion slammed into the houses. Very few remained standing. Many people were killed outright or trapped as they fell, and many more died in the fires that consumed what remained. MacMechan reported that the blast ripped much of the *Mont Blanc* into a "spray of metallic fragments" that rained down on both sides of the harbour; a cannon launched from the ship crashed down three kilometres away to the east, while its anchor catapulted in the opposite direction to the far side of Halifax, beyond the Northwest Arm. A mushroom-shaped cloud formed over the harbour, a kind of black, oily rain fell, and fires burned out of control. A tidal wave nearly five metres high slammed into Halifax, smashing tugs and small boats and lifting people as they walked on the

Looking south over Halifax on December 6, 1917, after the explosion. (NAC, C-019953)

lower streets. As the water drained back into the harbour, it swept more victims to their deaths.

The cities were not equipped to deal with the magnitude of the destruction or the huge number of dead, injured, and displaced people. The hospitals were filled with bloody victims, many of them blinded or seriously injured by glass flying from shattered windows. A rumour circulated that there would be a second explosion from the ammunition magazines ashore, and many believed the city was under attack by the Germans. Word went out for everyone to abandon their homes in favour of staying out in the open on the Commons, in Point Pleasant Park, or by Citadel Hill. Although the second explosion did not occur, many were forced to stay outdoors in the bitter cold, and some of the injured and elderly died of exposure. Most of the men who went to aid the *Mont Blanc* were killed in their heroic attempt to save the city from disaster.

Fear hung over the city, but compassion was apparent everywhere as the healthy tried to aid the helpless, sometimes carrying victims on their

backs to the overcrowded hospitals. Twenty-five thousand people were without shelter, and 6,000 lost their homes completely. The death toll reached nearly 2,000, while 9,000 more were injured, and many remained unaccounted for. A harsh winter storm arrived the next day, with snow and freezing rain followed by high winds, all of which hindered the efforts of the rescue workers who poured into Halifax from Canada and New England.

So great was the explosion that plates and glasses had fallen from the shelves as far away as Charlottetown and Sydney. Some Nova Scotians reacted by blaming the Germans. One newspaper said, "Practically all the Germans in Halifax are to be arrested," and editorials in the *Herald* fixed the responsibility on "that arch fiend, the Emperor of the Germans." But ordinary Haligonians, full of goodwill, countered the hate-mongering of the newspapers as they opened their homes to the injured and homeless.

Over the course of several years, court hearings tried to determine exactly who was to blame for the accident. Finally, the Supreme Court of

Canada ruled that both ships were at fault and that this terrible disaster truly was an accident. The Halifax Relief Commission oversaw the reconstruction of the shattered city, including the wholesale replacement of the wood frame buildings in the Richmond area with hydrostone homes. Physical and emotional scars remained among the victims, and the events of that apocalyptic day haunted the people of Halifax and Dartmouth for many decades.

CHAPTER TWENTY-THREE

On Hardship's Shores

Beacons of Salvation and Madness

LOOKING WEST on a clear night, I can see the beam from the light-house on Sambro Island, near Ketch Harbour, over thirty kilometres away. I can also see the lights of container ships the size of football fields, cruise ships, and jack-up oil rigs that come and go from Halifax harbour. As I stare across the expanse of water between here and Ketch Harbour, the thread of light I see connects me to the distant past, for Sambro is the oldest standing lighthouse in Canada. It was preceded only by the doomed lighthouse at Louisbourg on Cape Breton Island, which burned to the ground almost as soon as it was built. The replacement was smashed to smithereens by the British during the siege of 1758, and it was re-constructed, destroyed, and rebuilt a few more times until everybody gave up on it.

Another lighthouse visible from my back door is on Devil's Island, at the mouth of Halifax harbour. I canoed out to it once from Eastern Passage. On this calm summer day, as the lighthouse went about its automated business, I watched a huge container ship glide by in the deep waters of the harbour entrance. But all I had to do was turn my back and keep focussed on the old lighthouse itself to slip back a century or so in time. Life for the lighthouse keeper and his family here meant daily intimacy with the immense power of the sea and an overpowering res-ponsibility for the safety of strangers in ships passing by this rocky outpost in the Atlantic.

Shipping at the turn of the twentieth century remained a dangerous business, and lighthouses were often the only resource against disaster. In

The lighthouse at Estevan Point, British Columbia. (MMBC, 982.10).

earliest times, there was not much of a "house" involved, and ships were warned of danger by bonfires on headlands. The first indoor lights consisted simply of candles and reflectors, not much to work with on a foggy or stormy night. Oil lamps burning fish oil, seal oil, vegetable oil, or, preferably, whale oil (until Abraham Gesner's invention of kerosene spared the whales) became fairly sophisticated. Substantial lighthouses were in place on the east and west coasts of Canada by the 1860s, including such formidable structures as those at Bonavista Bay in Newfoundland, Seal Island at the mouth of the Bay of Fundy, and Race Rocks and Fisgard on Vancouver Island. Revolving lights floating in pools of mercury seemed like a good idea in the 1890s, when no one realized that the results of working around mercury fumes were poisoning, madness, and death. By the end of the century, electricity had started to replace kerosene. Carefully engineered lamps that included mirrored glass or metal, as well as refracting and concentrating lenses, created a brilliant and penetrating light.

The Atlantic and Pacific coasts of Canada became dotted with beacons of light, and the lighthouse keepers often served as weather reporters, rescuers of ill-fated sailors, enemy observers in times of war, and even, on Langara Island in the Queen Charlottes, lookouts for advancing tsunamis. While lighthouses may have been vital for shipping safety, lighthouse keepers were rarely treated with great respect and were paid meagre wages for their work. Nonetheless, "keeping the light" was an honourable, if not always well-paid occupation, often requiring isolation and hardship.

Characteristically, men and women worked together in lighthouses; usually the husband was the keeper and his wife worked with him, her labour counted upon but unpaid. At times, though, widows kept lights alone, and women participated in some of the most heroic rescues. Mary Ann Croft, a widow, tended the lighthouse on Discovery Island, near Victoria, all alone. She held her post at a meagre fee from 1901 right up until 1932. She lived utterly isolated, facing a variety of threats, not just from hostile weather but occasionally from wildlife as well. She survived on fish, food she grew in her garden, sheer dogged perseverance, and a visit from an itinerant nurse once per annum.

Minnie Paterson, of Cape Beale, on a remote section of Vancouver Island's west coast, worked with her husband around the clock to help the ravaged survivors of the SS *Valencia*, which foundered nearby in the raging sea. On January 22, 1906, the twenty-four-year-old steamship was heading north from San Francisco to Seattle. In the middle of the night, it veered off course and ran into the rocks off Pachena Point on Vancouver Island. The captain ordered the boats lowered and sent passengers out into the cold, heavy seas in hopes that they could find their way ashore. Some of the boats were smashed alongside the ship, and others were swept away. The rescue vessels that arrived could see the *Valencia*, but they could not get close enough to help those still alive. Some of those who had set off in the lifeboats did reach shore, and the next morning some of the crew made it to land by way of a lifeline. Minnie had the fortitude to nurse the survivors for over seventy hours without rest. Despite heroic efforts to save those who remained clinging to railings and rigging, 117 people perished in the wreck, including Captain Johnson, who went down with his ship. Ernest Jordan, aboard the *Salvor*, watched the demise of the *Valencia* close at hand. "It was terrible to stand off there and watch the wreck break up, and see the people who were in the rigging drop off into the boiling sea." For months afterwards, bodies and skeletons would be found along the shores and in sea caves along the coast.

Later that year, Minnie Paterson was again on hand when the *Coloma* met a fate similar to that of the *Valencia*. She undertook an arduous nine-mile journey in a driving gale at night to a homestead at Bamfield Creek. From there, she and Annie McKay set out into rough waters to reach a passing ship, the *Quadra*, in order to get help to the desperate *Coloma* passengers. As a result, thirty-eight people were saved from a watery grave.

James Henry Sadler took the lighthouse keeper's job on an island in Quasino Sound in 1915 for a wage of forty dollars a month. He had a wife and three small children, and they had Kains Island all to themselves. Sadler was obliged to row seventeen miles to get his mail if he wanted it, and more than once his family's food supply became perilously low, due to lack of funds or the difficulty in getting a boat to or from the island. Near Christmas in 1917, the situation had grown particularly desperate. Sadler tried to row his small skiff out through heavy surf to a vessel offshore, only to be pounded by killer waves that slammed him back to land and pinned him beneath floating logs. His wife, more than a little upset, suggested that an easier life awaited the family ashore somewhere — anywhere.

On a second occasion, Sadler failed to get off the island for supplies. In July, the family was living on starvation rations and very unhappy when a government ship brought relief. It took back a report that everything on Kains seemed just fine. Sadler, stubborn and/or loyal to his important task, decided to stick with the job even after his wife started to become mentally unstable following news of her brother's death in the First World War. In 1918, however, James finally admitted defeat: he sounded a distress horn, which was heard by a passing whaler. When rescuers arrived, both husband and wife appeared to be quite insane, and the family was finally ushered ashore. Sadler reluctantly quit his job, and his wife was sent to an asylum.

Isolation on an island in the ocean seems to be a reasonable cause for insanity. In 1919, William Hartin's wife was reported to have had a mental breakdown. The reason was said to be lack of mail delivery to their lighthouse on an island north of Queen Charlotte Sound, but one can guess that the problem went deeper than that.

Sometimes women proved physically and mentally stronger than men at enduring island life. Mr. and Mrs. Tom Watkins kept a lighthouse off the coast from Prince Rupert. Tom caught pneumonia and died. There was no soil on the island in which Mrs. Watkins could bury her husband, so she had to let his body freeze on the roof of their house until help arrived during that dreary winter.

Romantic as it may seem in retrospect, there was nothing idyllic about the life of lighthouse keeping families. The pay was pitiful, help could not be summoned easily in case of emergency, husbands, wives, and children drowned with some regularity, and madness was endemic — from isolation, mercury fumes, or both. Ultimately, automation did away with this hazardous occupation. There are virtually no regular lighthouse keepers left along the coasts of Canada; instead, technicians arrive twice a year by truck, boat, or helicopter to service the highly mechanized lights. Newfoundland has fifty-six lighthouses still standing, there are eighty-seven more spread around the Maritimes, and British Columbia has forty-one.

"Human Nature is Careless"

Despite the difficulties and deprivation some had to endure, the population of the British Columbia coast increased steadily. Part of the increase came through immigration, and not all of the immigrants came from eastern Canada, the United States, or Great Britain. While non-white labourers were welcome to do the lowest-paying, hardest, and dirtiest work, they weren't necessarily welcomed by all British Columbians. Some white people argued loudly and often about what should be done about people of colour. In 1903, the head tax on Chinese immigrants was raised from $100 to $500. In 1904, the first Sikh immigrants — 2,000 of them — arrived in Vancouver, took up low-paying jobs in lumbering and other industries, and settled down with their families.

In 1906, a Japanese firm opened a state-of-the-art copper mine, Ikeda Bay Mines, on ore-rich Moresby Island, complete with phone lines to the local hotel. Despite rampant prejudice against Asians, the Department of Mines praised the operation as a boon to the province. Nonetheless, the next year, paranoid legislators put forward the Natal Act to restrict Oriental immigration. It became law, even though the Queen's representative refused to sign it. Undaunted, the Asiatic Exclusion League of Vancouver, made up of working people opposed to admitting competitors willing to

Sikh immigrants arriving in Vancouver, about 1906. (GA, NA-303-252)

work for lower wages than themselves, maintained the pressure to keep immigrants out. The league members were angry and they were loud. Meetings were held, and fists were waved. Acrimonious marchers paraded through the streets, and 9,000 of them gathered at city hall to sing "Rule Britannia." The demonstration climaxed with an outright assault on Chinatown and Japantown: four hours of rioting and violent clashes with the residents. In 1908, Canada forged an agreement with Japan to limit immigration into British Columbia ports to 400 persons per year. In that same year, Canada banned the opium which had been filtering into the West Coast from China.

Regardless of the hardships and deterrents, new immigrants kept coming to British Columbia, and industry was still eager to import cheap labour. In the summer of 1914, the *Komagata Maru,* with 376 hopeful Sikh and Punjabi Muslim immigrants on board, tried to land its human freight. The ship sat in the harbour at Vancouver for two months before ultimately being sent back to Hong Kong. The rules were not to be skirted. Finally, in 1920, a ruling opened the door a crack to admit more East Indians who already had family in British Columbia.

The COASTS of CANADA

Vancouver and Victoria grew by leaps and bounds. Some consider 1908 to be the year the lucrative tourism industry got off the ground in Victoria, with the opening of the Empress Hotel. Many of the streets were still muddy trenches, and dockside brawls were commonplace, but now Victoria also boasted a seafront promenade, meticulous English gardens, and afternoon tea. Other communities flourished, too. In 1914, when the Grand Trunk Railway opened its terminus in Prince Rupert, the seaport town came to life as the halibut fishing capital of the world, and the new industry formed a basis for economic optimism. With rail and ships, Prince Rupert now had commerce with the world in two directions, although it continued to rely on sea rather than land routes for most of its supplies.

The Tides of Coastal Culture and Commerce

British Columbia's growing population increased the pressure on resources of all kinds, including good land. At the same time, rising imperialism combined with increasing numbers of non-white faces fanned racism. The coastal Natives suffered all the way around. White fishers and white-owned canneries decimated the salmon stocks, and indeed the Natives joined the fray as they acquired motors for their boats and better fishing gear to keep up with the white competition. In many communities, a mixed common language emerged, used for communications between cooperative Natives and non-natives. This ad hoc language blended Chinook, Nootka, or other tongues with French and English. Some Aboriginals tried to enter mainstream society, but they found ever-increasing barricades in their paths.

White trappers had the right to trap anywhere, regardless of traditional Native hunting and trapping territories. To hold onto any land rights at all, most Natives had to remain wards of the state. The Nisga'a, along with other Native peoples, pushed to strengthen the legality of their land claims, a struggle that, for some, would drag on into the twenty-first century. Due to an assortment of oppressive measures, they grew more vigilant, politically savvy, and militant about protecting their rights, and in 1909, they sent petitions to King Edward VII demanding better treatment by government officials.

Christian missionaries and Indian agents collaborated to impose federal policies to "manage" Natives with respect to land ownership, local politics, and education — often with devastating results. The turgid fusion of religion and government bureaucracy worked towards depriving Natives of their rights, language, identity, and sometimes even their children, and they exerted tremendous pressure on them to give up every aspect of their traditions. During the First World War, an Indian agent at Alert Bay threatened to arrest any Kwakiutl people who failed to hand over their masks and ceremonial clothing or cease having potlatches. Masks, headdresses, copper jewellery, and sacred items were impounded and sent to Ottawa, robbing these people of their most precious belongings as well as their self-respect.

In Victoria, the government snatched a whole reserve from the Songhees for the sum of $434,000. In 1913, a royal commission pompously declared that "a strong race had supplanted a weaker" and that "Indians must accept the inevitable." As the outcome of such astute observations, the commission prompted the further assimilation of Native peoples by "exchanging" about 50,000 acres of valuable land for about 90,000 acres of land that no white man had yet come up with a good use for. This pushed Native families into less visible and more inhospitable locations, while providing significant profit for white businessmen about to exploit the more valuable land. Even with this increase in acreage, Native people of British Columbia retained a mere 0.4% of the province which they once had all to themselves. By the onset of World War I, Aboriginals made up only 5% of the province's population.

A 1910 royal commission on forestry thought it might be wise to go easy on the trees because "human nature is careless of anything of low commercial value, especially when the supply seems inexhaustible and waste costs nothing to the waster." Wise words they were, but they went almost unheeded. By 1911, 80% of crown timberland had already been leased to the industry, and trees were cut at a hectic pace. Logs were transported by inland waterways or along the coasts with little if any concern for the ensuing damage. Lumbermen assumed that nature would generously repair whatever man ripped asunder, and if the land failed to revitalize itself, it really didn't matter much when there were so many acres of forest yet to be consumed. Where hillsides were too steep to set up camp, camps were established on rafts, ready to move on to the next patch of forest when the trees had been toppled and floated off.

Most men in the forestry industry found the warnings of a few bureaucrats laughable. Nor did any of the logic of the royal commission rub off on the fishing industry, especially when it came to canning salmon. The so-called "iron Chink" had been invented and by 1911 was replacing Chinese workers looking for a living wage. The device could decapitate and clean a fish at the profitable rate of one per second. Salmon cans could now be soldered two seams at a time as well — all the more reason to harvest even larger quantities of a seemingly inexhaustible resource, and harvest it even faster.

"Just Time to Say Goodbye"

Shipping on water routes could have remained a comfortably profitable venture for companies on both sides of the British Columbia-United States border in the early years of the twentieth century, but each side wanted a share of the other's territory, and so, in April of 1901, a trade war of rate-cutting ensued. As a result, everyone started losing money. Eventually, an agreement was reached to keep peace in the family: American vessels would trade primarily on the American side of the border, and Canadians would trade on the Canadian side.

By 1906, Canada had finalized taking over its own land defence on Vancouver Island and the mainland, and the Royal Canadian Navy had been established in 1910. Canada's entry into the First World War almost coincided with the purchase of two Chilean submarines, which arrived in the summer of 1914. The navy would use them to defend the coast from invaders if need be, even though the nascent war was in Europe, literally on the other side of the earth. At first, the war drew energy and money towards the East Coast, but when the United States became involved, British Columbia communities involved in the lumber industry benefited. Sitka spruce from the Queen Charlotte Islands, for instance, proved ideal for building fighter planes, and the jobs created by the demand attracted an influx of Swedish workers. British Columbians of all backgrounds, including 200 of Japanese descent, volunteered for active duty. By the end of the war, 6,225 men from the province had died, and at least 13,000 had been wounded.

A distant war, a flagging or a booming economy, political wrangling — nothing seemed to affect the endless list of shipwrecks. The *Capilano* sank off the coast in a snowstorm in October of 1915. Frances Keeper, daughter of the postmaster at Savary Island, recorded that it was "an awful sight to see a ship with her lights still glowing heading for the bottom, and at the last moment, just before she submerged, the whistle gave a final blast."

At around two in the morning of October 23, 1918, in another fierce early snowstorm, the Canadian Pacific vessel *Princess Sophia*, headed from Skagway to Victoria, ran aground on Vanderbilt Reef, along the Alaska panhandle. Her captain, F.L. Locke, a man with nearly thirty years of experience, radioed to report a serious but not life-threatening accident, and salvage and rescue vessels steamed toward the *Sophia* from Vancouver Island. The passengers grew increasingly annoyed by the delay, but, like the captain, they did not fear for their lives. The small ship *Cedar* arrived before dawn, but neither it nor other would-be rescuers could get close enough to the *Sophia* to rescue anyone, and they were beaten back to shelter by the weather. The *Sophia* sat on the reef without shifting as the storm raged, apparently in a stable if desperate state, but suddenly, at 4:50 in the afternoon of October 25, the ship lifted and turned from the reef. The rescuers were appalled to hear the *Sophia*'s final message: "Just time to say goodbye. We are foundering." When the *Cedar* could approach the next morning, only the foremast of the *Sophia* showed above the water. Three hundred and forty-three people had drowned or been killed by the exploding boilers, an irrecoverable loss for the coastal communities of Yukon and Alaska. The disaster sent a shockwave through a populace that had come to rely on what they considered routine and safe travel along this coast. On Armistice Day, November 11, 1918, the celebrations for the ending of a world war were diminished in Vancouver as the bodies of 157 of the *Sophia*'s victims were brought to the docks by the *Princess Alice*.

While coastal Native peoples continued to struggle for their rights, the Political Equality League formed chapters in Victoria and Vancouver to fight for equal rights for women, and leaders travelled around the province to get signatures on petitions demanding the right to vote. But they remained somewhat sluggish about sharing the rights they did have. In 1913 the Council of Women in Vancouver opposed allowing Oriental women into their discussion groups, and they told their masculine counterparts that they felt only married women should be allowed to immigrate to Canada from Asia.

During the war, women found their way into vacated jobs on farms and in offices, in the factories and canneries. As the war raged in Europe, the women in British Columbia stepped up their demand to vote, facing official as well as unofficial humiliation. During a 1916 crusade, when suffragists organized a march through Victoria to the legislature, police rerouted them, sending them through the red light district.

On April 5, 1917, the campaign succeeded, and white women received the right to vote in British Columbia. In 1918, Mary Ellen Smith became the first woman to sit in the provincial legislature. She declared effusively that she believed in "the faith, intelligence, honour and integrity of every member of this House," and she spoke in favour of the legislature working for the "best interests of all people of this province." Underpaid workers succeeded in getting the Minimum Wage Act for Women and Girls passed in 1918, the result of a good fight put up by garment and laundry workers led by Helena Gutteridge.

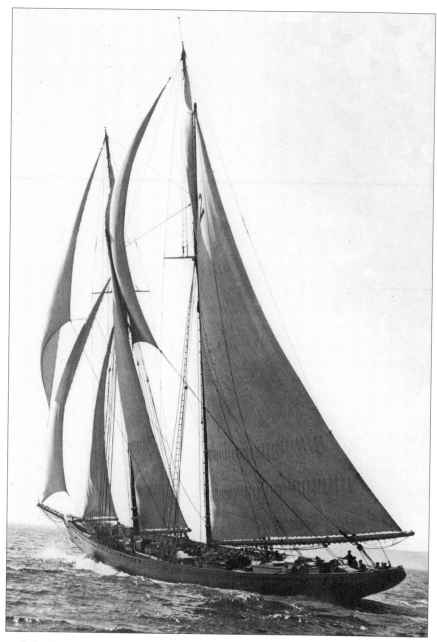

"The Grand Banks Fishing Schooner Bluenose," *by W.R. MacAskill.* (NSARM, 1987-453/98)

CHAPTER TWENTY-FOUR

Between the Wars

The Slightly Roaring Twenties

THE END OF WORLD WAR I brought relief everywhere, although repercussions from the war were felt for several generations. Such a large proportion of Canada's young men had been killed that unprecedented numbers of women remained unmarried. Over time and little by little, these independent women helped change the educational and social prospects for all women, but no baby boom followed World War I. The world-wide influenza epidemic of 1919, thought to have travelled from Europe to North America with returning soldiers, nurses, and other personnel, killed 50,000 Canadians; 66,655 had died in the war. At the Okak mission in Labrador, 300 Inuit died of influenza, including the entire adult male population of the community.

The wealth and freedom of the "roaring twenties" were enjoyed more vigorously in the urban centres of central Canada than on the coasts, but a degree of post-war relaxation was evident everywhere. A ruling in 1920 opened the immigration door to East Indians who already had families in British Columbia. Nonetheless, acceptance of "foreign" customs was not forthcoming. After the war, Mennonites and Doukhobors, religious refugees from Russia and Germany, arrived to build self-sufficient communities. Their hard work, their exclusiveness, and their religious devotion sometimes set them at odds with the more secular communities nearby.

Customs of British Columbia Native people also troubled the unenlightened white community. Chief Daniel Cranmer, a Nimkish chief, held a five-star potlatch in 1921. Despite the fact that the government had declared potlatches illegal, clandestine potlatches continued into the middle of the twentieth century. Some professed they'd rather die than give up the ceremony, while others devised clever ways to celebrate a

A Kwakiutl potlatch ceremony, Alert Bay. (GA, NA-1164-4)

potlatch without the authorities recognizing it for what it was. Chief Cranmer, however, didn't hide his potlatch. He threw a whopping party — a six-day feast that had taken nearly a decade to prepare. Blankets were almost a form of currency to West Coast Natives, and Chief Cranmer gave away goods equivalent to 30,000 blankets. Along with actual blankets, he triumphantly offered everything from sacks of flour to violins, motorboats, and pool tables. For this ostentatious generosity, the Mounties arrested the good chief, but when Cranmer got out of jail he was still smiling at the thought of his grand accomplishment. His potlatch would be remembered for a long time by his people; it has probably never been topped.

More sensitive to Native tradition and, indeed, inspired by it, was Emily Carr. Known as Millie to close friends and Klee Wyck to those who spoke Chinook, she was born in Victoria in 1871. She travelled north to remote islands and settlements to paint the landscape, the villages, and the totem poles. Observing the powerful impact of natural forces on the coastal people, she wrote, "Houses and people were alive. Wind, rain, forest and sea had done the same things to both — both were soaked through and through with sunshine, too." At first, she painted images of people as well

The COASTS of CANADA

as totem poles and trees, but an elder explained that a picture could trap a person's spirit, and when he or she died, the spirit might never be set free. For this reason, she stopped painting Native portraits. Carr travelled to France and England, where her work was highly regarded, but when she returned to British Columbia, she had to support herself by running a boarding house. The National Gallery bought some of her work in 1927, when other Canadians began to recognize her achievement in capturing the spirit and mystery of northwestern coastal life.

Behold the Bluenose

After World War I, some Nova Scotians turned their sailing expertise to a somewhat more peaceful enterprise: racing. Enthusiasm for sailing big fishing schooners continued long into the age of steam, and its most spectacular exponent was the *Bluenose*. A fishing vessel, the *Bluenose* was fast enough to compete in elite Canadian-American competitions funded by rich men racing sailing ships designed exclusively for speed. A couple of Halifax businessmen had established a race in which only legitimate fishing vessels could compete, and at first, American vessels had done quite well. But that all changed when the *Bluenose* took up the challenge.

Bill Roue designed the *Bluenose* with innovative ideas, and for the keel-laying ceremony, the Governor General, Sir Victor Cavendish, 9th Duke of Devonshire, came to Lunenburg to drive a golden spike with a silver mallet; the total cost of construction was $35,000. In March of 1921, the *Bluenose* was launched. Captained by Angus Walters, it proved itself by winning the 1921 International Fisherman's Trophy, racing against the Americans. Unfortunately, endless wrangling about qualifications and rules dogged these Halifax races, and some racers would do anything to get an edge, even forcing a competitor into dangerous waters like the ledges near Sambro. Through the 1920s and 1930s, the *Bluenose* won some races and lost some, and at the same time it worked the Grand Banks, hauling vast quantities of fish back home to Lunenburg. It ran aground only once, in Placentia Bay, but after repairs, it beat the *Gertrude L. Thibaud* in the next year's race. By the 1930s, the *Bluenose* had become the symbol of Nova Scotia seafaring and Canadian pride. Captain Walters sailed it up the St. Lawrence River and into to the Great Lakes for the in 1933 Chicago

World's Fair, and there he provoked some bad publicity. When a woman sightseer touched the wheel of his famous schooner, he reportedly said that she had "violated" his ship.

The *Bluenose* and its captain survived that embarrassment, but by 1939, the beautiful ship was not only obsolete but risky, as it was far too vulnerable to German submarine attacks. In that year, Walters bought the vessel he had once sailed for a mere $7,200 and tried to restore it, but he couldn't raise enough money from the government or public purses. Discouraged, he sold the *Bluenose* to the East India Trading Company in 1942, and it sailed off to haul freight around the Caribbean. On January 28, 1946, it hit a reef off of Haiti and went down. Nevertheless, the *Bluenose* achieved a degree of immortality. An untarnished image of the legendary sailing ship appeared on the 1937 ten-cent coin, and, except for brief intervals, it has remained on the "tails" side of the Canadian dime ever since.

Navies of Rum and Runners of Rum

Booze arrived in Canada with the Europeans. James Moreira, a rum historian, asserts that in the Maritimes in particular, rum "has made and lost fortunes; it has won and lost elections; it has fuelled riots and provided comfort in the wake of disasters; it has been a factor in rebellion." Long ago, rum found its way north from West Indian sugar plantations and distilleries, and in 1655 it was first used aboard British naval ships. In 1711, Colonel Samuel Vetch reported that it was the drink of choice for his men, rather than "beer, which due to the severity of the winter freezes." Eventually, as a part of his daily regimen, every British sailor was allotted half a pint of rum. During the Boer War, the Royal Navy issued a substantial quantity of over-proof rum three times a week to bolster spirits, and maybe it was at least partially the rum ration that tempted young Canadians to join the British fleet and head for South Africa. The navy maintained its time-honoured tradition on Canada's coasts, and when the Royal Canadian Navy was established in 1910, it followed suit, disbursing rum in a formal ceremony at 11:30 in the morning to all sailors over twenty. These rum supplements soothed the navy through two world wars and up until March 31, 1971, when the "last tot" was taken aboard *HMCS Saskatchewan*. Ending the tradition failed, however, to usher in a new era of total sobriety among Canadian sailors.

The rum trade bolstered the economies of many ports, including Louisbourg, Halifax, Saint John, and St. John's, and some merchants grew rich. In the middle of the nineteenth century, however, there was a backlash against "demon rum," and the growing temperance movement fixed battle lines between the wets and the dries, the drinkers and the teetotallers. Temperance societies were a springboard for all kinds of social improvement, but, in the United States, the temperance movement also spearheaded Prohibition. The Volstead Act of 1920 set off an unprecedented era of crime, built around the illegal importing and distribution of alcoholic beverages.

The thirst of the great American cities was insatiable, and their pockets seemed bottomless. Some of the criminal activity seemed to be of such a "family man" nature, and the money was so attractive that Maritime and Newfoundland fishermen as well as boat builders eagerly participated. Prohibition proved profitable for captains willing to transport booze by sea from the French island of St. Pierre, off the coast of Newfoundland, to American ports. The price of a quintal of cod had dropped from $13.62 in 1918 to $6.25 in 1927, so taking up smuggling seemed like a reasonable career move. Because the traditional sailing schooners proved to be too visible and too slow, too easily captured by the U.S. Coast Guard, special rum-runner boats were built in ports like Shelburne, Mahone Bay, Lunenburg, and Liverpool. They sat low and squat on the water, obscure if not necessarily fast. The rum runners would use anything necessary to avoid detection, including stuffing oily rags into the engine exhaust pipe to create a smokescreen to conceal themselves from their adversaries.

Entrepreneurial British Columbia boat owners joined the campaign to profit from Prohibition. They delivered, not only Canadian commercial liquor, but also high-octane moonshine from the stills along the northern coast. Fortunes were made smuggling booze to Washington state as adept navigators threaded their way through tricky northwest channels, eluding the U.S. Coast Guard while fulfilling their mission to supply the American public.

One of the most famous Canadian smugglers was the Nova Scotian rumrunner Jack Randell, whose motto was "once a scrapper, always a scrapper." He worked for a man named Jamie Clark, whose schooner, the

I'm Alone, equipped with two one-hundred-horsepower diesel engines, was well built for the purpose. In 1928, Randell loaded up 1,500 cases of liquor in St. Pierre and headed for the warmer waters of Louisiana. Here he unloaded his freight onto a waiting ship, and then he sailed to British Honduras to take on another load of booze for thirsty Americans. Before he could get this cargo ashore, however, the Coast Guard vessel *Wolcott* caught up with him and fired warning shots over his bow. They were in international waters, and Randell believed that the American Coast Guard had no business harassing him. Randell was courteous enough to allow the *Wolcott* captain, Frank Paul, to come aboard and discuss the matter; they agreed to disagree. The *I'm Alone* tried to sail away, but the *Wolcott* pursued, with Coast Guard artillerymen firing shells at the *I'm Alone* while sailors shot at it with their rifles. Another Coast Guard vessel, the *Dexter*, opened fire as well. Randell didn't stand a chance against what he later called this "cowardly attack."

Captain Randell was thrown into a New Orleans jail and charged with conspiracy, while back home in Canada he became a celebrity, "an international hero for upholding British naval tradition on the high seas." Some politicians saw this attack on a private vessel as an act of war, and this political pressure eventually caused the charges to be dropped. In 1935, the U.S. government apologized to Randell and paid Clark $25,000 in damages for sinking his ship.

Canada's relations with the United States were not all adversarial. Franklin Delano Roosevelt, scion of a wealthy family, spent his summers as a child on Campobello Island, just off the coast of Maine but part of New Brunswick. While fishing from the yacht *Sebalo* off the shores of Campobello in 1921, Roosevelt fell overboard. As the result of remaining in cold, wet clothes for the rest of the day, Roosevelt fell victim to the polio virus going around, and the disease affected his legs so badly that he could barely walk. Nonetheless, he overcame the hardships of polio to pursue his political career, trying to hide his infirmity from the American public, often with some success. When he became president of the United States in 1933, he returned to Campobello (accompanied by two navy destroyers) to be greeted by cheering islanders. He would come back to the island haven of his youth twice more before America entered World War II.

A Revolution in the Making

After a short post-war boom, the 1920s brought severe economic hardship to most Newfoundlanders and Maritimers, despite the glory of sailing races and the profitability of liquor smuggling. By the mid-1920s, a Maritime rights movement flourished. Maritimers felt cheated by decisions made by a federal government whose priority seemed clearly to be Upper Canada. At Confederation, Maritimers accounted for twenty percent of the new Dominion's population; by 1921, they made up less than twelve percent. Because they had fewer representatives in Parliament than Ontario and Quebec, they couldn't get what they felt was their due, and that made hard times that much harder. As well as resentment, a strong feeling of regional identity for New Brunswickers, Nova Scotians and Prince Edward Islanders fuelled this backlash.

Throughout the region, a branch plant economy was emerging, with steel mills, coal mines, and other large industries owned more and more by investors from away. Labour unrest that amounted almost to warfare erupted between the low-paid iron and coal workers of the Maritimes and companies such as the British Empire Steel Corporation, with directors in Toronto, New York, and London. Militant leaders like J.B. McLachlan led workers into bitter and often violent strikes. In 1922, for example, BESCO's decision to cut wages by forty percent so outraged the workers that some angry leaders called for the "complete overthrow of the capitalist system."

The governments of Nova Scotia and Canada responded on one occasion to this threat of "revolution" by sending 1,000 troops and 1,000 policemen to quell it, hinting that British warships might join the battle as well. Red Dan Livingston, another leader of the disgruntled workers, said he was forced to sign a deal on their behalf "under muzzles of rifles, machine guns, and gleaming bayonets." Cape Breton coal miners, who mined seams of coal reaching far under the sea, were continuously angry. They went on strike in 1923, 1924, and 1925. Their grievances against the government and the corporations, only partially settled with each new agreement, lasted for generations. BESCO went out of business by 1930, and Cape Breton labour poet Dawn Fraser wrote, "May Satan's imps attend your hearse — adieu, adieu, Cape Breton's curse."

Another labour movement of sorts was led by a Catholic priest named

Moses Coady. He saw that farmers and fishermen were getting a raw deal and would do better if they helped themselves through co-operatives. He believed that co-operation was "the only means in our day through which the masses of people can again have a say in the economic processes." Some labelled Coady a radical and a Communist, but the down-to-earth approach of his Antigonish Movement led to the creation of successful fishing and farming co-ops and community credit unions. His work proved so valuable in the region that later in the century, his ideas were taken to poverty-stricken countries around the world.

Women and people of colour were entrenched in the work force but earned very low wages. Women held most of the teaching jobs in British Columbia as well as in the East, partly because the pay was so low and the prospects so circumscribed that men with aspirations or dependents couldn't afford to accept the work. Often women teachers found themselves in the most difficult situations. Jessie Stott, of Saanich, British Columbia, arrived on Redona Island by steamer in 1922 to find that the schoolhouse was right next door to a smelly fish reduction plant. Because she was single and the island was primarily inhabited by married men and their families, she wasn't allowed to live there. Each day, she rowed back and forth between the island and the mainland until the fish plant went out of business and the school was abandoned. Nurses worked under similar economic conditions, and women who married were expected to quit their professions. However, this rule didn't apply in remote communities where there was no replacement. Kathleen Patterson, for example, a nurse in Bella Coola in the 1930s, had to "pull teeth, deliver babies and colts" and act as an undertaker when necessary.

Tsimshian fishermen, along with some other Aboriginal workers, formed the Native Brotherhood of British Columbia in 1931 in order to protect their rights and their livelihoods. Native employees were also an essential part of the logging, canning, and agricultural economies, and they fought long and hard to achieve a semblance of equality and reasonable wages in these industries.

"The Friendly Arctic"

In the first two decades of the twentieth century, Canada had established some degree of de facto sovereignty in the far North, with a few tiny RCMP detachments in place, the disruptive bowhead whalers sent home, and the government-sponsored exploratory voyages of Joseph-Elzéar Bernier completed. The next explorer on the scene to help expand and, to some degree, confuse understanding of the North was Vilhjalmur Stefansson, born in Manitoba of Icelandic parents. He took a couple of trips to the western Arctic, and in 1910 he claimed to have discovered "blond Eskimos." He travelled back south with the theory that these people, now known as the Copper Inuit, were perhaps descendants of Greenland explorers or even offspring from the Franklin expedition. Amundsen wrote Stefansson off as a charlatan, but others bought into the far-fetched notion. When the Americans began to lose interest in him, Stefansson found the Canadian government willing to back his expeditions.

Between 1913 and 1918, Stefansson undertook incredibly dangerous travels in the North, drifting around with sledges on ice floes, letting the currents take him and his men where they would. In the process, he discovered Lougheed, Brock, Meighen, and Borden islands. He retuned home with his vision of a "friendly Arctic" and published a book of that title in 1921. He promoted the North as a place to be exploited for its natural riches, and later he set up a reindeer ranch of sorts on Baffin Island and "improved" the trade in musk oxen. Unfortunately for this Arctic optimist and entrepreneur, neither domesticating reindeer nor trading in musk oxen worked out well.

Next, Stefansson took it upon himself to claim Wrangel Island, which lies north of Siberia, for Canada. This gave Ottawa a monumental diplomatic headache, for it embroiled Canada with the United States and the Soviet Union. As well, four members of the Wrangel expedition had died on that difficult journey. Now Stefansson was viewed in Canada as both reckless and troublesome, so he returned to the United States, and there he remained highly regarded as a brave explorer.

Meanwhile, in the Eastern Arctic, Norway was considering claiming all the territory explored by Otto Sverdrup. Not everyone in Norway thought owning Ellesmere Island was such a great idea, but Canada, worried about the Norwegian claim, re-established the Eastern Arctic Patrol. Beginning in the early 1920s, icebreakers worked through the short summer seasons, keeping navigation channels open, supplying a few settlements, and generally establishing a visible Canadian presence.

To complicate the situation, the U.S. Navy sent Richard Byrd steaming off in the *Peary* in 1925 to look for places to build American air bases in the far north. Canadians became nervous, and the Minister of the Interior asserted that anyone who wanted to root around in the Canadian hinterland had to get a permit first. The intrepid Captain Bernier was again sent north to give the Americans the unwelcome news that they couldn't traipse around without a license. When the Americans returned the following year, they did so with license in hand; Canada had effectively backed its claim.

In 1929, Canada set aside the worry of Norway's claim by chipping in $67,000 retroactively towards the expenses for Otto Sverdrup's trip of 1898-1902, which had, after all, provided Canada with excellent maps and knowledge. By then, Canada had effectively established both legitimate claim and control over the North. Aside from a few crackpots, visionaries, and military strategists, however, no one really had much sense of what to do with all that wilderness, now that it was internationally agreed to be Canadian soil.

The Bad Times, the Good Times, and a Rock in a Bad Place

By the early 1930s, the east coast forestry business was down seventy-five percent. Fish production was down by half, and the ending of Prohibition in the United States in 1933 cut off booze smuggling as a source of income. Farmers received a pittance for the crops they raised. Coal production and steel production both fell by over fifty percent, and the region fell into the throes of the Great Depression.

Throughout the Maritime provinces, many people were destitute during the dirty thirties. In the rural communities, people ate potatoes and fish and whatever else could be hunted or homegrown. Women sewed clothing from cotton flour sacks, and men built, rebuilt, and otherwise cobbled together the machinery, boats, and buildings they needed. Some local governments provided meagre help so the poorest of the poor could survive. In the coastal community of Guysborough, Nova Scotia, a dollar

CGS Stanley *escorting two sailing vessels in the La Have River near Bridgewater, Nova Scotia, 1910. Similar icebreakers were used in the north in the early 1920s to back up Canadian sovereignty claims.* (NAC, PA207009)

a month was the official "dole" for poverty-stricken families. Natives who had lost their lands and traditional hunting and fishing rights remained at the bottom of the economic heap, and Blacks also suffered from poverty coupled with racism that sometimes prevented them from gaining even the most menial jobs.

Newfoundland's economy, too, was in tatters in the 1920s and 1930s. Though it was still a British colony, it had its own elected government and operated most of its own affairs. Right up into the twentieth century, the French maintained fishing rights along the western shores of the island. This had riled Newfoundlanders for generations. In 1904, when the French Shore was turned over to Newfoundland, Prime Minister Robert Bond boasted that Newfoundland was now no longer tainted by "the blasting influence of foreign oppression." Newfoundland also had an ongoing boundary dispute with Quebec — that is to say, with Canada — over the ownership of much of Labrador. In 1927, the British Privy Council ruled in favour of Newfoundland, legitimizing its claim to this enormous tract of the mainland. This was all good news for development and for the existing communities. By the 1920s, logging, paper mills, and mining had created some diversity, but fishing was still the undependable engine that drove the economy. With the onset of the global economic collapse of 1929, the colonial government, already deeply in debt, was pushed into desperation. It was more than a little humbling for Newfoundlanders to revert to true colonial status, governed by a joint commission appointed by the British Parliament and consisting of three Newfoundlanders and three men from away.

The Depression took its toll on British Columbia as well. Although some families in the remote villages along the coast preserved some degree of self-sufficiency, in Vancouver the unemployed and homeless lined the streets, while in Victoria, over a quarter of the population was on some form of government assistance. Many canneries stayed open during those years, but the pay was pitifully low. In the small communities and in rural areas, bartering became the norm. Everyone from wharf builders to midwives might expect to be paid in chickens, fish, pigs, or butter. As in the Maritimes, the women turned cotton flour sacks, or even public fishing notices that were printed on fabric, into all kinds of clothing and household linens.

Despite the economic see-saw of the 1920s and 1930s, Union Steamships capitalized on the growth of Vancouver by offering cruises for Vancouverites to Cortez and Savary islands, Powell River, Sechelt, Gibsons, and up Howe Sound towards Squamish. Bowen Island was developed into a tourist spot, with dancing pavilions, swimming pools, cottages, and beaches with sand shipped in all the way from Scotland; oddly enough, it became a popular destination for trade union picnics and rallies. By 1937, over 170,000 people were travelling the coasts on day trips by ship.

By the 1930s, Canadian Pacific and the Boscowitz Steamship Company had started to threaten the Union Steamship Company with serious competition. In some cases, whoever could load the fastest won the cannery shipping contracts. The Union ship *Carenda* could take on 1,500 cases per hour, while the Canadian Pacific's *Princess Joan* could load only 500 cases per hour. Other times, whoever got to the dock first got the job. When a canner at Bella Bella sent out a message that a shipment was ready to go, the *Carenda* and the *Princess Joan* raced for the job. The *Carenda* won by shutting off its lights, taking a shortcut through the uncharted

Gunboat Passage, and sidling up to the cannery dock before the Canadian Pacific ship had a chance. When the *Princess Joan* did arrive, Andy Johnstone, the *Carenda* skipper, shouted back to his competitor, "Don't worry, Cap'n, we'll be out of your way in another hour!"

The infamous Ripple Rock was a navigational hazard that seemed to have been placed in the water by the Devil himself. In the middle of Seymour Narrows, it had wrecked at least fourteen large vessels and over 100 smaller ships and boats and drowned no less than 114 souls since Europeans had first arrived in these waters. The Americans were the first to propose that it be removed somehow, but in the early 1930s, a new idea was put forward: why not make it part of the foundation of a bridge between Vancouver Island and the mainland? A commission overruled this lofty notion, and it was decided Ripple Rock would be blown to bits. A couple of attempts failed, but not before the rock had taken the lives of nine more men, workers whose small boat had capsized. Finally, in 1955, a tunnel was drilled into the rock, and it was blasted away by nearly one and a half tons of explosive. Rock fragments and water shot 1,000 feet into the air, and a water shock wave coursed down the inlet and out to sea. With Ripple Rock reduced to harmless rubble at the bottom of the inlet, the channel was clear for shipping.

A convoy in Bedford Basin, Halifax, April 1, 1942. (NAC, PA-112993)

CHAPTER TWENTY-FIVE

The War Years

Sea Wolves

OTTAWA POLITICIANS were often more skilled at navel-gazing than constructing schemes of naval strategy, and only significant prodding awakened them to the need to defend Canada's shores. German U-boats had crept into East Coast harbours right through World War I, and they returned as an even bigger threat in World War II. Ottawa eventually began to see the inevitability of intrusion, if not outright invasion, on both Atlantic and Pacific coasts. Whereas in 1939 the Canadian navy had a mere thirteen warships and 3,000 men, by 1945 it had 365 ships and 100,000 men.

Some semblance of prosperity found its way back to Newfoundland's shores in the late 1930s and early 1940s as the United States, Canada, and Great Britain created five airports, several army posts, and a pair of naval bases on the island. U.S. military dollars poured into the economy. Many Newfoundlanders enlisted in the militia to defend their home shores, while others joined the British or Canadian overseas forces. For civilians, there was something close to full employment, the likes of which had never been seen. There would be a stiff price in loss of human life to be paid, however, for the economic benefits of war.

Newfoundland schooners were still plying the waters of the Atlantic during World War II. The German subs torpedoed anything of commercial or military value afloat in the northwest Atlantic. To avoid being easy targets, ships were obliged to sail or steam without running lights, and that posed other hazards, not the least of which was potential collisions with other ships. On June 13, 1942, while crossing the Cabot Strait from Newfoundland to Cape Breton, the coastal trading schooner *Eva U. Colp* found itself smack in the middle of an outgoing allied convoy.

Personnel of the Women's Royal Canadian Naval Service embarking at Halifax for service overseas, February 1, 1944. (NAC, PA-108181)

Even though the *Colp* was showing lights, it was accidentally rammed by the *SS Ann*. The crew had to abandon ship, but the larger vessel rescued them from the drink.

Later that year, the Cabot Strait became even more dangerous for shipping. In October, the *Caribou* — the ferry that made regular runs from North Sydney to Port aux Basques and back — was savagely torpedoed by the German sub U-69. Of the 237 people on board, 136 died, including thirty-one of the forty-six-person crew, most of them residents of the small community of Port aux Basques. Canadians and Newfoundlanders alike were outraged by what Newfoundland writer Jack Fitzgerald called an "unprovoked, cowardly attack on a defenceless ferry." The ferry had been escorted by HMCS *Grandmere,* which could not immediately drop depth charges because of the civilians in the icy waters. Later, the sub would be pursued by the naval vessels *Reindeer* and *Elk,* but it escaped.

American military ships also took a beating along Newfoundland's shores. The *Pollux* ran aground near Argentia; many died, although eighty men reached shore by a rescue rope and huddled together at the bottom of a thirty-metre cliff to await rescue. When the U.S. destroyer *Truxton* foundered in Chambers Bay, off the Burin Peninsula, some crewmen made it ashore in rubber rafts. As the ship broke apart in the hammering waves, residents from St. Lawrence lowered dories down a seventy-metre cliff to save the desperate American sailors. Between the two sea disasters, over 200 men died — collateral damage in a war where the indifferent forces of nature sometimes seemed to be on the side of the enemy.

In this war as in the last, ships travelled in convoys from the East Coast of Canada to Europe with men and supplies; the first convoy of eighteen vessels, escorted by British cruisers and Canadian destroyers, left Halifax in 1939. While convoys offered a certain amount of protection against U-boats, they weren't foolproof. In October 1942, Convoy SC104, with forty-seven ships, including two destroyers and four corvettes, came under submarine attack and lost eight ships in three days.

Subs in packs cruised the waters off the Atlantic coast of Canada like ravenous sea wolves on the prowl for victims. On July 19th, 1942, the Norwegian ship *Kronprinzen*, carrying steel, cotton, and flour, had been travelling in a convoy from New York on its way to Halifax. Eighty nautical miles off the coast from Yarmouth, it was gouged by two German torpedoes; one of the holes was "large enough for a trawl dory to row through." The captain would not abandon ship but called for tugs from Halifax and Boston to rescue his vessel. The men worked the pumps as the ship drifted toward shore at Lower East Pubnico. The impoverished people there requested a modest wage to unload the goods and carry the cargo ashore for safe-keeping, but the Norwegian captain refused. When he realized that the flour couldn't be salvaged, the captain ordered his men to dump it into the sea rather than allow the local people to carry it home to feed themselves. The Pubnico fishermen, knowing just how many hungry mouths there were along the coastline, ignored the captain, and they also ignored the Mounties, who shot water cannons to keep them away. Undeterred, they rowed their dories out to grab the sacks of flour before they could sink into the sea. The ship was eventually towed off to Halifax for repairs.

The merchant seamen who manned the supply ships sailing from St. John's, Halifax, and Saint John often found themselves exposed and vulnerable at sea. Although they were not members of the armed forces, they encountered extreme danger, and their death toll exceeded the norm for military men crossing the Atlantic. Yet, on the streets at home, they were sometimes called "zombies" and scoffed at by servicemen and civilians alike as cowards for not being part of the fighting units. The merchant seamen's fight for recognition continued right up to the end of the twentieth century; only in 2001 were these men truly honoured for their part in helping to win the war, and by then time had greatly thinned their ranks.

War in the Streets

World War II brought the Atlantic port cities back to life, especially Halifax, the town that British Admiral S.S. Bonham-Carter called, "probably the most important port in the world" in 1941. Historian Graham Metson noted that Halifax at this time "was no longer the wild, free city of the nineteenth century," but in fact was "poor and puritan." The city was unprepared for the thousands of soldiers and sailors that gathered to go off to war, and it was pushed beyond endurance. Chronicling the affairs of the Merchant Navy, F.B. Watt describes Halifax as "an overcrowded hell hole." There were shortages of everything, including accommodations for the military families that followed the men into the city, and those flocking into the city blamed Haligonians for their lack of goodwill and inability to accommodate the onslaught.

There would be no second Halifax Explosion, but there were some serious close calls as military ships jammed into the harbour. In April of 1942, the British ship *Trongate*, loaded with TNT and ammunition, caught fire in a harbour filled with 200 other ships, some of them carrying hundreds of American troops. The mine sweeper *Chedabucto* was ordered to fire on the *Trongate* and sink it.

In 1943, a fire broke out in Bedford Basin on the U.S. ship *Volunteer*, loaded to the gunwales with ammunition, dynamite, magnesium, and bales of tobacco. The officers and the captain were drinking and playing cards at the time. When the fire was discovered, some men abandoned ship, leaving the captain to protest the intrusion of the firemen as they jumped aboard onto an already red-hot deck. The brazen firemen used bales of tobacco to insulate the magnesium barrels and keep them from igniting, and they cut holes into the ship's metal deck plates to release the explosive gases, which they ignited with a rifle shot. Eventually, valves were opened, water poured into the hold, and the *Volunteer* was sunk to avert disaster.

On July 18, 1945, an ammunition barge exploded near the docks, close to a major ammunition magazine north of Dartmouth, in the Burnside area. Dartmouth and parts of Halifax were evacuated; everyone expected the entire magazine to go up in a blast similar to that of 1917. This time, however, despite several small explosions, there was no cataclysm.

Halifax did not survive the war completely intact, but once again, the assault on the city was not the doing of the enemy. On May 7 and 8, 1945, Canadian military men celebrating the allied victory in Europe went on a rampage and tore the city apart. Official VE Day celebrations were scheduled to take place in churches and on the parade grounds, but the men were in favour of something less formal. Thousands of them headed downtown, where they helped themselves to the entire stock of beer on hand at Keith's Brewery on Hollis Street. Many residents remember them as non-threatening, but not everyone would agree. Novelist Hugh Garner wrote, "The mob filled the street from one side to the other, breaking the windows of seventy houses." Three people died and 211 were arrested. Five hundred businesses were looted, liquor stores were raided, police cars were burned, and the rioters caused five million dollars in damage. But there was more to the rampage than a party out of control. Many military men felt that the city had treated them poorly as they swarmed the streets, the restaurants, and the movie theatres throughout the war, and for this they held a grudge against the city. The authorities were well aware of this grievance, but, Hugh Garner said, "Though everyone in authority knew it was coming, little was done to prevent the crisis brewing."

Admiral Leonard Murray and Mayor Allan Butler drove around town trying to subdue the drunken mobs with orders given over loudspeakers. The navy was blamed for starting the uprising, and Admiral Murray eventually accepted the responsibility for everything that had gone wrong. Those two days would long be remembered by Haligonians who had seen their city torn to pieces by the very men sworn to defend it. After the war, the navy had to contend with three mutinies in 1949, which, when scrutinized, led the brass to abandon some of the inhumane and irrational customs and rules aboard ship that had been inherited from the British.

Relocation of Japanese Canadians to an internment camp in the interior of British Columbia, 1942-1946. (NAC, C-046350)

Fear and Prejudice

In 1939, just in time for World War II, the Lions Gate Bridge was opened, linking North Vancouver to the main part of the city and opening it to a daily onslaught of commuting workers. Between 1940 and 1944, the number of British Columbia women employed outside their homes went from 30,000 to 60,000, due mainly to the fact that they took over the jobs of men going off to war. Up the coast, the Sitka spruce industry came back to life with the military need for wood. Hemlock, spruce, and cedar were in demand for aircraft manufacturing, and year-round logging left massive scars upon the beautiful Gulf and Queen Charlotte islands. An RCAF base was built at Alliford Bay as part of an elaborate but somewhat feeble plan to protect the coast against possible invasion from across the Pacific.

There was legitimate reason to fear invasion. Just a day after the attack on Pearl Harbour, Japan had assaulted the British port of Hong Kong. Almost 2,000 Canadian soldiers were on hand there to assist British troops in defending the territory, but it was a lost cause. Two hundred

Japanese Canadians arriving at an internment camp at Slocan, in the British Columbia interior, 1942. (NAC, C-046356)

Canadians were killed, and nearly that many again were captured and sent to prison camps. Later in 1942, it was discovered that the Japanese had also sent a few troops to remote islands in the Aleutian chain — American territory. No one was sure what the Rising Sun had in mind for Alaska or the coast of western Canada.

A heady concoction of fear and prejudice began to wreak havoc on Japanese-Canadian families. Newspaper editorialists and some religious leaders told the public they should be afraid of their Oriental neighbours, who were the same flesh and blood as the crazed armies who wanted to gobble up Asia. Some Chinese shop owners posted signs to remind their neighbours that they were *not* Japanese. Halford Wilson, a powerful Vanouver alderman, had proposed in 1941 that the government should impound fishing boats owned by Japanese families along the coast. When war was declared against Japan later that year, Wilson had his way, despite the fact that RCMP spies had discovered that Japanese British Columbians tended to be more patriotic than other Canadians. Nonetheless, livelihoods were snatched from fishing families, and some white fishermen were more than a little pleased by the summary removal of the competition posed by their very adept Japanese counterparts.

In February of 1942, the federal government announced that anyone of Japanese ancestry would be removed from what it called "protected" zones, and that would mean uprooting families from their homes along the coast and elsewhere. Twenty thousand people were "evacuated" and forced into internment camps in the interior of the province. It was a gut-wrenching experience. Worse yet, their fishing boats, houses, and farms were simply seized by the government and sold off at prices far below market value; often the true owners did not receive a penny. Although the term was not technically applied, Japanese-Canadian men, women, and children were prisoners of war.

Once Japanese families had been exiled from the coastal community of Steveston, the British Columbia government made an appalling decision: they released men from prisons and moved them there to take up fishing in the Gulf of Georgia. The result was drunkenness, arson, murder, and a general disregard for property and law, while the diligent, well-behaved citizens who had once lived there peacefully were themselves incarcerated many miles away.

Defending the Shores

The war dramatically changed the nature of the passenger ships on the Pacific inland waterways. The once lively and brightly lit Union steamships were painted grey, their radios were often silenced, and they required protection against underwater mines. The pilot houses were reconstructed of concrete, and guns were affixed to the sterns. While crowds of uniformed men swelled the passenger lists, recreational travellers still headed to and from the islands on their days off, now that gasoline for cars was rationed. Schedules were supposedly secret, and arrival and departure times were no longer posted, but anyone who didn't look Japanese or German could get an honest answer just by asking.

While a full-scale Japanese invasion of the West Coast seemed like a tactical impossibility, enough evidence of a serious threat remained to demand vigilance. The *Fort Camosun* was a 7,000-ton freighter built in Victoria to carry war supplies. In June of 1942, on its first voyage, it headed out onto calm seas, heavily laden with plywood, lead, zinc, and munitions supplies. Early in the morning of June 20, the voyage was interrupted when torpedoes slammed into the ship, tearing massive holes into its side. The torpedoes were launched from what is believed to be Sub I-25 of the Imperial Japanese Navy. At the helm was Commander Meiji Tagami.

The men on board the freighter had a rude wake-up call, and all thirty-one took to the lifeboats. HMN Corvettes *Quesnel* and *Edmundston* picked up the distress call and responded. The *Quesnel* began an attack on the sub, while the *Edmundston* picked up the distraught men from the boats. Eventually, the sub slipped off to sea, and the *Edmundston*, later aided by the *Dauntless*, a tug from Vancouver, tried to tow the sinking *Fort Camosun* to port. The wounded vessel stayed afloat long enough to reach Neah Bay, where, with part of the ship above water, it came to rest on the bottom. The cargo was salvaged, the ship was repaired, and it went back to work, surviving the war by more than fifteen years.

The night after the *Fort Camosun* was torpedoed, the same Japanese sub fired twenty-five shells at the lighthouse on Estevan Point on the western coast of Vancouver Island. Some people in the tiny community nearby fully believed the war had arrived: British Columbia was about to be invaded by the Japanese. Fortunately, however, none of the shells hit the lighthouse or the homes. George Bowering suggests that the metal casings of those shells "had once been scrap metal shipped from Vancouver to Japan during the thirties."

Back on the mainland in Vancouver, air-raid sirens had been set up and tested, mothers covered the windows with black-out curtains at night, and everyone grew more nervous about the enemy from across the Pacific. However, although the war was certainly bad news for Japanese Canadians and occasionally frightening for coastal dwellers, it was a boon to the British Columbia economy. Its per capita income became the highest of any province, and, as Canadians moved west to cash in on the boom, the population rose to over a million.

When the war ended, there was as much cause to celebrate on the West Coast as there was on the East. In Vancouver, however, the rowdy celebrations that filled the streets did not turn violent; unlike Halifax, it emerged from the war unscathed.

In Iqaluit, an Inuit man works on a traditional igloo in preparation for Nunavut Day, April 1, 1999, when Nunavut became a separate territory. (CP)

CHAPTER TWENTY-SIX

Winds of Change, Seas of Grief

"The Bludgeonings of Fate"

WHAT NEWFOUNDLAND had lacked in economic wealth over the years, it had cultivated in character. Ray Guy said, "Your average New-foundlander is waterproof, shockproof, dustproof, shock-resistant and anti-magnetic . . . he has been bred over three or four hundred years for durability." The second half of the twentieth century put this durability to the test.

After the war, Newfoundlanders wanted political freedom from Britain. Economic woes were diminished, temporarily at least, and many people felt frustrated with the Commission of Government, set up in 1934 and supervised from England. Most wanted Newfoundland either to become a Dominion, a full-fledged member of the Commonwealth, or to become a province of Canada, a proposal that had been on the table since before 1867. The American influence during the war had been so positive in so many ways that there was even considerable enthusiasm for becoming part of the United States.

In the referendum of 1948, which offered Newfoundlanders the choice between joining Confederation and becoming a Dominion, fifty-two percent voted in favour of union with Canada. The persuasive powers of Joey Smallwood were significantly responsible for this outcome. The last of Canada's fathers of Confederation and the first premier of the new province, Smallwood, a broadcaster and a savvy politician, remained in office for twenty-two years, swaying his countrymen with the eloquence of an evangelist. "After all the bludgeonings of Fate," he told them, "Newfoundland's head may be bloody but it is still unbowed. The economic blizzard has strewn the scene with considerable wreckage, but the spirit of the people is invincible."

Joey Smallwood signing the document of Confederation with Canada. (NAC, PA-128080)

Smallwood, loved by many and loathed by some, pushed for consolidation and modernization. Up-to-date fish plants opened, and more people worked packing more fish brought ashore by bigger boats with fewer crewmen. Supplying mid-twentieth-century services — health care, education, electricity — to remote outports was impossible, and Smallwood thought that moving the people to the services would have better results. Forty-nine communities were abandoned completely between 1946 and 1954, and, to speed up the process, the government funded a centralization program in 1953. "Burn the boats" was the battle cry of the government agents who urged families to leave their outport homes and move into larger towns. People from another 110 Newfoundland and Labrador communities were relocated; a few lucky ones could float their houses across bays or drag them over the ice to new foundations. Some outports became ghost towns immediately, and some were inhabited for a while by older folks who refused to leave their ancestral homes. In 1965, Newfoundland established the Fisheries Household Resettlement Program, and in 1967, the federal government joined the program. Until 1975, increased financial incentives lured families away from 150 more communities.

For some, the opportunity to leave the outports was a godsend, but for others it was disastrous. Critics now suggest that, quite apart from individual and communal grief over the end of a way of life, the cost to the economy of alienation, unemployment, and the breakdown of community and family support systems was too high. Some relocated families drifted back to their former communities, at least seasonally, to try to make a living as their parents had done from inshore fishing, but the downturn in the cod fishery made such a move a very difficult challenge indeed. The dramatic changes brought on by Joey Smallwood's vision will be blessed and cursed well into the twenty-first century by Newfoundlanders wherever they live.

Cold War and Cold Water

The mutual fear between the Western powers and the Communist Bloc after the war actually helped to sustain the economy of Halifax. The Cold War meant continuing military preparedness, and in Halifax almost a quarter of the jobs were related to the military establishment. Canada sent three destroyers to the Korean War and, during the Cold War, maintained over twenty destroyers, seventeen escort ships, and ten mine sweepers.

The economy in the North benefited from the Cold War, too. The air defence radar stations along the Atlantic and Pacific coasts that had guarded against attack from the Germans and Japanese were dismantled, but fear of attack by high-altitude Soviet bombers flying over the North Pole led to the building of the Distant Early Warning (DEW) Line in the mid-1950s. These radar stations, strung along the arctic coast between Alaska and Baffin Island, were paid for by the United States, but they were built by Canadian companies, often with Native labour. They were also owned by Canada and commanded by Canadians. Although changing military technology started to make them obsolete almost as soon as they were built, at least parts of the DEW Line contributed to the local economy for many years.

Although military forces had paid some attention to "guarding the coast" ever since the Europeans started to take an interest in Canada, the lion's share of the effort went into warding off enemies or harassing friends of the enemy. The idea of a military agency dedicated to protecting or rescuing those in trouble at sea is relatively modern, but nonetheless some early legal attention was paid to protecting navigational aids. In 1784, a Nova Scotia law was enacted to safeguard such devices. Even if a "navigational aid" was nothing more than a stone cairn on a headland or a wooden barrel anchored to the channel floor, a person could be sentenced to twelve months in prison for damaging these vital tools. Even securing a boat to a marker buoy could earn a six-month jail sentence or a £20 fine. Of course, the personal safety of sailors was of no great concern to the British Navy or commercial ship owners during the 1700s. This bit of common knowledge prompted Samuel Johnson to remark, "No man would go to sea who had contrivances enough to get himself into a jail."

The Canadian Coast Guard officially came into being in 1867 as the Marine Branch of the Department of Marine and Fisheries. It wasn't until 1962 that the branch was officially named the Coast Guard and moved into the jurisdiction of the Department of Transportation. Along the coasts, the Coast Guard has regional headquarters in St. John's, Dartmouth, and Vancouver. The service operates over fifty large ships, seventy-four smaller rescue vessels, thirty-five helicopters, and four hovercraft, and among the large vessels are the icebreakers that ply the north and east coasts. Canada has had ice-breaking operations since just after Confederation, when Prince Edward Island was guaranteed a year-round ferry in return for joining Canada. These ferries, of course, had to be able to plough through the stubborn Northumberland Strait ice.

In the 1920s, icebreakers took supplies to isolated northern settlements as a gesture of sovereignty over the Northwest Passage. By the 1930s, they kept the Hudson Bay port of Churchill, Manitoba, open as late in the year as possible to allow shipment of grain. During the Cold War, Canadian icebreakers supplied the American Distant Early Warning stations in the Arctic.

In 1969, the icebreaker *John A. Macdonald* sailed through the Northwest Passage both ways, escorting the American tanker *Manhattan*, the first commercial ship to make the voyage. Sixteen years later, when the American Coast Guard wanted to sail the *Polar Sea* through these coastal

The Coast Guard icebreaker CGS John A. Macdonald. (DFO, 100316)

waters, the *John A. Macdonald* protected Canadian sovereignty by providing an escort. This excellent icebreaker was decommissioned in 1991 after serving the Coast Guard for thirty-one years.

Despite the growing militarization and the anxieties bred by the Cold War, coastal Canada made some positive and lasting contributions to peace. Moses Coady's Antigonish Movement, flourishing since the 1930s, sent social activist priests such as Father Harvey Steele from Glace Bay, Nova Scotia, off to Third World countries to fight dictators on behalf of rights for the poor. In 1957, Cyrus Eaton, a vastly wealthy industrialist, convened the first of many Pugwash Conferences in the original "Global Village" on the shore of the Northumberland Strait. Supported by the likes of Albert Einstein and Bertrand Russell, philosophers, economists, scientists, and political thinkers from many nations gathered to work for worldwide disarmament. For the rest of the twentieth century and into the twenty-first, these conferences have continued, meeting in Pugwash, Nova Scotia, and in other places around the world to promote peace.

The Price of Fuelling the Economy

In 1953, the American magazine *Holiday* said of the Maritimes, "You'll find a friendly remoteness from the confusion of the world." Many small coastal communities had gravel roads at best right up into the 1960s, some rural areas had no electricity until then, and telephone party lines were common around the Bay of Fundy into the 1970s. Cape Breton Island was linked to the mainland of North America by the Canso Causeway in 1955, improving the highway system that allowed Maritimers to pour westward out of the region, seeking economic salvation in Montreal, Toronto, Alberta, or British Columbia. In 1959, the St. Lawrence Seaway was finished, allowing ships with cargos bound for the interior of the continent to bypass east coast ports entirely. This dealt the regional economy another serious blow. Many Maritimers had annual incomes one- third below the national average, and 82,000 workers left the four Atlantic Provinces in the 1950s. Maritime Union was again discussed, resuscitating the Maritimes Rights movement of the early years into an anger that historian W.S. MacNutt called a potential "Atlantic Revolution."

Provincial and federal agencies tried to counter this economic decline in the 1960s and 1970s by pouring money into a handful of industries and mega-projects. Some of these, including Volvo and Michelin plants, succeeded in creating long-term jobs. Others either proved themselves abysmal failures right away, like the heavy water plant in Cape Breton, or failed gradually after a long period on life-support. Despite decades of strenuous effort, Cape Breton coal mines could not survive the mid-twentieth-century shift in energy use. Coal-fired steam engines gave way to diesel engines, and coal was replaced by oil and electricity for home heating. Electricity, once produced by burning coal, was now produced by hydro, oil-burning, and nuclear sources. The steel mills established to take advantage of the nearby coal took many years to die, but perish they did by the tail end of the twentieth century.

In addition to consolidation and modernization, Joey Smallwood's program for Newfoundland also included heavy industry. Massive iron mines were opened in Labrador in the 1950s, and work began on the Churchill Falls hydroelectric project in 1966. It wasn't finished until 1974, with a final price tag of over a billion dollars. Since the Churchill River has its origin in Quebec, Newfoundland couldn't retain all the benefits of the dam. Deals were made with the Quebec government allowing the province to resell its share of the power to American utilities, and Quebec profited mightily. These deals were hotly contested for several decades, and many Newfoundlanders still feel cheated out of considerable wealth.

From the 1960s into the 1990s, a weak economy and high unemployment drove young Newfoundlanders, like their Maritime counterparts, to find work in other parts of Canada. However, Mobil Oil's announcement that it intended to tap into the Hibernia oil deposits, off the coast of Newfoundland, and the gas and oil fields near Sable Island, off Nova Scotia, brought some back. In spite of the dangers, hopeful young men and women earned — and continue to earn — big money working far at sea on the enormous rigs.

In February 1982, the *Ocean Ranger* proved, if proof were needed, that the sea respects oil rigs no more than ships. Mobil Oil had chartered the *Ocean Ranger* to drill in the Hibernia oil field, 180 miles southeast of St. John's. A raging winter storm, with 145 kilometre per hour winds, churned the North Atlantic into eighteen-metre waves. Designed to withstand harsh conditions, the *Ocean Ranger* could not handle the excesses of this storm. The rig tilted, windows in the control rooms shattered, and water flooded into the delicate electronic equipment. All hell broke loose as the rig tipped on its side, capsized, and went down, drowning eighty-four men, fifty-four of them Newfoundlanders. There were no survivors, and only twenty-two bodies were recovered.

The deaths shocked Atlantic Canadians, and the loss of a state-of-the art $120 million oil rig to the whims of nature sobered a petroleum industry that was charging full steam ahead into offshore exploration. Three inquiries, two American and one Canadian, analyzed the fate of the *Ocean Ranger* and recommended, among other things, that considerably more effort go into improving lifesaving gear, such as sealed rescue boats and survival suits, even for oil rigs considered unsinkable.

Despite the hazards, some still felt that offshore oil would be the biggest economic windfall for Newfoundland since the building of military bases during the Second World War. But first, Newfoundland had to duke it out with the federal government to see which had jurisdiction over the resource. In March of 1984, the Supreme Court of Canada ruled that the continental shelf — the seabed and everything under it — was an "extra-territorial manifestation of external sovereignty." In other words, it came under federal jurisdiction; while Newfoundland would see some profit from offshore oil, it would do so with Ottawa more or less in charge of development, a grave disappointment for many Newfoundlanders.

In the mid-1970s, sizeable reserves of natural gas and oil were discovered near Sable Island, and drilling began. An undersea pipeline was created to bring the gas ashore, and in the late 1990s a land line was laid to transport it to New England. In Nova Scotia and New Brunswick, squabbling continued well into 2002 to determine just how this valuable commodity could be distributed in the Maritimes.

Unclean Harbours and Unhappy Exile

The concept of sustainable development seems not to have occurred to the political mind until the last quarter of the twentieth century; the coastline everywhere was seen as a massive disposal system for every kind of waste. Coastal cities dumped raw sewage into the harbours, and some continue to do so. The Metro Halifax area pours over twenty-five million gallons of sewage and untreated waste water into the harbour every day. In 1994, the Metro Coalition for Harbour Cleanup pointed out that both the city and the Department of National Defence were breaking the Fisheries Act by illegally spewing untreated sewage into the ocean, but the pollution has yet to be curtailed. Plans to solve the problem and clean up the mess keep being made and remade, but with a price tag nearing half a billion dollars, progress is pitifully slow.

The West Coast waters are subjected to similar punishment, and progress comes in tiny increments because governments and taxpayers begrudge the necessary capital investment. Pristine Victoria discharges its sewage into Juan de Fuca Strait, often to the chagrin of the Americans who find it washing up on their shores. Although some work has been done to lower the levels of toxic chemicals in the mix, it still contains the bulk of the city's daily flushings. Vancouver and Nanaimo are only slightly ahead, giving their sewage some primary treatment that involves sedimentation before piping it into the ocean. Contamination from sewage and the run-off from highways and farms is a constant threat to British Columbia's commercial oyster production, eighty percent of which is in Georgia Strait. The highly toxic "red tides," which infect shellfish and then people with life-threatening illness, are believed to be increasing due to city run-off and sewage.

In the 1950s, the automobile-dependent urban lifestyle caught up with British Columbians near Vancouver. They demanded more and better bridges for all those cars to cross so much water — the Lions Gate Bridge could no longer host the long line of commuters coming from North Vancouver and beyond. New bridges needed to be built. But there was a price to be paid, and not just in dollars. A section of the bridge under construction at Second Narrows collapsed on June 17, 1958, killing more than twenty men. Other workers fell into the water far beneath and made their way to safety on boats or by swimming ashore. Divers spent days trying to recover the bodies of those less fortunate, and one searcher perished.

In the east, the dream of linking Prince Edward Island to the mainland was still discussed and debated. Before and during the construction of the Confederation Bridge, between 1994 and 1997, arguments raged over whether it would be an environmental asset, providing new lobster habitat and eliminating the pollution caused by the ferries, or whether it would be a liability, increasing motor traffic while disturbing the undersea environment irreparably. Efforts were made to build the thirteen-kilometre bridge in as environmentally neutral a way as possible, but with what success remains to be seen. Only five years after the bridge's completion, fears that easier access to the island would bring more criminals and criminal activity had already proved to be well founded.

As always, those who have suffered the most from rampant industrial development have been the powerless. At Churchill Falls, money and technology poured into Labrador, while Newfoundland and Quebec indulged in endless wrangling. Native land claims and rights were ignored or abused, and the Aboriginal peoples lost more than they gained.

In Nova Scotia, the Scott Paper pulp mill in Pictou County was allowed to pour its effluent into Boat Harbour, adjacent to the local Mi'kmaw community. The pollution virtually destroyed Boat Harbour, and it would be many years before the Pictou Landing Mi'kmaq received restitution for their financial losses. The community also happened to be downwind of the pulp mill; aside from everyone's having to endure the stench, the children began to suffer severely from respiratory illnesses.

On Cape Breton Island, the Sydney tar ponds are an apparently permanent legacy of unchecked heavy industry. They contain 100 years' worth of by-products from the Sydney steel mill: 700,000 tons of sludge, laced with heavy metals, PCBs, and other contaminants. Some of this toxic soup leaks into the harbour and on out to sea, while the rest poisons the working-class people who live nearby: the local neighbourhood has one of the highest cancer rates in the country. Efforts made since the 1980s to burn this toxic waste have failed. At least $52 million went into one incineration project that didn't work, and no action has been taken on a proposal to simply encase the ponds in concrete. The problem is so terrible and so huge that no one really knows what to do about it.

Blacks, too, have borne the brunt of economic and industrial development. They have lived in the Maritimes for centuries: Matthew da Costa arrived in Port Royal from France in 1605, and in 1686, a freed slave lived near Cape Sable. The first wave of Black Loyalists came to Nova Scotia and New Brunswick as early as 1782 and 1783, followed by the Maroons, who arrived in Halifax from Jamaica in 1796. More came north from the United States during the War of 1812, and by 1850, nearly 5,000 Blacks lived in Nova Scotia alone.

By the middle of the twentieth century, there were several all-Black communities scattered around the province, but the most famous was Africville, on the shore of Bedford Basin at the north end of Halifax. Through the 1940s and 1950s, Africville families were supported by men who worked as stevedores, stonemasons, and makers of barrels, while women worked at a nearby bone meal plant or cooked and cleaned in the homes of the well-to-do. Although many were poor, others were not. Africville included many fine dwellings, and Black clergy and educators bolstered the strong community spirit. In the 1950s, the city opened a dump on the edge of Africville, which was viewed as a place of little

Africville, 1965. (FORMAC)

consequence. Fires took their toll on the community, and health hazards including the lack of clean drinking water caused diseases easily prevented elsewhere. In 1959, Africville workers earned, on average, less than $1,000 per year; the Reverend William Oliver, a community leader, portrayed Africville as "a picture of neglect." The city blamed the community itself and attempted to solve its problems by relocating the residents. Africville had a strong sense of pride, however, and many people did not want to move. Unfortunately for them, the gospel of urban renewal was sweeping North America, and at the same time the harbour-front land had become increasingly attractive for industrial development. In 1962, Africville residents were ordered to leave; those who would not cooperate were forcibly removed, some of them carried off with their belongings in garbage trucks. One of the last residents to vacate was Aaron "Pa" Carvery. He had refused to accept a suitcase of money offered by City Hall, only to find his home bulldozed without his consent. The bitterness over this assault remains strong today in the Nova Scotian Black community. Africville will long remain in the public consciousness as a symbol of institutionalized racism and the product of urban development run amok.

A Requiem for Fish

Big questions are raised continuously on all coasts of Canada about the welfare of marine life. Easterners speak of the "death of the fisheries" as a fact of life and grieve for the monumental losses to the sea and the people. Indeed, unemployment caused by the decline of the fishery is one of the factors making the jobs generated by the offshore oil and gas industries so attractive.

The perception that fishing "isn't what it used to be" seems to have existed for a long time, but people have never backed off from their relentless harvest of the sea; as technology has improved, fish stocks have dwindled. The first attempt to control fishing in the northwest Atlantic began 1949, but there was little regulation until 1970, when the Gulf of St. Lawrence was decreed a Canadian-only fishing zone. By 1974, the fishing industry and the government finally realized that the cod stocks were dropping along the Labrador coast and on the Grand Banks. Ships from more than twenty countries helped themselves to as much cod as they wanted. The Soviet fleet was considered to be the worst offender, and Canadian ports were temporarily closed to Soviet ships in 1975 in response. Canada soon declared a 200-mile limit, asserting its sovereignty and its right to control how much fish could be harvested from these waters.

Fishing actually improved in the Atlantic for a few years, but by the late 1970s and into the 1980s, federal cutbacks put a crimp in fisheries research. At the same time, corporations began to propose their own methods of "managing" the resource without government intervention. Ironically, 1987 was the "best year ever for the Atlantic Fisheries," according to the Atlantic Provinces Economic Council, as fishermen landed $791 million worth of fish. It was an anomaly, however, and bad years followed. In May of 1990, as the fish stocks dropped almost out of sight, APEC declared, "The scale of social disruption caused by proposals to rationalize the sector is unprecedented." Because there were so few fish, coastal communities withered, fishermen hauled their boats ashore, and the processing plants laid off employees.

While the industry continued to argue for maximizing profits — after all, they caught only what the market demanded — genuine research continued to decline. The Harris Report suggested some alternatives in 1990, including, on the one hand, extending the 200-mile limit, or, on the other, giving up on any kind of control beyond that perimeter and sending Canadian vessels to ravage the international "nose" and "tail" of the Grand Banks along with the foreign vessels.

Government funding for research declined even further just as everyone in the industry realized that no one was looking out for the best interests of the undersea resources. The Department of Fisheries and Oceans tried to get a handle on the nature the problem. Inshore fishermen screamed that the big draggers were killing the sea and had been doing so for decades, and in the late 1980s, many nations continued to harvest fish near or within the 200-mile limit. At the same time, inshore fishermen commonly ignored quotas. The Halifax *Chronicle-Herald* reported that probably fifty percent more fish were landed by inshore fishermen than what they actually reported.

Some blamed the grey seals for killing the cod and wanted to kill more seals, but researchers at Dalhousie University suggested another alternative: a contraceptive vaccine to be administered to female seals on Sable Island. A University of Guelph zoologist argued that the seals would naturally decline soon anyway; they would starve to death due to the lack of fish. Still other researchers argued that the seals alone were not the problem; the seas themselves were changing. Global warming, they said, compounded the overfishing problem because, as the polar ice melts, the water in the North Atlantic becomes colder, creating an environment less conducive for breeding.

In 1991, when Newfoundland politician John Crosbie was federal Minister of Fisheries, he expressed his despair at the sorry state of things by borrowing Samuel Johnson's famous remark about a dog walking on its hind legs: "It is remarkable not because it walks poorly, but that it walks at all." Another Newfoundlander, Brian Tobin, who took over Crosbie's job, officially closed down the Atlantic flatfish and cod fishery in 1994, putting 35,000 people out of work. The government tried to bandage the economic wounds with a combined retraining and subsidy program that provided some sustenance for fishing families for a few years. Occasionally, newspaper headlines declare optimism about recovering cod stocks, but few envision a return to the traditional way of life for those who relied upon inshore fishing.

On the East Coast, and especially in Newfoundland, "cod" and "fish" are synonymous, but the cod stocks are not the only ones in drastic decline. The commercial Atlantic salmon fishery ended in 1984 because the salmon had virtually disappeared, and the wealthy fly fishermen's associations brought tremendous pressure to bear on governing bodies at every level to save their sport. On the West Coast, the situation is different. Although there is a significant sport fishery for coho salmon, sockeye salmon has been British Columbia's most important commercial fish.

On the West Coast, the United Fisherman and Allied Workers Union had spoken up on occasion about limiting licenses to protect their jobs and to help limit the catch. In 1968, a federal fisheries minister outlined a plan to protect the fishermen by issuing fewer licenses and thus protecting profits. Between 1975 and 1985, the commercial catch of Pacific salmon tripled, and it seemed as if the fish would replenish themselves indefinitely. But in the early 1990s, the fish went missing, and in 1996, the salmon catch had shrunk from a recent twenty-seven million fish to a mere seven million. The Fraser River spawning runs decreased drastically; in Georgia Strait, the coho stopped biting for the sports fishermen; and some species seemed to have almost vanished from British Columbia waters. Who was to blame? Partly the loggers for damaging rivers and estuaries, partly the polluters, perhaps partly global warming, but most likely a cocktail of all these and more.

West coast battles between commercial fishermen and the Department of Fisheries and Oceans have continued into the twenty-first century, even though both sides argue that they want what is best for the fish. On August 26, 2002, more than 130 boats gathered in Johnstone Strait, near Campbell River, to protest the DFO decision to close the late summer fishery. According to the DFO, spawning sockeye experienced mortality rates as high as ninety percent in their efforts to enter the Fraser and other rivers up and down the coast. The resource was at risk, they claimed, and the fishermen would have to back off. Some fishermen went to work harvesting the sockeye anyway, under the threat of $100,000 fines. The *Vancouver Sun* quoted Howe Sound fisherman Lorne Thames, who said, "It's a really bad year"; he expected to take home a mere twenty percent of his normal pay. Many fishermen think the DFO statistics are wrong. While erring on the side of caution seemed to be the right thing to do, a lot of unhappy fishermen wondered how they could stay in business with so few days available for fishing.

On both east and west coasts, the business of fishing the oceans is changing. When *National Geographic* writer Tom Melham visited Newfoundland in 1991, he observed that the connection of the people to the sea was intact despite impending doom in the fisheries. "Newfoundland fishermen don't build houses back from the sea," he noted, "but right at its edge . . . these people are farmers of the sea."

True farming of the sea — aquaculture — seems to be a reasonable alternative on both coasts to fishing the open seas. In the east, the Atlantic salmon is the most important farmed species. In 1988, it was said to be worth $48 million per year in the region, with fish farmers in New Brunswick leading the way. In the mid-1980s, fish farms began to appear along the British Columbia coast, their pens stocked with imported salmon varieties that seemed to grow faster, healthier, and meatier in captivity than the native species. Aquaculture has become a business similar to raising any other kind of livestock, with nearly 100 west-coast farms employing nearly 3,000 people.

Economically, aquaculture seems to be advantageous, and it reduces or eliminates pressure on local species. On the other hand, early studies suggest that uneaten food, medicines, and droppings from farmed fish are pollutants, and that aquaculturists should dispose of them responsibly instead of simply counting on the sea to flush them away. In addition, fish escape from farms when the pens inevitably give way due to accidents and storms. In theory, the farmed fish are sterile; in practice, there is speculation that escapees not only compete with native species for food and space, but also interbreed with the wild stock and produce genetic changes damaging to the species.

Self Government and Beyond

The Nisga'a people had lived in the Nass Valley, on the northern coast of British Columbia, for over 10,000 years. In the summer of 1998, they won a land claim battle they had been fighting for well over a century. Leaders had first travelled to Victoria in the nineteenth century to demand ownership of their ancestral lands, but generations of politicians dismissed their claims. A more recent round of negotiations began in 1976. Twenty years later, the Nisga'a had hammered out a deal with the provincial and federal governments, and two years after that, all parties signed on the dotted line, returning to the 5,500 Nisga'a people nearly 2,000 square kilometres of land, along with self-government and $190 million. Criticized by many white British Columbia taxpayers who fear a landslide of other claims, the Nisga'a Treaty has been celebrated by First Nations people across Canada.

In the North, the influences of urban, industrial, and technological culture have been hard on the old ways. When Inuit abandoned traditional housing for the apparent comforts of southern-style homes, families often ended up living in ragtag shacks. Alcohol ravaged many families as the economy became cash-based and the traditional occupations that grew out of fishing, trapping, and hunting could no longer provide a livelihood. As dependency on the government grew, so did the problems.

Education was a priority for many leaders, however. Between 1962 and 1994, the number of students in school nearly tripled, partly because the Northwest Territories had the highest birth rate in the country; in 1994, 1,253 teachers taught 16,252 students. Aurora College grew out of the former Arctic College in 1995 to bolster post-secondary education, and the school had an enrollment of over 4,000. In 1998, plans were solidified for an even more advanced arctic university, primarily for Aboriginal students in Canada but also for their neighbours in Greenland, Iceland, Russia, Sweden, Norway, and Alaska.

Inuit in smaller communities still try to eke out a living through hunting, trapping, and fishing, but those who work in the mining and petroleum industries earn considerably more money. While fears of environmental disaster cloud the optimism of many Northerners, some see a bright economic future in oil, especially in the offshore fields. In the Beaufort Sea, the Amaulgak Field alone is said to contain at least fifty-four million cubic feet of oil and natural gas. As in the days of old, the riches of the Arctic draw a familiar parade of entrepreneurs and exploiters, fools and visionaries to compete for them.

While outside influences continue to reshape Inuit and other Native cultures in the North, a very significant influence has filtered south. Throughout North America and Europe, collectors have developed a craving for the traditional art of the Inuit. James A. Houston, an artist from Toronto, began to popularize Inuit art in the late 1940s, and interest materials increased the scope of Inuit art, so that paintings, wall hangings, and especially limited-edition prints have become popular, as well as the prized soapstone and ivory carvings. Their commercial value has increased to the point that artists, artisans, and craftspeople can make a living from their traditions. Much of the work by Inuit artists tells stories of hunters, fishers, and the wildlife that provided spiritual and physical sustenance for their ancestors.

In the 1990s, the government of the Northwest Territories underwent a radical change. From 1905 until the end of World War II, government decisions were all handed down from a commissioner and a raft of civil servants based, not in the North, but in Ottawa. In 1951, a few council members were elected, and the proportion increased each year until, in 1975, all were elected. In 1967, the seat of government was moved from Ottawa to Yellowknife.

Even in the face of difficulties and deprivations, about half of the population of the Northwest Territories was Native, and nearly half of them spoke languages other than English or French. In 1993, the passage of the Nunavut Land Claim agreement in Parliament set in motion the division of this enormous and varied tract of land. On April 1, 1999, the eastern part became the separate territory of Nunavut, with Iqaluit (once Frobisher Bay) as its capital, and with a population of 27,000, eighty-five percent of them Native. Governed and run by Aboriginal people, Nunavut is the first territory of its kind in North America. Its founding was a landmark occasion for other indigenous peoples around the world; in fact, the remainder of the Northwest Territories is considering a similar change for its 41,000 people.

Nunavut consists of 1.6 million square kilometres, stretching from the community of Sanikiluaq, on Hudson Bay, to Grise Fiord on Ellesmere Island, 2,000 kilometres to the north. Most of the land is Arctic tundra, and the strong sense of isolation comforts many Inuit who wish to maintain the traditions of their ancestors. Inuit politician John Amagoalik, who hails from Resolute Bay, suggests that isolation has its advantages: "Our luck was to inhabit a land that no one coveted." At the same time, Iqaluit, now a town of a 4,200 people, has two Kentucky Fried Chicken outlets. No road connects it with the south, and the only road leading out of town is dubbed "The Road to Nowhere."

Concerning Nunavut's new political status, Amagoalik said that the people are "exhilarated . . . but also we are a little fearful." Unemployment remains at thirty per cent, illiteracy is not uncommon, and substance abuse creates constant near-crisis situations in many communities. At the same time, there is a renaissance, not only of traditional art, but also of traditional sports, culture, and spirituality. Going out on the land or on the ice has become a way of connecting with the past and reconnecting with the natural world, and, at the opposite extreme, events such as the international Arctic Games emphasize connections to the larger community.

CHAPTER TWENTY-SEVEN

A Northwest Passage of the Heart

IT'S MAY 25, 2002, and I'm walking down a path towards the beach at Cox Bay, just south of Tofino on Vancouver Island. I haven't surfed the Pacific Ocean for six years. Rain is falling — well, not rain really, just drizzle. Tofino gets a lot of precipitation — 3,295 millimetres per year. It holds the Canadian record for the most rain in a twenty-four-hour period: 489 millimetres in 1967.

Today is the day I kiss my first slug. I had been giving a talk to the sixth-graders from Wickaninnish School and asked for their advice: what unusual and uniquely West Coast thing should I do before flying home to the East? "Kiss a slug," a girl said, and they all agreed. The rain has brought out a whole family of banana slugs, and I pick up the largest one I see. It is a thirteen-centimetre-long yellow and black torpedo that has left a shimmering trail of ooze over the gravel. I hold it up to my face and kiss its back. The other surfers in their wetsuits on the path to the waves are watching me, and they shake their heads.

That challenge accomplished, I return the creature to the forest floor and walk to the beach, the great west coast trees towering all around me, the sound of Pacific waves drawing me towards them. The wind is out of the southwest, and on nearby Long Beach the waves are choppy, but in Cox Bay, sheltered from the wind, the waves are glassy and shoulder high. I paddle straight out to sea — west, heading for Asia. The water is cold. I'm wearing a full wetsuit, with boots, hood, and gloves. I paddle out past where the waves are breaking and turn to face the shore. Before me is the long, arcing sandy shoreline, with massive logs scattered along the high tide mark. Beyond them stands the great rain forest of Vancouver Island, giant hemlock and red cedar and Sitka spruce. A low cloud obscures the mountains to the east. Amidst all this grandeur, I hardly bother to notice

285

that the rain has increased. It's not much of an issue if you're sitting in the Pacific Ocean in a wetsuit.

I scoop up seawater and taste it. I've been told the Pacific is less salty than the Atlantic. The taste test bears that out. On this particular day in May, my guess is that the Atlantic off Nova Scotia and the Pacific here are about the same temperature: six degrees Celsius. There are at least twenty other surfers in the water nearby — all in wetsuits, men and women in equal numbers. Canada breeds cold-water surfers. We may not be the best surfers in the world, but we surf the coldest water during the coldest weather. In Nova Scotia, this means January, when the water temperature hovers near zero and the air temperature drops to minus twenty degrees.

Here at Cox Bay, the shoreline is relatively undisturbed. Aside from two "wilderness resorts" tucked into the forest, the land looks unscathed and unchanged. The Nuu-chah-nulth people say that their ancestors lived here for more than 10,000 years, in harmony with the environment, well fed by the riches of the sea and land. Before Europeans brought the smallpox and other diseases that destroyed nearly eighty per cent of the population, as many as 100,000 Aboriginal people, lived on this coast. Young men and women undoubtedly paddled out in sturdy handmade craft and saw the same vista as I now see. Making for shore, they would have tapped the power of the waves for an exhilarating ride in to the beach. If they were the original surfers here, then my foray into the waves today is just part of an ancient tradition.

On his last voyage, Captain James Cook passed this bay, and his navigator may have taken note of its potential protection from the winds. Cook had sailed east from the Hawaiian Islands to this coast, and then he headed north in search of a west-to-east version of the Northwest Passage. Just 224 years and two months before I kissed my slug and paddled to sea here, Cook pulled into Nootka Sound, north of Tofino. There he struck some bargains with the local inhabitants and repaired his ships before sailing north. Failing to find his shortcut back to England, he returned to Hawaii, where he met his demise.

Today, Tofino is a quiet fishing community and home to a dozen or more ecotourism businesses. It's a town of sea kayakers, surfers, mountain bikers, and nature lovers of all kinds, as well as commercial fishermen and Native craftspeople. But this part of Vancouver Island has a long

Tofino, British Columbia. (ALISON HUGHES)

legacy of dispute. In nearby Clayoquot Sound, John Jacob Astor's merchant ship the *Tonquin*, under the control of its harsh captain, Jonathan Thorn, came to trade with the people known to the outside world as the Nootka. Thorn so angered them that they seized his ship and killed most of his crew. The following day, the *Tonquin* was blown to smithereens, possibly by the surviving crew members, and so ended Astor's vision of economic dominance here.

In the twentieth century, horrific logging practices had ravaged and scarred much of this coast, and in 1993, a British Columbia government plan to allow continued logging of old-growth forests led to large-scale protests. Thousands of individuals poured into Tofino from many parts of the world, and over 800 were arrested for civil disobedience. To this day, the Clayoquot Sound area is a focal point for outrage over the loss of irreplaceable coastal forests.

Not all of the local disasters were brought on by greed. At least one resulted from an ill-conceived act of exuberance. As I look to the south of Cox Bay, towards the boundary of Pacific Rim National Park, I face the crash site of a Canso A aircraft that smashed into the forest in August of 1945. Amid the celebrations of victory over Japan at the Tofino RCAF station, a drunken airplane mechanic lured a nurse into the plane and, whisky bottle in hand, took off for a joyride over the Pacific. Unfortunately for them both, the plane was nearly out of fuel, and the woozy mechanic turned back towards land. He was sober enough to jettison the depth charges on board, pockmarking the forest with explosions that left craters six metres across. The plane itself soon crashed into the forest, and the two people inside may or may not have survived. No remains of the pilot or his passenger have ever been found beneath the canopy of the giant evergreen trees.

Sitting in the centre of the bay, Cox Point to the south, Frank Island to the north, I paddle to catch wave after wave just beyond the shore of the Canada's most westerly coast. The waves generated by the Pacific follow the same laws of physics as the waves generated by North Atlantic storms. The cold soon seeps into my bones, despite the protection of neoprene, reminding me always that Canada's coasts require care and caution.

But there is a constant lure to that cold water. A map of this area is full of seductive names that send the enquiring mind and spirit wandering to discover what it would be like in Cypress Bay, Mosquito Harbour, Browning Passage, Father Charles Channel, Bedwell Sound, Herbert Inlet, White Pine Cove, Shelter Inlet, Templar Channel, Grice Bay, and Fortune Channel.

The road to Tofino across the mountains from the island's east coast was not completed until 1959. In many ways, this remote, wet, Brobdingnagian coast of raw beauty still feels a world apart from Victoria and Vancouver and civilized points east. It's possible, of course, to wake at my home at Lawrencetown Beach, Nova Scotia, watch the sun come up out of the Atlantic, catch a flight west, and see the sun set over the Pacific — should the clouds miraculously open up — on the same day. But there's still a big fat continent in between. Like the early mapmakers, informed more by optimism than fact, I almost wish I could compress the great chunk of Canada and discover an easy and convenient water route east to west. Until then, I have to settle for a Northwest Passage of the heart that allows me to feel in my chilly bones the powerful link that tethers all of Canada's coastal people together. We soldier on with our busy and often trivial lives, but the awesome power of the sea will not allow us to forget the forces that continue to shape the land and the lives of those who live near its shores.

Selected Bibliography

Africville Genealogical Society. *The Spirit of Africville*. Halifax: Formac, 1992.

Allen, Patricia. *Metepenagiag: New Brunswick's Oldest Village*. Fredericton: Red Bank First Nation and Goose Lane, 1994.

Armour, Charles. *Sailing Ships of the Maritimes*. Toronto: McGraw-Hill Ryerson, 1975.

Bancroft, Hubert Howe. *The History of British Columbia, 1792-1887*. San Francisco: The History Company, 1887.

Barman, Jean. *The West Beyond the West: A History of British Columbia*. Toronto: University of Toronto Press, 1991.

Beeby, Dean. *Deadly Frontiers: Disaster and Rescue on Canada's Atlantic Seaboard*. Fredericton: Goose Lane, 2001.

Berton, Pierre. *Seacoasts*. Toronto: Stoddart, 1998.

Bodsworth, Fred. *The Pacific Coast*. Toronto: Natural Science of Canada, 1970.

Bowering, George. *Bowering's B.C.: A Swashbuckling History*. Toronto: Viking, 1996.

Bremner, Benjamin. *Tales of Abegweit*. Charlottetown: Irwin Printing, 1936.

Brody, Hugh. *Living Arctic: Hunters of the Canadian North*. Seattle: University of Washington Press, 1987.

Brown, Craig, ed. *The Illustrated History of Canada*. Toronto: Lester and Orpen Denys, 1987.

Callbeck, Lorne C. *The Cradle of Confederation*. Fredericton: Brunswick Press, 1964.

Careless, J.M.S. and R. Craig Brown. *The Canadians 1867-1967*. Toronto: Macmillan, 1968.

Choyce, Lesley. *Nova Scotia: Shaped by the Sea*. Toronto: Penguin, 1996.

Coates, Ken, and Bill Morrison. *The Sinking of the Princess Sophia: Taking the North Down with Her*. Toronto: Oxford, 1990.

Comeau , Pauline and Aldo Santin. *The First Canadians: A Profile of Canada's Native People Today*. Toronto: Lorimer, 1990.

Dawson, Joan. *The Mapmaker's Eye: Nova Scotia Through Early Maps*. Nimbus and Nova Scotia Museum, 1988.

Dickason, Olive. *Canada's First Nations*. Toronto: McClelland and Stewart, 1992.

Doane, Benjamin. *Following the Sea*. Halifax: Nimbus, 1987.

Fingard, Judith. *The Dark Side of Life in Victorian Halifax*. Porters Lake: Pottersfield, 1989.

Fisher, Robin. *Contact and Conflict: Indian-European Relations in British Columbia, 1774-1890*. Vancouver: UBC Press, 1977.

Fitzgerald, Jack. *Newfoundland Disasters*. St. John's: Jesperson, 1984.

Francis, Daniel. *Discovery of the North: The Exploration of Canada's Arctic*. Edmonton: Hurtig, 1986.

Francis, R. Douglas, et al, eds. *Destinies: Canadian History Since Confederation*. Toronto: Holt, Rinehart and Winston, 1988.

Francis, R. Douglas, Richard Jones and Donald B. Smith. *Origins: Canadian History to Confederation*. Toronto: Holt, Rinehart and Winston, 1988.

Francis, R. Douglas and Donald B. Smith, eds. *Readings in Canadian History: Pre-Confederation*. Toronto: Holt, Rinehart and Winston, 1986.

_____. *Readings in Canadian History: Post-Confederation*. Toronto: Holt, Rinehart and Winston, 1986.

Friesen, J. and H.K. Ralston, eds. *Historical Essays of British Columbia*. Toronto: Gage, 1980.

Garod, Stan. *The North*. Toronto: Fitzhenry and Whiteside, 1980.

Gould, Jan. *Women of British Columbia*. Saanichton, B.C.: Hancock House, 1975.

Griffiths, Franklyn, ed. *Arctic Alternatives: Civility or Militarism in the Circumpolar North*. Toronto: Science for Peace, 1992.

Gunn, Gertrude. *The Political History of Newfoundland, 1832-1864*. Toronto: University of Toronto Press, 1966.

Halpenny, Frances, ed. *Dictionary of Canadian Biography*. Toronto: University of Toronto Press, 1974.

Hill-Tout, Charles. *The Salish People*. Vancouver: Talonbooks, 1978.

Humber, Charles J. *Canada: From Sea to Sea*. Toronto: Loyalist Press, 1986.

It Happened in British Columbia: An Illustrated Review of Some Aspects of B.C.'s First 100 Years as a Canadian Province. Vancouver: B.C. Centennial Committee, 1970.

Johnston, Hugh J.M. *The Pacific Province: A History of British Columbia*. Toronto: Douglas and MacIntyre, 1996.

Kilian, Crawford. *Go Do Some Great Thing: The Black Pioneers of British Columbia*. Vancouver: Douglas and McIntyre, 1978.

LaPierre, Laurier. *Canada, My Canada: What Happened?* Toronto: McClelland and Stewart, 1992.

Larsen, Henry et al. *The Big Ship.* Toronto: McClelland and Stewart, 1967.

Lower, A.R.M. and J.W. Chafe. *Canada: A Nation and How it Came To Be.* Toronto: Longmans, 1948.

The Lower North Shore. Québec: Gouvernement du Québec, 1984.

Mackay, Ian. *Quest of the Folk.* Montreal: McGill-Queens University Press, 1994.

MacMechan, Archibald. *At the Harbour Mouth.* Porters Lake: Pottersfield, 1988.

Major, Kevin. *As Near to Heaven By Sea: A History of Newfoundland and Labrador.* Toronto: Penguin, 2001.

Marsh, James H., ed. *The Canadian Encyclopedia.* Year 2000 Edition. Toronto: McClelland and Stewart, 2000.

Marlatt, Daphne and Maya Koizumi. *Steveston Recollected: A Japanese Canadian History.* Victoria: Aural History Provincial Archives of B.C. 1975.

Maud, Ralph A. *A Guide to B.C. Indian Myth and Legend.* Vancouver: Talonbooks, 1982.

McGhee, Robert. *Ancient Canada.* Ottawa: Canadian Museum of Civilization, 1989.

McNaught, Kenneth. *The Pelican History of Canada.* London: 1983.

Miller, J.R. *Skyscrapers Hide the Heavens: A History of Indian-white Relations in Canada.* Toronto: University of Toronto Press, 2001.

Morrison, James H. and James Moreira. *Tempered by Rum: Rum in the History of the Maritime Provinces.* Porters Lake: Pottersfield, 1988.

Morton, James. *In the Sea of Sterile Mountains: The Chinese in British Columbia.* Vancouver: J.J. Douglas, 1974.

Mowat, Farley. *The Farfarers.* Toronto: HarperCollins, 1998.

_____. *This Rock Within the Sea.* Boston: Atlantic Monthly, 1968.

Newton, Norman. *Fire in the Raven's Nest.* Toronto: New Press, 1973.

Ormsby, Margaret A. *British Columbia: A History.* Vancouver: Macmillan, 1958.

Parsons, Robert. *Lost At Sea*, Volume 1. St. John's: Creative, 1991.

Paterson, T. W. *British Columbia Shipwrecks.* Langley: Stagecoach, 1976.

Paul, Daniel. *We Were Not the Savages.* Halifax: Nimbus, 1993.

Robinson, L. B. *Esquimalt: Place of Shoaling Waters.* Victoria: Quality, 1948.

Rowe, F. A. *A History of Newfoundland and Labrador*. Toronto: McGraw-Hill Ryerson, 1977.

Rushton, Gerald. *Whistle Up the Inlet: The Union Steamship Story*. Vancouver: J.J. Douglas, 1974.

Russell, Franklin. *The Atlantic Coast*. Toronto: Natural Science of Canada, 1970.

Soucoup, Dan. *Historic New Brunswick*. East Lawrencetown: Pottersfield, 1997.

_____. *Maritime Firsts*. East Lawrencetown: Pottersfield, 1996.

Thurston, Harry. *Atlantic Outposts*. East Lawrencetown: Pottersfield, 2002.

Watkins, Mel, ed. *Canada*. New York: Facts on File, 1993.

Weihs, Jean. *Facts about Canada, Its Provinces and Territories*. New York: H.W. Wilson, 1995.

Woodcock, George. *British Columbia: A History of the Province*. Vancouver: Douglas and McIntyre, 1990.

_____. *The Canadians*. Toronto: Fitzhenry and Whiteside, 1979.

York, Geoffrey. *The Dispossessed: Life and Death in Native Canada*. Toronto: Lester and Orpen Denys, 1989.

Zaslow, Morris. *The Opening of the Canadian North 1870- 1914*. Toronto: McClelland and Stewart, 1971.

Illustration Credits

Permission to publish the illustrations in *The Coasts of Canada* has been generously granted by many institutions. Their full names appear below, along with the abbreviations used with below the illustrations.

BC   Peary-MacMillan Arctic Museum, Bowdoin College, page 218.

CMC   Canadian Museum of Civilization / Bill Holm, page 28.

CP   Canadian Press Picture Archive, Kevin Frayer, page 266.

DFO   Fisheries and Oceans Canada, page 271.

GA   Glenbow Archives, pages 205, 236, and 244.

GNL   David Preston Smith and Department of Tourism, Culture and Recreation, Government of Newfoundland and Labrador, page 136.

GSC   Minister of Public Works and Government Services Canada, 2002, courtesy of Natural Resources Canada, Geological Survey of Canada, pages 23, 214; Earth Sciences Information Centre, Natural Resources Canada, Geological Survey of Canada, cover and page 138.

MAV   Museum of Anthropology, Vancouver / Bill McLennan, page 31.

MM   Mariners' Museum, Newport News, Virginia, page 46.

MMA   Maritime Museum of the Atlantic , page 192.

MMBC   Maritime Museum of British Columbia, Victoria, BC, pages 106, 107, 154, and 232.

MU   John Bland Canadian Architecture Collection, McGill University, page 75.

MUNL   Centre for Newfoundland Studies (Hettasch Collection), Memorial University of Newfoundland Library, page 134.

NAC   National Archives of Canada, pages 51, 54, 57, 65, 70, 84, 90, 92, 95, 98, 101, 104, 109, 114, 116-117, 140, 169, 194, 268; MacLaghlan Collection, 228-229; Department of Fisheries and Oceans, 253; Canadian Press, 256 and 258; Tak Toyota, Canadian Press, 262 and 263.

NBM   New Brunswick Museum, page 180.

NLC   National Library of Canada, pages 68 and 74; Cartographic and Architiectural Division, page 56; Website Images in the News: *Canadian Illustrated News* (13:25, 139), page 132, (16:11, 172), page 161, and (3:7, 108), page 224.

NSARM   Nova Scotia Archives and Records Management, page 242.

NSM   Nova Scotia Museum, Halifax, page 38.

PAM   Hudson's Bay Company Archives, Provincial Archives of Manitoba, page 150.

PANL   Provincial Archives of Newfoundland and Labrador, page 62.

PAPEI   Public Archives and Records Office of Prince Edward Island, page 184.

PC   Parks Canada, (Brian Molyneux) page 36; (J. Steeves) page 44.

SHF   Ship Hector Foundation, page 119.

YCM   Yarmouth County Museum, page 176.

YU   Beinecke Rare Book and Manuscript Library, Yale University, page 42.

Acknowledgements

A book like this owes a great debt to all the historians and authors who have come before, providing me with articles and books brimming with facts, opinions, anecdotes, clues, hunches, and best intentions. History is not static, and what we know of the past changes as new evidence arises and as our own horizons widen.

A special thanks to my researchers, Peggy Amirault, Nadine Flagel, Stephanie Mason, Andrew Richardson, and Therese Hebert. I also appreciate the support of my wife, Terry, and my daughters, Sunyata and Pamela, who helped lighten my spirits when the weight of history seemed almost too great to bear. My thanks to the coastal Canadians of so many varied shores. I found generosity, warmth, friendship, and good stories in such diverse communities as Arisaig, Mutton Bay, New World Harbour, Saint John, St. John's, Sheshatshui, Nanaimo, Tofino, Inverness, and West Chezzetcook, to name a few. I am especially indebted to the people of Nova Scotia, who have given me so much.

I began writing history in earnest when I researched and wrote *Nova Scotia: Shaped by the Sea* for Penguin Canada. That experience granted me the opportunity to become acquainted with the pleasure (and pain) of intimacy with history. The parts of *Coasts of Canada* that touch on Nova Scotia draw substantially on my earlier research.

Great rewards in publishing heaven should be showered upon all the folks at Goose Lane Editions.

Index